D0620840

THE TRIBE THAT HIDES FROM MAN

The Tribe
that Hides from Man

ADRIAN COWELL

STEIN AND DAY/*Publishers*/New York

First published in the United States of America by
Stein and Day/*Publishers* in 1974
Copyright © 1973 by Adrian Cowell
Library of Congress Catalog Card No. 73-92187
All rights reserved
Printed in the United States of America
Stein and Day/*Publishers*/Scarborough House, Briarcliff Manor, N.Y. 10510
ISBN 0-8128-1690-0

FOR

Pilly, Boojie and Xingu

CONTENTS

Introduction, 13

I
XINGU

1 The Visit, 23
2 The Killings, 37
3 The End of the Trumai, 47
   A list of the Indians mentioned in Chapters 1 to 3, 52
4 The Txukahamei, 53
5 The Frontiers of Killing, 64
6 The Search Starts, 70
7 Cachimbo, 78
   A list of the Indians mentioned in Chapters 4 to 7, 84

II
THE KREEN-AKRORE EXPEDITION

8 The First Clues, 89
9 The Captured Children, 96
10 Parliamentating, 104
11 The Massacre, 110
12 We Find the Village, 119
   A list of the Indians mentioned in Chapters 8 to 12, 125
13 The Trail, 126
14 The Trail Halts, 136
15 Waiting for the Air-drop, 146
16 The Stones, 154
17 The Kreen-Akrore Village, 161
18 The Unknown Man, 173
19 Waiting, 180
   A list of the Indians mentioned in Chapters 13 to 19, 188

III

THE AFTERMATH

20 The End, 191
   Postscript, The Attack on the Parque, 197

APPENDICES

 I The Exploration of Xingu, 219
 II Tribes of the Xingu Area, 225
III Decree Governing the Parque, 243
IV Txukahamei Expedition to Pacify the Kreen-
   Akrore, 1969–70, 246
                    Acknowledgments, 250

ILLUSTRATIONS

BETWEEN PAGES 38–39

Claudio Villas Boas.
Orlando Villas Boas.
Aerial view of River Xingu.
The road crossing the Xingu near Diauarum.
A village of the Kuikuro.
A Suya family.
Urua flute-dance.
A Kuikuro leader wearing a necklace of Jaguar claws.

BETWEEN PAGES 54–55

Diauarum: Txukahamei mother brings sick child to dispensary.
Diauarum: Claudio with Indian child.
A Kamayura canoe on Lake Ipavu.
Txukahamei mourning by a grave in the jungle.
Javaritu.
Pionim.
Rauni.
Bemotire.
A Kamayura fishing with bow and arrow.
Indian shooting with his feet.

BETWEEN PAGES 70–71

The air-strip at Cachimbo.
Brazilian parachutists recover Richard Mason's body.
Mekrenoti family returning from the trek.
Mekrenoti carrying tortoises tied in frames.
Txukahamei hunting with club and bow.
Txukahamei on the hunting trail.
Artefacts taken from the Kreen-Akrore.

BETWEEN PAGES 102–103

Typical unexplored jungle.
Bebgogoti with the captured Kreen-Akrore child.
A Kreen-Akrore plantation.
A Kreen-Akrore village.
A Kreen-Akrore hut.
Antonio.
Pripuri.
The Expedition travels up the R. Manitsaua.

ILLUSTRATIONS

BETWEEN PAGES 134–135

Cutting the trail in Kreen-Akrore territory.
Claudio checks the trail by compass.
The Kayabi dance after killing a rubber-tapper in 1961.
Claudio with hundreds of sweat bees on his hat.
Claudio holds up presents at night to invisible watchers.
Claudio crossing a river in Kreen-Akrore territory.
Building a bark canoe for the expedition.
Building a canoe out of a solid tree-trunk.

BETWEEN PAGES 150–151

Claudio and Pripuri examine a sapling broken by the Kreen-Akrore.
Cutting through driftwood blocking an unused river.
Hauling the canoes overland.
Hauling the canoes through rapids.
Jungle on the river's edge.
Claudio and Orlando lead the expedition descending the unknown R. Peixoto Azevedo.
Orlando measures a Kreen-Akrore footprint.
Orlando examines a twig broken a few moments earlier by one of the Kreen-Akrore.

BETWEEN PAGES 166–167

Marching into the Kreen-Akrore village waving presents.
Hanging up presents in a Kreen-Akrore hut.
Claudio hangs up presents for the Kreen-Akrore in the jungle.
Examining one of the "present sites".
Kretire and other Indians examine baggage left by the Kreen-Akrore.
Kretire demonstrates the bones of a victim of the Kreen-Akrore.
Kreen-Akrore tree carvings of a tortoise and a snake.
Kreen-Akrore stone axe.

BETWEEN PAGES 182–183

The abandoned Kreen-Akrore village.
A Kreen-Akrore "oven" and grave.
Working on one of the three air-strips built by the expedition.
One of the air-strips.
Brazilian parachutists check remains of a government expedition wiped out by the Atroari Indians.
A Brazilian boy demonstrates the straw wig taken from the village of the Cabecas Peladas.
Imitations of axe, scissors, needle and knife left by Cinta Larga Indians as a "shopping list" for the Chico Meireles expedition.

[viii]

MAPS

General Map of Central Brazil, situating the National Park
of Xingu and showing the Trans-Amazonian roads under
construction, p. 15

The National Park of Xingu, p. 22

The Area of the Search for the Kreen-Akrore, p. 88

The Expedition to Contact the Kreen-Akrore, p. 127

The Timbira Area and Tribal Migrations, p. 179

General Bandeira de Mello, President of the Indian Foundation, has himself made a surprising attack on the Xingu National Park ... using a time-honoured Brazilian expression, the General said that the Xingu was *"para Ingles ver"*—"for the British to see"— meaning that it was just for show. When visitors left the reservation the Indians discarded their feathers and other ornaments and slipped on their "civilised" clothes. "The Indians are not museum pieces," the General went on. "They need freedom."

The Daily Telegraph, May 4th, 1971

INTRODUCTION

A few days before the intended deadline for this book, two despondent letters arrived from the Brazilian whom the book is largely about.

"Claudio and I are tiring," Orlando Villas Boas wrote. "What inspires us at the moment is the attraction[1] of the Kreen-Akrore, but what disheartens us each passing day is to see the prospects of the Indian declining . . . Friends are helping us to retire. Pray God, it will be soon."

A week later a note came from a close friend of the two Villas Boas brothers: "Last week Orlando was transported from Cachimbo to São Paulo. He had a heavy heart attack. He wanted to join Claudio at the Kreen-Akrore front."

Since then, Orlando Villas Boas has recovered and, with his brother, has resigned from the Indian Foundation (FUNAI); but for me these three letters represented the end of some sort of dream. In 1958, I had arrived in the Xingu jungle in Brazil and had spent seven months learning to live and hunt with the Indians at a time when Orlando and Claudio Villas Boas had been trying to create what was a last retreat for the Indian. The brothers were recognised even then as Brazil's greatest living explorers, and for more than a dozen years they had been 'pacifying' jungle tribes and sheltering them from the first shock of civilisation. Xingu was the only place I had visited where the Indians did not seem crushed or demoralised, and its ten thousand square miles of jungle, river, lake and savannah were a magnificent wilderness where the tribes travelled and hunted without barriers in space or time. It had seemed just possible during that short period that the Villas Boas brothers might achieve something for the Indians that no one else had achieved. And like many other people I tried to do what I could to help, and returned to Xingu several times during the next ten years.

In the spring of 1971, however, the military government of Brazil drove a road through what had by then officially become the "Parque Nacional do Xingu" the Xingu National Park. There were protests from all over Brazil, and from scientists and anthropologists throughout the world. The Parque's frontiers had earlier been defined by Presidential decree, and Article 198 of Brazil's Constitution states: "The Lands inhabited by Indians are inalienable in terms set out by Federal law, and to the Indians pertain the permanent possession of, and acknowledged right to, the exclusive usufruct of the natural riches and all the utilities on them."

A few months later, the lower half of the Parque was sold off, and though the government have promised to replace this with a poorer and already part-inhabited area to the south, there is no evidence that they will keep this promise any better than the one they broke.

"The Parque has been mutilated," a letter from Orlando said. "Each time the situation is worse. This will bring the Indian rapidly to destruction."

*   *   *

Despite what has happened, the purpose of this book is not to defend something that has been destroyed; and it may even seem strange that someone who loved the Parque, and is a friend of the Villas Boas brothers, can only remember his last two years in Xingu—from January 1967 to January 1969—in the light of vendettas, epidemics, tribal quarrels and massacres. The reason lies in the peculiar nature of the campaign that brought the Parque into existence. While there was hope, most of the people who helped the Villas Boas were guilty of propagating what can only be described as the dream-side of Xingu,[2] publicising and emphasising the great beauty and innocence of Indian life. The Indian's only defence against the *civilizado* is his appeal to our sense of justice, and so we reported how the Indians were shot, or died of disease, not how their own tribal traditions of murders hindered the people who were trying to help them. The campaign for their survival was desperate enough without admitting that tribal society was so complex that not even Orlando

[14]

right across the watershed and down into the river system of the Tapajoz. But the brothers never forgot the Indians they had met in Xingu and they returned so often that eventually their Post at Leonardo[4] became their home.

During their first years, they had time for little beyond protecting the Indians from waves of invading prospectors and surveyors, and from the epidemics that began to sweep through the villages. But gradually Orlando and Claudio Villas Boas developed a plan for a "National Park" in which the Indians could progress towards civilisation during a transition period of two to three generations. They had critics who said this would be keeping the tribes in a human zoo, but anyone who watches the Parque Indians giving injections to the sick, driving tractors, stripping generators and running the Post's radio station, knows this to be untrue. The real point is whether the Indians should be allowed to develop towards civilisation in a way of their own choosing, and at a speed suited to their interests, or whether the speed and manner of their progress should be dictated by interests other than theirs.

During the two years covered by this book we were in Xingu making a film for Associated Television that was eventually called *The Tribe that Hides from Man*. On previous visits I had also made films (for the BBC), but this was meant to be a more ambitious project, and Orlando hoped it would help the Parque and the Indians in the political struggle that would soon threaten the existence of the Parque.

Our film unit consisted of Jesco von Puttkamer, a Brazilian photographer who had already spent several years in Xingu, and Charles Stewart, Erno Vincze, Chris Menges, Richard Stanley, Bruce White and Gareth Heywood. They were cameramen and recordists who worked together in England, and who flew out to Xingu from time to time, to relieve one another for contracts and other commitments at home. For three months Pilly, my wife, cooked our food on camp fires, and Boojie, our six-year-old daughter, ran round the villages teaching the Indian children how to be "ponies". As most of them had never seen a horse, this was not as easy as she thought.

We had our "moments". A mouse chewed through Bruce's hammock; Charles was marooned with five prospectors, five

[17]

secret police and several naked Txikao Indians; I jumped into a hornets' nest, and also set fire to one of Claudio's storesheds; Jesco fell down a bank into the River Jatoba; the Kayabi tribe adopted Richard Stanley (who is a friend of Peter Townshend's) and learnt from him some of The Who's current music. But what happened to the film unit was insignificant compared with the whole tragedy of what was happening in the Parque, and so we only come into the story as onlookers.

What we learnt of this story, we learnt through the medium of Xingu's peculiar language, a form of pidgin Portuguese. Some of the fifteen tribes in the area have languages that are related, so the Kayabi and Kamayura tribes, and the Txukahamei and Suya, can understand each other. But most conversation between tribes is in pidgin, helped out with whatever the speaker knows of the other's dialect. This is so much a part of Xingu that at first it was impossible to convince the newly contacted Txikao tribe that Portuguese was not a second language, common to all Indians except themselves. The result is that most Xingu conversation is limited by and very much tied to the crudities and implications of pidgin. For instance, the Xingu word for home is "Cuiaba", because the first *civilizados* to enter Xingu came from the town of Cuiaba. To tell someone that a journey is long, you say "loooooong" and try to look tired. It meant that when one of us talked to, say, a Txukahamei, we would be using about 800–900 words of pidgin Portuguese to about 50–100 words of their language, and our hands would be moving up and down like a semaphore. Most conversations were, therefore, cruder and more drawn out than described in the book.

*   *   *

The background to what was happening in Xingu was the scandal about the Indian Protection Service that started to break towards the end of 1967. Although this government department had originally been founded with the declared aim of protecting the Indian tribes, the Villas Boas brothers had always attacked its incompetence and corruption. A new Minister of the Interior asked their advice and ordered an investigation. The Report that followed described "assassination and massacre of entire Indian tribes, mediaeval tortures, abuses, slave labour . . . pimping, immorality and sexual perversions, including the prostitution of very young Indian girls". Extracts from the report were published in newspapers throughout the world and for a time every plane seemed to bring half a dozen journalists into the jungle. The *Sunday Times* headlined its investigation GENOCIDE, and the *News of the World* called theirs RAPE OF A SIMPLE PEOPLE. The scandal produced an upheaval in the whole Indian policy of Brazil, and put an end to the Indian Protection Service. But its effect was not very marked in Xingu, except in that it drew attention to what was, by contrast, the Parque's staggering success. An Indian Foundation was established, and its first President declared: "The only model in the world that provides the perfect nucleus for the conservation of indigenous culture is the National Park of Xingu, which will serve as the model for future projects of the Foundation."

While the reforming fervour lasted, the jungles of the Parque were safe.

Finally, the background to the expedition which forms the subject of this book was the Indian Foundation's decision to send out three parties in the dry season of 1968 to "pacify" three war-like tribes in Amazonia. This policy of pacification, of making friendly contact with primitive tribes and preparing them for the first shock of civilisation, was central to the whole policy of the Villas Boas brothers, and of the Foundation. One party went to the Atroari tribe in the north, and although the entire party was wiped out, except for one man who had left earlier, a follow-up expedition succeeded in contacting the tribe and making peace. The second group was sent to the Cintas Largas in Rondonia, where they had to wait in the jungle for almost two years, eventually persuading some of the tribe to come out of hiding. A year followed in which progress was made, but at the end of 1971 the tribe attacked and killed the two men who were looking after the Post.

The third expedition, under the leadership of Orlando and Claudio Villas Boas, was sent to the unknown jungle of Cachimbo, and the tribe we approached was the Kreen-Akrore.

NOTES TO INTRODUCTION

1. Term used for the contact and pacification of Indian tribes.
2. As a television producer, I was more guilty than most.
3. Appendix I gives a rough list of dates covering the exploration of Xingu.
4. Posto Leonardo is named after Leonardo Villas Boas, a third brother who was with Orlando and Claudio on their expeditions. He died in 1961, and the Post, until then known as Capitão Vasconcelos, was renamed in his memory.

I
Xingu

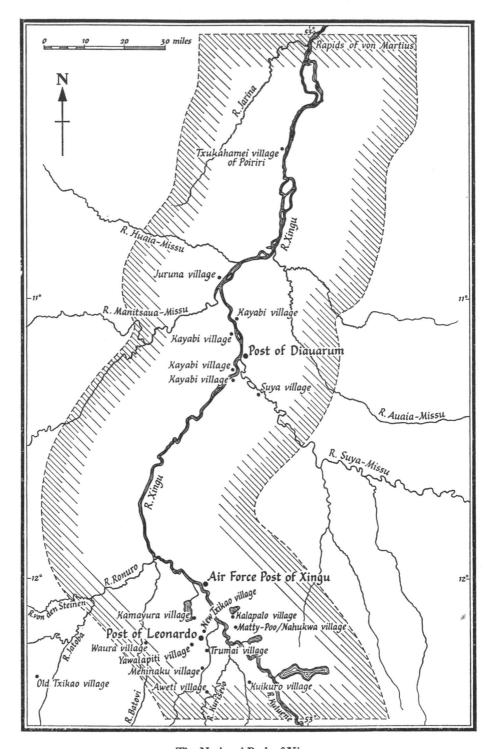

The National Park of Xingu

I*

THE VISIT

In January, 1967, Bruce White, Jesco von Puttkamer and I loaded five hundred kilos of our equipment into a 'plane, standing on the runway at Brasilia. It was the rainy season, and the contrast of the black clouds made the administrative buildings of Brazil's capital look unusually clean and white as we took off. The pilot banked towards the north-west, and after an hour and a half of flight we began passing over the open savannahs of the Serra do Roncador, which the three Villas Boas brothers had been the first to cross. A further three-quarters of an hour brought us to the first dark patches of forest, and in the next half hour we began to pass over the territory of the Xingu National Park. We landed to refuel at the main Post, Posto Leonardo, and later flew on for a further hundred miles to the Parque's northern base, Posto Diauarum.

This Post was then not much more than a score of thatch huts looking across a view of the River Xingu. Claudio had just added an extra hut for us to live and work in, and for the next month we were busy planning and starting the film. Orlando was in Brasilia dealing with the change in administration from the government of Marshal Castello Branco to the government of Marshal Costa e Silva; Claudio was recovering from the very bad malaria of his last expedition.

The Parque's policy has always been to keep the tribes in the jungle and to leave them as undisturbed as possible, and so the Indians only came to the Post when they themselves wanted to. There was therefore little to see, except for an occasional canoe which would come gliding across the water with a request for fishing-line or medicines. Of the Indians living at the Post, half worked for the Parque, and the other ten or twelve were being

---

* To help the reader, the Indians mentioned in Chapters 1–3 are identified in the list on page 52.

treated by Diauarum's nurse, Lotte. The only visitor besides ourselves was Aurore Monod, an anthropologist studying the Trumai tribe.

*   *   *

It was on a particularly rainy morning during our first month in Xingu that a canoe slid into the landing-place and two Indians walked up to Claudio's hut through the mud. They were the first to bring the news that the Kamayura tribe that lived not far from the up-river Post of Leonardo was about to visit Diauarum, but almost immediately we became aware of a strange sense of nervousness that seemed to ripple out from the Post to the surrounding villages in the jungle. For several days canoe after canoe beached on the landing-place and though the visitors would start with a casual remark or two they invariably cleared their throats and said something like:

"Are those Kamayura really coming?"

To begin with it was not easy to understand what was worrying them. But several days of almost continuous talk and story-telling followed, and gradually we too began to live a little in the past. For centuries, Xingu had been a cauldron of invading tribes. The Trumai had come from the south, the Suya had invaded from the west, the Kamayura from the east, and the Juruna from the north. Most of them had been withdrawing from the advancing white man, but where tribe had met tribe they had ambushed, retreated, massacred and defended. The jungle around us was, in fact, little better than a graveyard of extinguished peoples[1]: the Anumania wiped out by the Trumai, the Yaruma by the Kuikuro, the Maritsaua by the Suya.

As the different Indians told their different tribal stories, it became increasingly obvious that many of the massacres were not the result of battle but of treachery. The bowstrings of the Anumania were cut while they were bathing; the Yaruma were held during a wrestling competition so that the other Kuikuro could club them. And the Kamayura—who were about to visit us—had been inspecting the guns of some Juruna, one of the Diauarum tribes, when the rest of the Kamayura beat their weaponless visitors to death. The Kamayura had not been down-river since, and by the end of that week even we could

[24]

appreciate why the motives of the intending visitors should raise doubts in the minds of the prospective hosts.

The only person at Diauarum who seemed unconcerned was Claudio.

"It's what the Parque is about," he said, swinging in his hammock. "When we first came here, it was a struggle to keep the Indians alive, fighting epidemics, trying to defend the land. But that's over for the time being."

Claudio brooded on this for several swings of his hammock.

"Should we keep them in a zoo? Of course not. The Indian must learn to adapt to civilisation. But the disturbing thing about civilisation is not the atom bomb or the computer. It is the *civilizado* himself. One man alone can destroy a tribe's self-respect, unconsciously he can shatter its confidence."

Claudio said that this was especially true of the down-river tribes. They had hidden in the jungle, and had barely met any stranger until they made friends with either him or his brother. The first task was to teach them to adjust to other people, and obviously it was easier for them to adjust to Indians before they tried to adjust to *civilizados*.

"Of course it's good that the Kamayura should come," he ended. "They are more self-assured and sophisticated, and the meeting could be valuable."

For several days after this, Diauarum seemed like a Roman amphitheatre. Here we were, facing the wide sweep of the river, and one day, from behind an island about two miles away, the "lions", so to speak, would appear, paddling their canoes. Of our waiting "Christians" only one[2] of the five tribes of Lower Xingu had not fought the Kamayura before; and day after day, the almost ritual re-telling of massacre and persecution went on. The Juruna had lost virtually all their men during that last visit and another one preceding it. The Suya had been their enemies for almost a century, and in 1960 the up-river Trumai tribe had fled to Diauarum because the Kamayura had been about to avenge a case of alleged witchcraft. Even the Kayabi had had a man murdered on a sandbank early in the 1950s.

And yet, as Bruce and I walked round Diauarum with its airstrip, radio, motors and generator, with its anthropologist, nurse and film unit, we found it impossible to take the tension seriously. The Indians' fear seemed meaningless amidst the trappings of civilisation, and yet—looking back—it is curious that it never occurred to either of us that the trappings of the jungle were equally present. The ring of Macauba palms around the Post was where the vampire bats lived, and only a few months before, the bats had for some reason issued from their caves of decaying palm fronds and in a matter of weeks slaughtered every pig and chicken in Diauarum. Even the black earth of the paths (Xingu's soil is light-brown except in previously inhabited places) was a reminder that Diauarum was once the home of the Suya tribe until unknown raiders rushed out of the jungle and killed every Suya who failed to swim the river.

A few days later, a flash appeared on the southern arm of the river. Canoes lie low in the water and are hard to see, but the moisture on a paddle catches the sun like a mirror. We all drifted down to the shore to watch flash after flash coming down the river. Gradually, we made out several tiny dots that seemed to appear and disappear beneath the water. Eventually they grew bigger and steadier, and resolved themselves into three canoes. They crept down the far bank, swung out along the contour of the flooded sandbank, then caught the current to sweep across the river and on to the landing-place.

Half a dozen men and a few women and children got out. There were packages of food and hammocks, and bows and arrows. It was a typical visiting party, except that the Kamayura themselves were visibly different from the people of Lower Xingu. They wore their hair in a circle round their heads, cut rather like helmets, and they were naked except for bands of cord round their calves and biceps. (In Xingu it is the Indians with the longest experience of civilisation who do not wear clothes, and the most recently contacted tribes that show evidence of *civilizado* influence.) As the Kamayura stepped out of their canoes, they looked lithe, alert, and much more assured than the Indians who were with us on the shore.

"Have you come?" one of the Diauarum Indians asked.

"I have come," the first Kamayura answered. He then walked up the slope to Claudio's hut.

I had met this Kamayura, Takuman,[3] before; in 1958, when he had been the champion wrestler of Upper Xingu, manoeuvring for the chieftainship of his tribe. His father, the old chief, had just died, and he had been involved in the campaign for influence and prestige that is the contest for chieftainship. It is usually a long struggle, requiring subtlety and patience. Now, ten years later, he had passed the summit of his physical strength, but he was still powerfully built and had a shrewd face with eyes that were more aware than those of the Indians of Diauarum.

After a few minutes Claudio came out with Takuman, and allotted the visitors a hut. Thus began the chain of events that was to dominate Diauarum for the next six months. And looking back, probably each of us would say that the hardest thing to understand, in spite of all that Claudio said, was his attitude of restraint. Not many men move more calmly or appear more gentle than Claudio, and visitors occasionally say that he looks like a dishevelled saint. It therefore seems strangely out of character to remember him crouched in the dark, at least once a week, oiling revolvers by the light of a paraffin lamp. The collection of fifteen Colts, Smith Wessons and Walthers represented most of his savings from a very meagre salary of £30 a month. In Brazil, where inflation is chronic and guns have a permanent re-sale value, they are a good investment. But there was a passion in the way Claudio polished and oiled, cleaned and rubbed the metal that seemed greater than a normal investor's care. In a country where men swagger about with their holsters a revolver is an obvious masculinity symbol. But Claudio was unostentatious when he went hunting with his long-barrelled Colt .22 Magnum, knocking bird after bird out of the trees at forty yards. He drew his revolver slowly, clamped his left hand over the right where it held the trigger and butt, and in this undramatic position very deliberately, and with rocklike steadiness, raised his barrel and fired.

The only way I can describe his stance is one of stubborn humility infused with an instinct for violence, and perhaps this was not unlike his handling of the more dangerous tribes. Once, about this time, when a Brazilian magazine published an article about him, he fumed to Jesco:

"He describes me like a mediaeval saint. Like a priest in a Confessional. But this is the jungle, a place of force, where sanctity is just a cloud in the sky. I have rolled on the ground beating men with my revolver, I have . . ."

[27]

He broke off, surprised at his own anger. But I have often wondered since whether Claudio's gentleness needs a setting of violence. Like Gandhi, perhaps he can only be an apostle of non-violence in a situation of threatened volcanic explosion. And if this guess is correct, then it is not so difficult to understand how he may have suspected the outcome of the Kamayura visit, and yet, during the weeks that followed, continued swinging calmly in his hammock, left to right, right to left.

*   *   *

Next morning we watched the Kamayura scrape away at the weeds and leaves in the middle of the Post. In Upper Xingu the villages are built as a ring of huts, and the centre is smooth from the continual movement of dancing feet. The Indians of the lower part of the river are less preoccupied with ceremonial, however, and so the centre of Diauarum was undanced and very much overgrown.

The Kamayura scraped for several hours until a large area was smooth and clean. Then they began to paint each other with the bright red of *urucu*[4] and the black of the forest dye, *jenipapo*. They painted strong rippling designs across their bodies and faces.

Walking to and fro through the Post, the other Indians pretended not to be too interested. Suddenly a Kamayura leant forward, staff in hand, chanting in a sombre voice. He stood in the middle of the cleared patch in the centre of the Post, and then crouching, flailed the air with a *shack-shack*. Before him, another Kamayura pounded a thick bamboo pipe on the cleared and beaten ground. And swooping and dancing, leaping and pirouetting, the Kamayura began to rush in and out with leaves on their arms whirling like birds. They yelped and shrieked in joy, but anyone could see that their faces were impassive beneath the paint.

The air is so clear in the middle of the rainy season that it seems to shine like crystal, and the oiled paints on the Kamayura gleamed and flashed in the sun. Their skirts of straw swirled, their feathers waved and shone. The other Indians watched, and

[28]

there was an occasional rumble of thunder from the rain clouds building up across the river. The chanting grew deeper, the dance more fervent. Here, in the centre of the Post, something like a bright and formal happiness had begun to gyrate above the black earth. Then, finally, the batch of clouds came up overhead, the rain poured down, and the Kamayura stopped to drink the porridge-like liquid which is part of the ritual of the Tawarawana dance.

Takuman, the chief of the Kamayura, had been one of the dancers, and he came over and sat down beside me. He had been very friendly during my first visit to Xingu, and now he seemed to be asking for some sort of sympathy in return.

"We have come to talk hard about that Tuvule." His face looked sombre. "When I sit in my village square, all the Kamayura sit at the other end. When I live in the village, they all go and live in the plantations. That Tuvule makes my life sad. So I have come to say to Claudio 'Let Tuvule be chief. I will go and live with my brother-in-law at the Yawalapiti village.' "

Takuman's huge shoulders were accentuated by a wrestler's sash of coloured cotton, and his face was armoured by two bars of black paint across the eyes and cheeks. His appearance did not seem to fit the resignation in his words.

"Claudio says to me, 'Takuman, you are a great chief. Your father was a great chief. Why are you frightened of a young man?'" The painted snake leapt angrily across Takuman's muscles. " 'Claudio,' I say, 'I am not frightened. I have talked hard to this Tuvule. Do not kill the otter, I say, Orlando says the otter must not be killed.' But Tuvule laughs and lives in the village, pointing and talking about me. All his men have .22 rifles and .38 revolvers. And we have none." (Takuman was talking about Orlando's effort to save the great river otter of Amazonia from extermination—efforts that were frustrated by the workers at the Air Force base in the Parque, who offered the Indians a gun for every skin, and then smuggled them out. Takuman's point was that he was losing influence by supporting Orlando.)

"All Tuvule's men have guns," he added bitterly. "And now Tuvule says they will let the otter live."

[29]

That night I told Claudio what Takuman had said and asked if he would take sides.

"Of course it's a temptation," he snapped. "To interfere is always a temptation. But we must not. Between *civilizados* and Indians, yes—to correct the balance. But between Indians, interfering ends by crushing."

Incensed by the idea, he leant forward in his hammock.

"You know Takuman's father was chief. But do you know that Tuvule's father was one of the greatest chiefs? So his line is purer, and perhaps he will win. What right have I to interfere, just because Takuman is our man?'

Three figures swayed out of the darkness at the other end of the hut, moving to a strange, rhythmic honking, ponderous but also surprisingly gay. When you hear it for the first time, it seems an almost preposterous noise, like an anaconda on a motor-scooter, or like the parrots that sit beside the Xingu and imitate the outboard motors as they go by.

"The lord and owner of rituals, that is a chief," Claudio said. "Takuman made those pipes and he is the best pipe-maker in Xingu. But he cannot punish, he has no power, and what authority there is in the village lies with the head of each hut. The chief is just the head-man with most influence. But when we come to a tribe, we *civilizados*, what do we look for? We look for an important man to be the channel of our business. So, of course, we make him more important in the eyes of the tribe, and eventually he becomes just that—a chief. But in the nature of Indian society, it is not so. And in the long run, our interference harms."

We sipped at tin mugs of Brazilian cane spirit, *cachaca*, and sat there half the night, listening to the sound of the four-foot laughing pipes. Most *civilizados* find Indian music monotonous, but Claudio was deeply stirred.

"What magnificence. How beautiful." His hammock swung with enthusiasm. "I have been here twenty years, and I have never heard *Jacui* like this."

Jacui is the spirit who lives beneath the water, and his pipes are usually sad and sometimes mocking. The pipes may never be seen by women, and that was why the Kamayura were dancing up and down in the concealment of Claudio's hut.

[30]

"I told you the Kamayura are a mystic, devious people," said Claudio. "That is why I know Takuman has not come about Tuvule."

Much later, Jesco, Bruce and I went back to our hut, and across the Post we could still hear the pipes taunting, but growing sadder. Yet when I awoke next morning, the Kamayura were whooping in the dance of Tawarawana. Suddenly the whole thing began to seem too gay, too incessant, too bright and feverish. They had danced all the previous day and had then piped all night. Now they were dancing again. Like a man who stares up at an empty sky, it was the sort of persistence that arouses curiosity. I wondered whether it was to conceal their nervousness, whether it was to persuade the spirits to protect their visit, or whether there could be some other reason.

Whatever it was, in his cleared space at the centre of the Post, Takuman had become a ringmaster, and his audience was already hypnotised. On the black earth of Diauarum he was conjuring up a humming-bird world of light and rhythm, and wherever they were, whatever they were doing, the other Indians were drawn towards his spinning, coloured magic.

Every day in the weeks that followed the tension rose and fell, growing and relaxing according to the clouds in the sky. Early in the morning we would watch these clouds pile up in a great rampart across the other side of the river. Then the water would turn from pewter to slate grey, and as the sky pressed down, the terrific heat became almost unendurable. The "Eiffel Tower" of Xingu, a raised platform with half a dozen petrol drums that provided the Post with water, would make exploding noises as the air in the drums expanded. Gradually, the clouds edged across the river. The water turned jet black and the air became so hot that it seemed as solid as glass. Then—a streak of silver lightning, a rush of black waves, the banana leaves clattering like rattles in the wind, and the clouds would lunge across.

Rain poured down, the dancers ran, the pressure dropped. The dancing always seemed to start in a period of rising pressure and it nearly always ended with sudden, driving rain. This rising and falling tension seldom varied, except when a cloud floated over but did not drop its load of rain. Then the tension held for another two or three unbearable hours.

[31]

The Indians from the other tribes would paddle in from the surrounding villages, watch, move away, and then return to look again. They seemed fascinated and yet uneasy. Pripuri, the Kayabi leader, was standing near me one day when Takuman stopped dancing and came to watch beside us. After a long pause he said to me, but loud enough for Pripuri to hear:

"Pripuri is a friend. When we are canoeing down the river, Pripuri calls to us, 'Come here. Rest in my house.' " Takuman smiled reflectively. "He gives banana and mandioca and potato, and we rest. But we also know that my enemy Tuvule sent a message to Pripuri to kill me." Takuman paused for emphasis. "And so we are happy Pripuri is our friend."

Takuman went back to the dance and Pripuri stood almost rooted to the ground. Claudio said he was the shrewdest politician in his tribe, and that he had been one of his right-hand men in building up the Parque. He had led most of his Kayabi people into Xingu from the rubber-tapping territory of the Teles Pires River, and Pripuri liked to think of himself, with his Biblical ringlets and prophetic face, as the Moses of his people. But Takuman, the Kamayura, came from a more subtle and intricate culture, and we could almost watch him playing with the Indians of Lower Xingu like a snake with a rabbit.

"That relative of yours, a few years ago," I asked Pripuri. "Was it Takuman who killed him?"

"Not Takuman," Pripuri replied. "A relative of his."

As the days grew hotter and the dancing more intense, the atmosphere seemed almost Neapolitan with intrigue and rumour. The Kamayura had asked to visit the Juruna village. But the Juruna had refused because Takuman was a witch-doctor. Pripuri had taken the lead and paid Takuman to witch Diauarum's vampire bats away.

One day, Kaluene, the strongest of the Trumai men, began to put on his paint, and not long after, the whole Trumai tribe was dancing in the cleared space with the Kamayura. The Trumai were the tribe that had fled to Diauarum to escape the Kamayura, and it was Takuman's father who was said to have been killed by the Trumai witch-doctors. Yet in the short time since the beginning of the visit, several Trumai girls had succumbed to Kamayura wooing, and the two old witch-doctors of

[32]

the tribe had succumbed to Takuman's flattery. Only they, Takuman told them, truly remembered the ancient legends; they would be much appreciated in their true and ancient home up-river. The pregnant girl said that in no circumstances was the father of her child returning up-river without her.

The Trumai put on their wings of leaves and their skirts of rushes and danced with the Kamayura. They whooped and chanted, since Tawarawana was really their dance and their spirit. They had originally brought him from the east, and had taught his dance to the other Indians of Upper Xingu. Now these last descendants of a tribe that numbered only twenty, the guardians of an ancient language like no other in South America, were dancing with their declared enemies, the Kamayura. They stamped on the black earth of Diauarum, black from the refuse and blood and buried bones of countless villages before them.

Claudio came out of his hut to watch in the battering sunlight. He was stooping, and he looked worried. If the friendship of the dance could become a friendship of reality. . . .

The only Trumai not there was the witch-doctor's son. He was ill, lying all day in the gloom of his hut crippled with, I think, paralytic arthritis. Indians tend to conceal the sick, much as we hide a corpse. His limbs were wasted into sticks, joined unnaturally by knobs at the knees and elbows, and his father would say: "Every day I have to go out fishing because I have no son to fish."

He called his son ugly and unbeautiful, and we knew that Claudio was watchful in case the father's resentment reached the stage where he might kill. If the Trumai left the village and went up-river, Claudio could not watch so closely.

Across the river, the temper of the clouds was rising, and as the heat beat its way into the body and rose to the eyes, the tension seemed to grow alive within each person. There was Takuman, his face visored in black, his body painted like a leopard. Once the greatest wrestler, now the greatest witch-doctor. What did he seek in this dancing myth?

There was Kaluene, the strongest of the Trumai who could out-wrestle Takuman. He had two Juruna wives, and stole and beat his women. With arms like wings, he looked happy, floating on the music. The Trumai girls danced, with their hair completely covering their faces, and with little rush tails sticking up behind. One of them had a pale skin; she had been kept from the light of day in the traditional six months' seclusion of puberty. But unlike the whirling men, the girls and women in the dance were without colour and almost without movement. With heads bowed they just jogged their legs in time to the *shack-shack*.

The river was like a sheet of plate-glass, so polished that the sun seemed to skate across its surface. The light was so vivid that the Kamayura shone like coloured fire. Everyone was turning and gazing at the clouds, waiting for that first moment when the rain would pour down—an expected but unpredictable release. The tension of all the sky would sheet down into one narrow column of rain. It would drop here, or two miles away. Why? Why, for years, did the chickens increase, until suddenly the vampires massacred them? Why was this Indian struck by magic and that tribe wiped out by disease?

At the time, we explained all the tension as nothing much more than imagination stimulated by the unknown. The arrival of the visitors had released Indian fears inherited from thousands of years of jungle fighting. But since then I have begun to realise that we had also been watching something as close to the ancient pattern of war and festival as we would ever see. And what makes an Indian war hard to understand is our concept of absolute hostility. To the Indian, war is a sport, with trophies for the victor. They spy on an enemy for years, then attack and kill, capture and marry his women. Even when the arrows are flying, there is an almost game-like intimacy between the opponents, and they shout each other's names, learnt from captives or from spying on the enemy. Often the periods of war are interrupted by periods of festival when the enemies dance in each other's villages.

In the great isolation of Xingu, where hundreds of miles of jungle insulate the tribes from each other, war is one human group reaching out to another in the excitement of death. The excitement is increased when you walk in paint and music through the ranks of your enemy. You blaze in colour, vibrate to music, tingle with the imminent possibility of death. And, of course, many of the dances, like the spear-hurling Javari, are merely a sublimation of battle.

War is a communion with other men. So is a festival. And so Takuman danced. And so the Trumai were hypnotised, and danced, too. Until a few days later a distant whoop came floating across the roof of the jungle.

"Suya!" the Indians shouted. "Suya—Suya!"

The Kamayura had asked to visit the Suya village. Now, everyone said, the Suya were coming to Diauarum to forestall that visit. Takuman was a witch-doctor, and one of the endearing limitations of Xingu magic is that the witch-doctor had actually to put his packet of "medicine" in the village to be witched.

Whoop after whoop travelled faintly over the mile of forest between the tributary Suya-Missu and the main arm of the Xingu. Eventually nine canoes debouched into the main river, paddling fast. One Suya, painted red and black, stood up in a canoe waving his hand to blow the rain clouds away; the others whooped and whooped while they paddled, racing to beat the rain.

As they came into the shore, we saw that Javaritu was seated in the bow of the first canoe, cross-legged and red with *urucu*. He was a trusted henchman and ally of Claudio's, reliable, watchful, a man of obvious moral strength. If Kaluene could be called the Achilles of the Trumai tribe, Javaritu was their Ulysses. He had married two Suya girls, and though as a Trumai he could never be their chief, everyone knew that he virtually carried the group by his sense and steadiness.

Javaritu stepped out of the canoe, and soon his deep voice was chanting the Tawarawana, and the Suya were dancing with him. Thus on the bright *civilizado* stage of Diauarum, there were now five tribes—the Kamayura, Trumai and Suya swirling in the dance, the Kayabi and Juruna watching. The sun beat down. The dust rose above the oil drums on the water tower.

Claudio turned to me. "For fifty years," he said, "the Suya hid on their river. From all Indians, from all *civilizados*. When we contacted them, they were so disturbed that they stopped planting. Do you realise what that means? For thousands of years the Suya had planted mandioca—it is the basis of their

[35]

existence. Then we come, and it takes two seasons to teach them to start planting again. That is how cataclysmic was their meeting with strangers, how important it is that they should learn to associate with other tribes."

That night, the Post shook to a new dance, one that was part of the Feast of the Dead. Chanting in deep, rhythmic voices, the Indians moved from hut to hut, round and round the Post. Not only the Kamayura, but also the Trumai and the Suya, who had fought in Upper Xingu and had partly absorbed its culture. And the Juruna and the Kayabi, too, who had no part in that culture at all.

It was a remarkable crumbling of tribal barriers, a merging of isolated and hostile peoples. In face of the approaching white man, it was this inter-tribal hostility that was the Indians' greatest weakness. Now the five tribes danced together from the hut of one tribe to the hut of another, as sheets of lightning flickered in the distance.

So it had been in the last days of the Buffalo on the Great Plains to the north. Desperate, pressed by the white man, the prairie tribes of America had been drawn by the Ghost dance into a common and increasing friendship. For those prairie Indians, the innovation had come too late. For the tribes of the Xingu, we all hoped that it would come in time.

NOTES TO CHAPTER I

1. See Appendix II on extinct tribes.
2. The Txukahamei. They lived too far away from Diauarum to be involved.
3. See *The Heart of the Forest* by Adrian Cowell. Gollancz.
4. A dye made from a seed-pod grown in most Indian plantations.

2

THE KILLINGS

Indians can sometimes dance for a week or even longer, but there are always one or two who slip away to catch fish or fetch mandioca. Amongst those who set out in their canoes next morning were Javaritu the Trumai and Tapiokap the Kayabi.

In the middle of the afternoon, a low wailing began to ebb to and fro across the Post, and when we asked what was the matter, we were told that it came from the wives of Javaritu. They were crying because he had not come back. And no interpretation that I have heard since then has been able to explain why the wives should have been alarmed so early. Many of the other men were still out fishing and, even by sunset, it was unreasonable to fear the worst. Javaritu had spent forty years in the jungle, and was known for his skill and courage.

Next day Aruyave, Javaritu's brother, strapped on his revolver. He lived with us in the "film hut" and looked after the film unit's outboard motors and generator. He picked up Bruce's .22 rifle, and took our boat up to the Suya village, saying that if Javaritu's boat had sunk, his brother would be waiting on the bank; and if he had gone back to the village, he would be glad of a tow.

Aruyave returned that night, but he had seen nothing except a cloud of vultures circling over a sector of the jungle.

Claudio called us to his hut and tried to persuade Aruyave that it was more likely that Javaritu had broken a leg, or had been wounded by a snake or jaguar. He was probably lying helpless in the jungle, and Claudio promised that he would send all the canoes next day, and they would find him. Aruyave and the other Trumai did not argue. They just said that Kaluene, who had left on the same day for the Juruna village, was also dead.

Next morning we all paddled through the forest that separates the Xingu from its tributary, the Suya-Missu, where the ground was four or five feet under water. The river had been rising with every storm, and the water was sliding further and further into the jungle, dark green and mossy. We could see leaves and branches held below, in a strange winter of unfrozen ice, and we paddled weaving between the tree trunks that were nearly jet black with rain. Where a missing person would have left a trail in the dry season, there was nothing to be seen but tunnels of water.

"Don't look for Javaritu," Claudio had ordered. "Look for his canoe. It will be the only sign."

Instead of searching the rim of dry land where the canoe might have been left when Javaritu got out, I noticed that most of the Indians paddled about aimlessly, calling and whooping in the gloom.

"Javaritu!" The paddler behind me burst into a shriek. "Javaritu!" The word banged about between the trees.

"Don't call his name," said a voice out of the tunnel to the left.

"I do not call," was the reply. "I call to his spirit."

We came out at last on to the open grey water of the Suya-Missu, and returned empty-handed in the rain.

At Diauarum Claudio was beginning to face a situation approaching hysteria among the Trumai. Whenever I went to see him, whatever time of the day or night, there were always two or three dark figures in a corner of the hut, and Claudio would be talking to them, his white shirt looking ghostly in the darkness.

"Javaritu was Claudio's friend," one of the Trumai said to Jesco. "But we are weak and other tribes are more important. Claudio will let them kill us."

Aruyave had gone to where the vultures were hovering and had found only a dead tapir, but still the panic grew. The Trumai seemed to be feeding on each other's fears and a single rumour sometimes became a wave of near-hysteria overnight. Next day news arrived that Kaluene, the other missing Trumai, was dead; he had gone to the Juruna village on the morning that Javaritu went fishing, and after beating his wife had

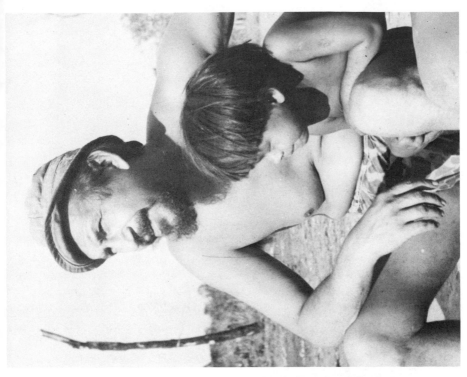

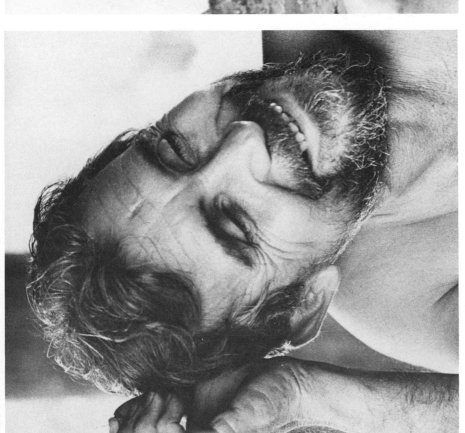

Left Claudio Villas Boas. (*Chris Menges*) *Right* Orlando Vilas Boas. (*John Moore*)

Above Aerial view of River Xingu. (*Jesco von Puttkamer*)
Below The road crossing the Xingu near Diauarum. (*Jesco von Puttkamer*)

Above A village of the Kuikuro, one of the largest tribes on the Xingu reserve.
(*Jesco von Puttkamer*)

Below A Suya family. (*Chris Menges*)

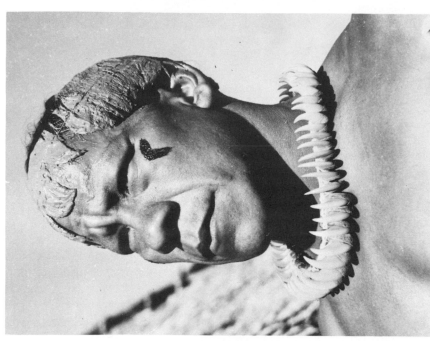

Left Urua flute-dance. (*John Moore*)

Right A Kuikuro leader wearing a necklace of Jaguar claws; his hair is plastered with red *urucu* paint. (*Jesco von Puttkamer*)

tried to seduce a girl in the plantation. A young Juruna boy who was a relative of the girl had hit him from behind with a branch, and had then clubbed him to death. It was a terrible end but an expected one. Several Indians had told us that only Claudio's intervention over the last few months had kept Kaluene from being murdered. But the rumour that came with the news was that the killer had a new .22 rifle, and who could have given it to him but Takuman?

Almost immediately the Kamayura left Diauarum, paddling their three canoes swiftly up-river. That night, shot after shot exploded in the dark.

"Who is it?"

"It's Aruyave."

"What's he shooting at?"

"He is shooting at the night."

During the next few days the little group of Trumai swung from anger to fear and back again, but the only one who seemed likely to act was Aruyave, and he was only eighteen. Whether the killing in the Juruna village had or had not been deliberately provoked, the Trumai had lost their two most effective men. And the sick young chief spoke for all of them when he said:

"We will go upstream. Why should we hide? We will go to our old village and the Kamayura will kill us. We will die in our home."

Claudio countered by talking calmly and confidently. The Trumai were safe while he was there; an attack on the Post was unthinkable. In any case, there was no definite news to indicate that Javaritu had been murdered. As always, Claudio faced the situation quietly. When he was not talking to the Indians, he would be playing with one of the Kayabi children. At other times he lay in his hammock, reading Teilhard de Chardin or Bertrand Russell's *History of Western Philosophy*. And on the occasions when he left his hut he seemed to move absent-mindedly, like an ageing academic. It was not easy to reconcile the role of an explorer with the spectacled, very gentle recluse who was handling the crisis in Diauarum.

That this handling had kept things under control was shown when the 'plane flew in a few days later. Claudio was needed for a more urgent crisis in another part of the Parque, and the

[39]

'plane had come to take him to the Post of Leonardo. Immediately he had gone, most of the Kayabi went back to their village. That night, the tension in the Post seemed greater than usual. The crickets whined, the frogs croaked. When the sun set, the water lay in livid grey and purple patches which seemed to seep and ooze towards the village. The night scene was much as it always was—but no one appeared to be asleep.

The tension was explained when Javari, the second of the two Indians who lived and worked in our film hut, told Aruyave that he knew where Javaritu was buried. Apparently the murderer had talked, and the leader of his tribe had chosen Javari to pass on the information. Next morning, the old Trumai witch-doctor paddled off in his canoe, and later reported to Aruyave:

"It is a small grave. They have cut the head, and the arms and the legs."

That afternoon, a crowd packed into the radio hut at the time for the daily link-up with the Post of Leonardo. Aruyave shouted into the microphone:

"I am going to get the body."

"Aruyave, do you hear me?" Claudio's voice was distorted in the speaker. "You must take Cuyabano or Pripuri." They were Claudio's most trusted men in the Kayabi tribe. He must have hoped they would guarantee the Trumai's safety.

"I will not take one of the tribe that killed him," Aruyave replied.

"That's an order, Aruyave!"

Aruyave's heavy Trumai face became heavier. "That is not an order I will obey."

Claudio had virtually brought up Aruyave since he had been orphaned as a boy, and had great personal authority.

"Aruyave, do you hear me," he repeated. "I order you to obey."

"I do not obey."

The speaker sputtered as Claudio switched off, a hundred miles away, and everyone filed out of the hut.

Next morning, the black earth of a grave was fresh outside the Trumai hut, a deep round hole extended at the bottom so that a body could lie facing east. We assembled by the landing-place, and I saw that all the Trumai had guns. But if it was meant to be a war party, then it was a tragic sight. Here was the entire fighting power of the great Trumai tribe who, a century before, had debouched into Xingu like a horde of Attila. At that time they had had four or five villages. Now their battle strength consisted of Aruyave, two feeble old witch-doctors, a ten-year-old boy, Diauarum's cook, Ahahi, and Sauku, who was in his thirties but a bit simple. There were two outsiders; one was a Juruna who had married a Suya girl and was thus related to the dead man's wives. The other was Petti, a Suya, who, also through the wives, was the dead man's brother-in-law. Aruyave was the only effective man beside the two outsiders.

Aurore, the anthropologist, and I had been asked to go, too, Aurore because she worked with the tribe, and I because Aruyave worked with me. Respecting Claudio's principles, we could not interfere, but at least we would be there to show our sorrow. Years before, Javaritu had been my guide on a month-long trip to the River Batovi, and he remained a reliable, undemanding friend ever since.

Javari was the only member of the tribe that had committed the murder. He had been invited because he had given the news, but I wondered whether he had done this out of friendship, or because the leaders of the Kayabi had asked him to do so—and if the latter was the reason, was it because of some plan of theirs? Or was it Indian fatalism: "We have killed your brother. Come. You may now kill us."

We got into the boat, and using the outboard, towed two smaller canoes up the Xingu. The sky was a brazen blue. On the most distant bank to the right we could see the sun gleaming on a paddle, and once there was a white shirt against the dark line of the jungle. We watched the far-off canoes but they barely moved; they were fishing, or too far away to worry us.

On the right bank of the River Suya-Missu we transferred to the two canoes we had been towing, and set off through a patch of white skeleton trees. Soon we arrived at a lake filled with rushes, a sea of green and yellow grass. In places, the rushes were so thick that we had to pull our way through. Then they opened into wide lanes of olive-green water, and we paddled in white fields of *aguape*, as graceful as lily leaves, curving like the fingers of a Siamese dancer. It is from these leaves that the Suya burn and distil their crystalline salt.

We skirted an area of dry land, and suddenly there was a canoe ahead. As we approached, we saw that it was half-full of water. There were bright patches where chips of wood had splintered from the side. The old witch-doctor pointed.

"They shot him here. He ran there." He knew from the tracks and broken rushes he had examined the day before. I could not understand Trumai, but Javari, who was sitting beside me in the canoe, quietly repeated the version he had heard from the Kayabi.

"This was the fishing-place of Javaritu. He came over from there." Javari pointed to a gap in the rushes. "Tapiokap the Kayabi is in a canoe over *there*, and calls 'Stop. Stop. Come and talk to me.' But Javaritu has fear and paddles away. 'I must catch fish for my nephew,' he says. 'Pah!' Tapiokap raises his .22. 'Pah. Pah.' He shoots two bullets in Javaritu's back. Javaritu falls and the canoe turns into the water. Over there Javaritu stands with the water around his stomach. 'Why do you do this?' he calls. Tapiokap fires two more, here and here." Javari pointed at his chest. "Then the bullets are finished and Tapiokap takes a shotgun. Javaritu calls on Pripuri. He calls on Cuyabano. He calls on all the Kayabi, his friends."

This was the worst part of the story—the thought of Javaritu begging for his life in that shallow swamp. Unlike most Indians, he usually never asked for anything, not even a fish-hook.

"Javaritu calls," Javari went on, "but Tapiokap shoots here," indicating his throat. "And the water swallows him."

This account differed from the witch-doctor's. In his version, there appeared to have been two attackers, and apparently Javaritu fired back. But whatever the details, Javaritu had been shot down without mercy.

One of the Trumai started to wail a moaning chant. The Suya brother-in-law, Petti, sobbed. Aruyave bent to his knees and bowed his head. All the others were silent. Then Aruyave and Ahahi, the only close relatives, began to dig beside some mauve flowers in a patch of jungle that was very bright with sunlight. When the loosened earth released a smell of decay, the other Trumai turned and sat in the canoes. Aruyave and

[42]

Ahahi continued scraping softly with their hoes, answering questions that were called up to them.

"Is the head still there?"

"It has not been cut."

"Are the arms off?"

"The arms are here."

"Is there flesh?"

"The flesh is here."

Apparently it was the possibility of mutilation that had most disturbed the Trumai. Reassured, the two witch-doctors and Sauku paddled away in one of the canoes, and Aruyave continued slowly performing his last duty to his brother. Soon he would be torn between the tribal obligation of revenge and the *civilizado* principle of compassion. It therefore seemed incredible that at this moment he should remember one of Claudio's lessons. He came over to me.

"Is it dangerous to touch?" he asked.

"No, Aruyave. But you should wash afterwards."

He went back to the grave and gently uncovered the body, now black with moisture. He came over to me again.

"Can you give me .20 bore cartridges? I want to make a present to Petti. I have always liked the Suya. Now I hate the Kayabi and like the Suya more."

The men of the Suya tribe, with their large lipdiscs, can appear brutal or frightening at a distance; but they have very gentle eyes, and charming, child-like faces. Petti was standing a few yards away, much more noticeably upset than anyone else, even more than Aruyave, whose face was heavy and did not show much expression. The murdered man was not even a blood relative of Petti's, but Javaritu's commonsense had helped and guided the Suya through the most difficult years of their early contact with civilisation. Like children, the Suya felt helpless and deprived by his death, and tears were running down Petti's face.

The body was wrapped in a red hammock and laid in a canoe. Aruyave got in, and paddled away through the trees and across the expanse of rushes. His voice rose in a strange, wailing chant, that was one of the most tragic and beautiful sounds I have ever heard. An Indian song of mourning is emotion finding instant

[43]

release, a wild and spontaneous sound which can never be repeated afterwards. Aruyave poured out his sorrow as he paddled his brother's body through the waves of rushes and past the nodding flowers of the *aguape*. His song flowed and flowed. It was a spilling tragedy, like the release of blood.

We returned to Diauarum in the boat. The red hammock, with the body, was laid before the grave that had been dug earlier. The Trumai began a ritual yelping that was disturbingly artificial after the mourning song in the canoe. Aruyave widened the grave, and as the body was lowered in, a woman came out of a hut and gave two pancakes of mandioca to be thrown on top. Aruyave turned the black face in the red hammock in the direction of the rising sun, and bent over his brother, one arm shielding his eyes as he started to sob. His free hand slowly swept earth on to the eyes below. Then he moved back, and the others pushed earth into the grave, faster and faster, until it was full, then they pounded it down.

Inexplicably, the tension of weeks vanished. We all felt relieved, and even Aruyave seemed happier. Claudio had often said that the myths and dances of the Indians were a means of dispersing the terrors of life, that ritual is the Indian release from sorrow and affliction. Now all emotion seemed to have vanished. Aruyave was only sorry, he said, that there had not been enough Trumai to perform the ceremonies in full.

*   *   *

Claudio returned to Diauarum a few days later, and he talked night after night, session after session, with Tapiokap. Afterwards he would call us for a drink, and occasionally his frustration showed.

"All Tapiokap says is, 'It was just so, Claudio. In the lake I talked to Javaritu. Then I went and killed him. Just so, Claudio.' 'But that is ugly, man. Is there no better reason?' 'No. I am like that.' 'But that is beast-like, Tapiokap.' 'Claudio, such I am. I am just like that.' "

At these times Claudio would appear at his most controlled and rational. He said that most Indians were quite open about what we regard as their weaker or more evil motives.

"If he's a coward, he just says, 'I was frightened. I ran away.' Or if she's killed a child, she just says, 'I did not want it. I buried it.' The Indian is a more natural man," Claudio repeated more than once. "And we have to remind ourselves of it. He behaves according to his nature, without limit."

It seemed as if Claudio was restating his theories to remind himself that they were the truth, and that no amount of disappointment could modify that truth.

During Pripuri's next visit, we asked for his interpretation of the killing.

"Surely Tapiokap, who is your relative, did not kill Javaritu, who is your friend, just like that?"

"Like that," Pripuri said.

"Isn't it true Javaritu witched Tapiokap's relatives?"

"I have not heard this. But when our people lived on the River Teles Pires, Tapiokap killed many Kayabi." Pripuri held up one full hand and the thumb of the other. Six. "Once he killed a father. He said, 'The son will grow and kill me.' So he throws the son into the rapids and he dies drowning. 'Tapiokap,' I say to him, 'the child was my relative. I, Pripuri, would have raised him in my house. Why did you do it?' 'I do it,' Tapiokap says. 'I did. I am like that.'"

Pripuri then told us about the background to Javaritu's murder.

"This drytime before you came back to Xingu, Cueca comes and says, 'Pripuri, that Tapiokap is going to kill.' So I ask, 'Who will he kill?' He says, 'Whatever one. A Suya or a Trumai.' So I say to Tapiokap, 'Our chief is dead. I, Pripuri, am in the place of a chief. I must say to you, you must not kill. The Trumai like me. The Suya like me. They give me bananas and potatoes. You must leave my village.' Then Tapiokap goes to the other side of the river and builds a house. But when the dancing starts, Cueca comes again. 'Tapiokap is roaming in the jungle,' he says."

Could it have been as meaningless as that? A psychopathic killer roaming the forest, excited by the dancing and the tension?

A few days later, returning from hunting with Pripuri, I arrived at the edge of the forest and peered out through the screen of leaves. There across the water was a sandbank, and I watched a vulture above circling in the sky, spiralling in lazy,

[45]

graceful curves until he pitched his wings up and plop, landed on the golden sandbank. Three vultures were already there. Vultures are normally solitary birds, each patrolling a stretch of jungle, until one locates a piece of carrion, and they follow one another down to feed.

But the sandbank was clear, without a hint of food. Looking up, I could see another ten vultures piled in the sky, all circling like 'planes stacked above an airport. The lowest one would drop and spiral faster than the others. Gradually, vulture after vulture dropped on to the sandbank and sat silent and unmoving.

"Pripuri," I asked, "when the sand has nothing to eat, why do the vultures come?"

Pripuri laughed. "This is their place," he said. "Vultures are such, like this."

3

THE END OF THE TRUMAI

The summer of Xingu is a time of dry days and desert nights, and during this period nothing changed. The rain drained off, leaving the sandbanks clean and yellow, and the duck flew in, calling happily, as if trying to make us forget the tragedy in Xingu. All the sandspits seemed to have their pairs of jaribou storks standing about, like neatly married couples, and even anacondas were easier to see as the water fell and the pools grew clearer.

Towards the end of the dry season, there is a week of light showers which ripen the fruit of the Caju. And it was in this gentle time of the *Cajuinha* that a Kamayura canoe came down the river carrying one of Takuman's more rebellious henchmen called Mapi. He stepped out of his canoe wearing cast-off Air Force uniform, white gym shoes and a light blue forage cap.

"A bad element," Claudio muttered, as we watched. "Always intriguing and hanging round the Air Force Post."

But Mapi proved to be an effective emissary. After months of vacillation the Trumai tribe agreed to abandon Diauarum and travel up-river to join the Kamayura.

"It's not the Trumai the Kamayura want," Claudio grumbled, "but the women. Four beautiful girls, and they are short of women. Takuman will probably have one. She's the daughter of a Kamayura and was promised long ago."

And so the Trumai were about to break up as a tribe. The young men, Aruyave, Ahahi and Sauku were married to Suya women and would have to stay in Diauarum. The girls would go up-river to marry Kamayura. And that would leave two old men, two boys, an old woman and a cripple to continue the ceremonies of the tribe.

"Why does the young chief agree?"

"He says, 'I am going to die. I leave it to my father.' "

"Why does the witch-doctor agree when the Kamayura threatened to kill him?"

"He's a vain old fool. They tell him he is the only one who knows the legends."

If we had not already learnt something of the strange magnetism that links an Indian to his enemy, it would have been a baffling decision.

A few days later Claudio stood on the black mud bank at Diauarum and watched the frustration of years of work for the Trumai. He was lending a canoe. He had given Mapi bullets, fishing-line and other supplies. But it was a bitter moment.

The break-up of a tribe does not necessarily imply the death of its members, but it does mean the end of a culture. And an Indian's vitality is connected with his understanding of himself through that culture. He works and lives, hunts, marries and dances because his ancestors did so before, because his children will do so after. He can live in someone else's village, but, like colonial government, it degrades a man and saps his vitality. For twenty-five years one of the main features of Claudio's work had been the prevention of the very thing that was about to happen.

The Kamayura and Trumai loaded themselves into three canoes. With head shaved like a Buddhist monk, the young chief sat propped between them.

"Goodbye." His face was wry with suffering. "Maybe Tapiokap is roaming there in the middle of the way."

*   *   *

In the weeks that followed, Aruyave occasionally walked about the Post with his .38 strapped to his waist. And one day Tapiokap arrived, as if daring his avenger to kill. Shouting and struggling, Tapiokap had to be rushed off to one end of the Post before Aruyave could get his gun from his hut. It was like a scene from Italian opera, but it led to a killing—and a killing that threatened the Parque's future.

In Javaritu, Claudio had lost a man who worked within the Suya tribe, so it had been the Suya, rather than the administration of the Parque, that was the loser. But Aruyave was one of the three boys who had been virtually adopted by the Villas Boas, and who now ran all the day-to-day administration of the Parque. Everyone hoped that eventually they would become the leaders of some sort of modernised Indian society.

These three boys were Aruyave, Mairewe and Pionim. Pionim was married to Aruyave's sister, and so he was not only Aruyave's brother-in-law but the murdered Javaritu's as well. This gave him an obligation to kill Tapiokap in vengeance. It was a vicious stroke of fate that made the last of the trio Tapiokap's brother. Mairewe was about twenty years old and Aruyave's closest friend, but by tribal custom, if Aruyave or Pionim executed Tapiokap, then Mairewe would be equally obliged to kill them.

And so Claudio went on talking in his hut, week after week. He had deliberately educated Mairewe, Pionim and Aruyave so that they were not divorced from the Indians they were being trained to administer, and, though one part of their minds agreed that it was tragic to kill a fellow Indian, another part reacted in a typically tribal way. A relative's obligation is the elimination of the murderer, and this is essential to the whole pattern of interlocking duties which makes up tribal society.

Claudio seemed very tempted to interfere; possibly he was thinking of removing Tapiokap from the situation by force. For he kept saying:

"Interfere? Certainly not. It's the temptation of all *civilizados*. You see the approaching disaster, and by a swift act of surgery you think you can save the Indian from himself. Then, of course, it's not the Indian who recognises the problem and finds its solution. And the next time the problem appears, he is no further towards solving it. They become the passive morons of civilisation, waiting for decisions to be taken on their behalf. Amazonia is full of them—witless, detribalised, remnants of a once vital people." The policy of the Villas Boas was to interfere as little as possible.

At the end of the summer we flew out of the Parque with Orlando and Claudio to spend six weeks on a government expedition near the mouth of the Xingu, and when we got back Tapiokap was dead.

[49]

"My people are sad," began the Kayabi who told us. "Pionim has killed the brother of himself." (Tapiokap and Pionim were members of the same Kayabi group.) "Pionim took a canoe across the river, and he took a mosquito net to the village. 'Look,' he says, 'Claudio has left a net, but it is too small for me.' So he gives it to the brother of himself.[1] 'Come,' that Pionim says. 'We will go to the Post and I will arrange ammunition for you.' On the way he shoots, then cuts the stomach so the body will lie under the water.' "

On Claudio's order, Pionim and Aruyave were now at the Post of Leonardo, and Mairewe was a hundred miles away at Diauarum. Every day we would hear the killer and his potential avenger talking to each other in the emasculated language of the radio.

"Diauarum calling Leonardo. Diauarum calling Leonardo."

"Leonardo replying. Leonardo replying. All well here. All well. Do you need a doctor? What about supplies?"

The subject that chained them like prisoners to each other was never mentioned.

Once Claudio flew Pionim down for a few hours and asked Mairewe to talk to him in a hut. They wept and embraced and said that they came from the same grandfather. But Claudio kept them apart, and he still went on talking and talking to the other Kayabi.

"That Tapiokap was mad. Just look what lunacy he did among the Kayabi. He killed the father of—" (I didn't catch the name). "Was it with an axe?"

"It was an axe," said Pripuri.

"There, you see, you are lucky to be without him. And now Pionim is sad. He is a Kayabi and talks your language. He is a Kayabi but he cannot talk to the Kayabi. He wants to come to Diauarum, but he cannot pass amongst his relatives. Surely the Kayabi should not kill him?"

Sitting in the dark, I wondered if this time Claudio would succeed, if this would be the occasion when the chain of revenge and counter-revenge would be broken by the Indians themselves. With such justice on the side of Pionim, with so much intelligence in the mind of Mairewe . . .

* * *

The rest of the tragedy had also unravelled itself in Upper Xingu. All the Trumai girls had been married, and though at first the old witch-doctors were honoured guests at the Kamayura village, gradually their hosts forgot to bring even their daily fish and mandioca. The two old men made their way over to the Post of Leonardo.

"Takuman, look at the Trumai," Claudio reproached, when we flew to Leonardo for a visit. "They have no plantation, they have no house. They are no longer a family, and you say you called them up-river to save them from Tapiokap?"

Takuman was wily enough to reverse Claudio's own arguments.

"Claudio, I am an Indian," he said calmly. "Don't talk to me like a *civilizado*."

Claudio persuaded the old men to build a hut and cut a plantation near the Post, and there they are still, a small fragment of a tribe about to pass into extinction.

The incident affected Claudio deeply. For nearly two decades he had been the centre of such spirals of Indian intrigue on which had often hung the life and death of a man or the extinction of a tribe. He was clearly upset by what had happened. Yet when the chieftainship of the Kamayura passed from Takuman to Tuvule, and Tuvule pressed his advantage, Claudio did not give up.

"I am going to Diauarum," Tuvule announced. "I have five young men without women, and we will dance and marry the Suya."

"It's your life," Claudio replied. "This is your land. You go and marry whom you want. But the Suya are like children, and I am not going to let them be overwhelmed. 'Go and dance,' I will say to the chief. 'But don't sit with your mouth open while those Kamayura with their paint and their talk carry off your women.'"

Perhaps Claudio had failed with the Trumai. But the Yawalapiti and Matipuhy now have villages, when they were fragmented groups as far back as 1946. And several other tribes have come as close to disaster, and either Claudio or Orlando have staved off their collapse.

"Save a few families," Claudio once said, "and the tribe has a chance. Look at the Juruna. Down to twenty, ten years ago, and now Jibaoh alone has eleven children."

NOTE TO CHAPTER 3

1. He would not mention Tapiokap by name.

INDIANS MENTIONED IN CHAPTERS 1 TO 3

Ahahi Trumai relative of Javaritu married to a Suya girl. Worked as cook at Diauarum.
Aruyave Young Trumai trained to help run the Parque. Javaritu's brother. During this period worked for the film unit.
Cueca Kayabi. Relative of Tapiokap.
Cuyabano Kayabi leader.
Javari Young Kayabi who worked for the film unit. Told Aruyave where his brother's body was hidden.
Javaritu Middle-aged Trumai married to two girls of the Suya tribe. Killed by Tapiokap.
Kaluene Young Trumai married to two girls of the Juruna tribe. Killed by a Juruna.
Mairewe Young Kayabi trained to help run the Parque. Brother of Tapiokap.
Mapi Kamayura sent by Takuman to bring the Trumai tribe up-river.
Petti Influential man in the Suya tribe. Brother of Javaritu's wives.
Pionim Claudio's principal Indian assistant. A Kayabi, and brother-in-law of Javaritu. Killed Tapiokap.
Pripuri Influential leader in the Kayabi tribe.
Sauku Trumai, married to a Suya girl.
Takuman Chief of the Kamayura tribe. Instigator of the visit to Diauarum.
Tapiokap Middle-aged Kayabi. Killed by Pionim in vengeance for killing Javaritu.
Tuvule Replaced Takuman as chief of the Kamayura.

Appendix II, page 225, gives a list of the tribes with brief notes about each.

4*

THE TXUKAHAMEI

The Txukahamei are the least complicated and at the same time the most carefree people of the Xingu. After the months of intrigue with the Kamayura, it was like a holiday to set out for their village.

Our boats roared down the river, past the Kayabi village with its great plantations, and past the huts of the Juruna, yellow on their bluff. Yells floated from one river bank to the other, and the Indians with us yelped and yodelled (a euphemism) as we rushed through the water.

"To the Txukahamei! AAAaaaayyyeeeee! Txu-ka-ha-mei!"

For a whole day we passed through a tangled wilderness of lakes and islands. A herd of wild pig trotted away from the sound of our motor; an Indian in the bows of our boat caught a swimming deer, held it up for Bruce to see, and threw it back. Alligators yawned, egrets flapped, ducks clattered, jacubim lounged and watched us pass. On every side the river was rippling away to the rim of the jungle, making it look like a dark and limitless land. And if anyone is the master of the unknown lands of Southern Amazonia, his name is "Txu-ka-ha-mei!"

The nomadic Txukahamei tribe once ranged five hundred miles from the River Araguaia across the River Xingu as far as the River Tapajoz, plundering everyone and everything they encountered. Under their frontier name, the Kayapo, they were the most feared tribe in Amazonia, and between 1943 and 1953 they killed so many rubber-tappers that the trade on the Lower Xingu is said to have fallen by ninety per cent. But the Villas Boas made peace with them in 1953, and one of their main groups eventually settled in the Parque at the village of Poiriri.

* The Indians mentioned in Chapters 4-7 are identified in the list on page 84.

[53]

Now, behind some cases of Jesco's equipment, there was a huge locked crate in the stern of the boat that held presents for the Txukahamei. Seated on top, delicately shading his lipdisc from the rays of the sun by means of a red and yellow golfing umbrella, was Rauni. He was Claudio's right-hand man among the Txukahamei and an old friend of both myself and Jesco.

I had first met Rauni in 1958, soon after the Villas Boas had made peace with the tribe. Orlando had persuaded two of the younger men, Rauni and Bebcuche, to visit his Post and learn Portuguese, and it was they who helped introduce me to the jungle—who taught me to "search for the little bees and gorge with honey", to kill the tapir and eat "'til sick". I had also gone on a long journey with the Villas Boas to visit one of the nomadic sections of their tribe, and there Bebcuche had said:

"When you come back we will catch the trail to the other Txukahamei that quarrel with us. We will tell them we are savage no more. Then all Txukahamei will live together, and we will sing the song of corn, and the song of water, and the song of the puma, and there is much beautifulness, and we will slaughter the Kuben Kran Kegn[1] dead."

Now I was back, and Rauni told me that it had been the Kuben Kran Kegn who had slaughtered most of Bebcuche's group, and that Bebcuche, together with his brother, had been mercilessly shot down by a prospector on a journey to the east. Bebcuche had been something of an elder brother to Rauni, and, to a much lesser extent, to myself. To change the subject Rauni held out his hand. "Pass the sunburn cream."

There was a pause while he applied a white film round the outer strip of his lips, which held his wooden lipdisc very much like a rubber band. The saucer-like disc stretched his lip more than six inches in front of his face, and it was therefore very exposed to sunburn.

"Do you think I should operate my lip?" Rauni spoke like a woman applying lipstick. "Krumare says the *civilizados* will laugh."

I asked why that should matter.

"When I am treating," Rauni said seriously, "it matters. With *civilizados*, treating is better if they do not laugh."

Rauni finished applying the cream, and probably to divert

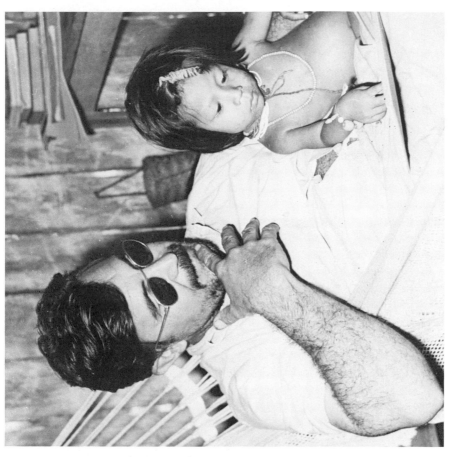

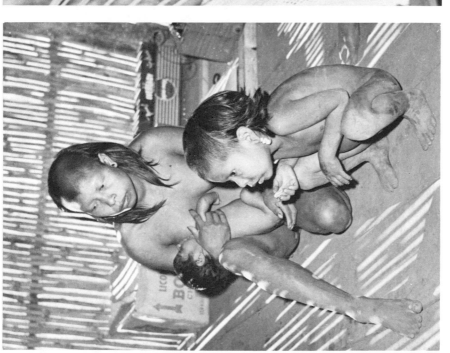

Left Diauarum: Txukahamei mother brings sick child to dispensary. (*Jesco von Puttkamer*)

Right Diauarum: Claudio with Indian child. (*Jesco von Puttkamer*)

Above A Kamayura canoe on Lake Ipavu. (*John Moore*)

Below Txukahamei mourning by a grave in the jungle (p. 59). (*Jesco von Puttkamer*)

Above left Javaritu, a Trumai killed by Tapiokap. (*Jesco von Puttkamer*)
Above right Pionim, a Kayabi, killed Tapiokap to avenge his brother-in-law. (*Adrian Cowell*)
Below left Rauni, a Txukahamei, Claudio's right-hand man. (*Pilly Cowell*)
Below right Bemotire, a white Brazilian captured as a boy and adopted by the Txukahamei. (*Chris Menges*)

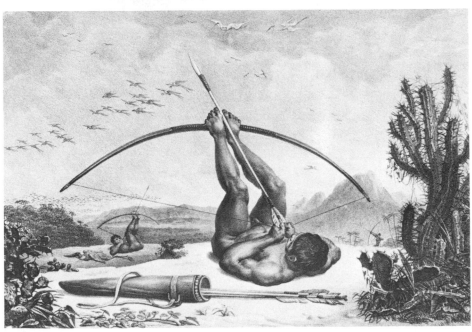

Above A Kamayura fishing with bow and arrow. (*Jesco von Puttkamer*)
Below Indian shooting with his feet (p. 76). (*Drawing by J. B. Debret—British Museum*)

my attention as the tube went into his pocket, he pointed at a little clearing on the western bank.

"See where the otters have worn the bank. Two rains ago, the skin-hunter who is camped there shoots with his .44." (The 1870 Winchester repeater which is still the standard weapon in the Amazon.) " 'Why do you shoot at a civilised Indian who has been to Rio de Janeiro?' I call from my canoe. And then when we are having coffee, I kill him with my paddle and take his .44."

As Rauni said this, his white "lipstick" and dark glasses looked particularly unnatural. Earlier on, the pink shirt and golfing umbrella had matched the warmth of his character, but now his eyes had grown beady and frightening, and it was a real shock to be reminded of the hybrid personalities that civilisation and the jungle breed along their frontiers. But the unusual thing about Rauni was that he knew exactly the impression he had made, and I could see the humour and deep intelligence with which he was watching me.

*   *   *

When our boats ran into the Txukahamei village at the end of the two days' journey, Rauni led Bruce and me up to the central square. We could hear the coughing and spitting that means an epidemic, but Rauni took no notice. Without a word he swept his arm in a circle, taking in the score of log and thatched huts.

What we saw would have been a cluster of shabby huts to most people, but Rauni and I knew that I had last seen the Txukahamei in a nomadic camp of flimsy shelters. Now thatched roofs kept out the rain, reducing the chances of pneumonia. There were hammocks and wooden platforms, so no-one slept on the damp earth. Nets kept out the mosquitoes, there were blankets for the cold nights. Pigs, chickens and ducks chased each other round the village square; there was even an optimistic lemon sapling. And where the Txukahamei had once scavenged for food to survive, returning only occasionally to small, haphazard plantations, now they grew crops on a large scale. They had steel axes, hoes, machetes—and it seemed to us that they

[55]

had lost all sense of agricultural proportion. They grew two or three times as much as they could eat.

"Corn, mandioca, potatoes, rice, beans, melons, sugar-cane, pumpkin, peanuts, bananas . . ." Rauni seemed to repeat the litany three or four times a day. They had also learnt to use canoes and fishing-line, and caught ten times as much fish as before. Guns trebled their consumption of meat.

To a casual glance this settlement was a primitive village, but we realised that what Rauni was showing us was that the nomads had passed through a more violent revolution in their first decade than anything that the future could bring. And I also realised that since Orlando and Claudio never forced change on a tribe, this amazingly swift transition—for Indians—must have come from the leadership of Rauni. Bizarre he might appear, but for his two hundred people on the brink of an alien world, he obviously had some of the importance of a Peter the Great.

*   *   *

That evening, the coughing roared as we moved through the village behind a flailing brand that sparked and lit the way with flame. As each cough exploded, it set off its own chain of reaction from hut to hut. The sound of 'flu was everywhere— the high treble hack of children, men booming with a deeper sound, and a sharper, willowy bark from women.

As we entered a hut, someone would throw dry palms on to the fire, and a dozen faces would be lit up by the flame. Those with shivering fits lay in the ashes by the fire; those burning with fever poked their heads out of dirty blankets, their eyes dead, their faces slack. Some shivered so much that their lipdiscs quivered like leaves in the wind. Some of the children's faces had been so softened by fever that it was difficult to tell boys from girls. Mothers lay on their backs surrounded by pieces of potato or crushed banana, where they had obviously tried to feed some child and failed.

It had always seemed to me that the great beauty of Indians flows from their natural animal grace, and so the epidemic gave a terrible impression of despair. Influenza deadened their vitality. Malaria burnt in their eyes. Pain slumped their limbs

[56]

into unnatural positions. Some were even too apathetic to crawl into a hammock, or to brush the dust from someone they cared for.

We moved from hut to hut, taking temperatures and jabbing injections. Jesco had fought many epidemics during his seven years with Indians, and, ear pressed to a sick woman's back, he listened for the first bubble of pneumonia. A calabash of water for those with fever. A potato or bunch of bananas for others whose fevers had dropped.

"Has she had fever, Rauni?"

"Only this morning. Now she coughs, and says she has pain. Give *Aralem*."

Aralem is a suppressant for malaria, which usually comes out with 'flu. But our *Aralem* was in the form of pills, and it was not popular with the Txukahamci, who prefer injections because they hurt and accordingly must be effective. When someone on the verge of pneumonia had to have antibiotics—also pills—we bribed them with nose-drops. With a showman's gusto, Rauni would squirt the drops into surprisingly submissive, upturned nasal holes. They were deeply appreciated.

Claudio sometimes says that the main problem with an Indian epidemic is the loss of the will to fight. The Indians feel the evil is too strong to resist and they give up the struggle. Our battle was thus psychological as well as physical, and it was important that manifestly *civilizado* remedies should be used to fight the *civilizado* disease. The Indians examined every piece of medicine paper, every coloured packet we threw away, and these were nearly as important as the drugs they had contained, and the comfort we offered. In such a campaign, nose-drops play their part.

The morning round usually took three to four hours, and then we would return to our hut, where convalescent Indians sat on a carpet of discarded pill papers, waiting for a meal of rice and beans. Medicines soon ran out, and we sent the boat up to Diauarum for more. Unfortunately there was little chance that it could get back in less than five days; and it seemed like a miracle that afternoon when we heard the distant hum of a 'plane. Almost shouting with joy we ran to the air-strip. The scarlet 'plane came roaring down the river and circled the air-

[57]

strip, but as it continued to circle and circle, we realised that to the pilot it looked too wet to land. Suddenly the 'plane tilted its wing over the jungle, and we stood and watched it fly straight back, into the grey distance.

Soon after, we were called to a woman lying on the ground, blood spewed right across the floor, her limbs writhing in the pool. Suddenly her stomach convulsed in spasms, and she began to groan deeply. In complete despair I thought of the 'plane, and the doctor who had probably been in it.

A final groan, a last desperate spasm, and the body stiffened.

"Dead," said Rauni, in a matter-of-fact tone. He stood up and went out. But Jesco held the woman's hand in his own, and after about twenty minutes her breathing became noticeable. Within an hour she was sitting up, and there we were in that Indian hut with no idea of what had been the matter, or whether it would return, or whether there was any treatment that could help if it did. Probably no role is more desperate than that of the *civilizado* given absolute trust by Indians, who does not possess the knowledge or the means to meet that trust. It is no coincidence that people like the Villas Boas brothers started their life work in just such a situation.

That evening, another desperate case. A young girl held her son in her arms and coughed black blood on to the floor as we watched. Beneath the hammock the pool of blood looked ominous.

"The wild sickness," said Rauni sadly. The girl was very beautiful.

"It's the fast TB," Jesco agreed. He had seen a lot of it amongst the Karaja tribe, two hundred miles to the east.

By evening the girl was lying in a complete coma on her back, and as we were going to examine her, someone called us to the other end of the hut. Another woman had blood pouring from her nose, and when she tipped back her head, the blood spouted from her mouth.

"This is not that wild sickness," said Rauni. It was humiliating that we, the *civilizados*, could only hope that his diagnosis was right.

Later that night the coughing increased as the air grew colder, and we were about to go back to look at the girl a third time when a high-pitched wailing rose above the village. A sudden silence: not a voice, not a movement. But only for a minute. Then the usual ripple of coughing rose to a crescendo.

Next morning the girl was lying on the ground, her narrow, athletic body and young breasts tragically beautiful, but curving inwards and empty. Her teeth were bared in an inane grin. She was carried in a hammock slung under a pole, and her legs swung to and fro, left and right. Her husband was standing in a deep hole he had dug in a forest clearing, and on either side of his feet a tunnel had been dug out from the hole, so that she could lie straight and extended. Without a word, the body was lowered into the husband's arms, and he laid it in the tunnel. He then climbed out and began to drop her possessions into the grave.

"They throw her pot," Rauni explained. "Then afterwards they do not see it. They throw her mat. Then afterwards they do not see it. They throw her comb. Then afterwards they do not see it."

The husband cracked open two or three gourds and let the bits drop into the grave. He scattered a handful of red and yellow feathers, the pathetic jewels of a feminine life. Then a few handfuls of unspun cotton. And that was all. The traces of the beautiful girl, whom we had seen holding her son so desperately, were gone. Logs were laid over the hole, and with grave faces, but without a tear, the husband and the dead girl's elder sister piled the earth into a mound. The machete she had used in the plantation when she took on the responsibility of a wife, only a few months ago, was stabbed into the nearest tree, and on it was hung the basket in which she had carried the food for her family.

The clearing was about twenty yards in diameter, and contained half a dozen similar mounds.

"It's for children and girls only," said Rauni. "The men are in another place."

I had seen these mounds of the nomads beside some of the trails in the forest. When the Txukahamei approach during their nomadic journeys, the wife or son or granddaughter of the dead person goes to the grave and clears back the encroaching jungle. The mourner crouches beside the grave, bends his head

[59]

and stays for a day. There is no Indian who feels more love than a Txukahamei, or who shows a more real sense of grief.

On the day after the girl was buried, there were crossed arrows round her house. Her old father had shaved his head and, feeble-limbed and shaky, was staggering up the path carrying a bucket. Nobody, according to custom, might help. Over the next two weeks we watched him and his grandson becoming more and more dependent on each other, the old man breaking potatoes for the boy, the child rolling and playing round his grandfather.

The epidemic had passed its climax. As if the disease had worked itself out in the single death, everyone seemed to be getting better. A 'plane landed, the boat returned with medicines, and another boat brought Lotte, the Diauarum nurse. Within six months, Dr Noel Nutels and his National Tuberculosis Service cured the TB among the six Txukahamei who were discovered to have it.

This was all very much in the pattern of the Parque, which has fought Brazil's most successful campaign to keep the Indians alive. In 1946, when the brothers first arrived in Xingu, twenty-five Indians died in a single epidemic, and the population was falling at a terrible rate. Now a death is rare, and Xingu is the only Indian area of Brazil where the population of a whole group of tribes is on the rise.

But success is an ugly word when someone in your care has died, and though we were not responsible for the epidemic, some *civilizado* was.

"If the *civilizados* are friends," Rauni asked, "why do they bring disease?"

Sometimes I have been asked, in Brasilia and São Paulo, how I can ignore some of the obvious faults of the Villas Boas brothers. And the reply that usually comes first is that if Claudio occasionally drinks, and Orlando cracks with temper, then this is not merely the result of twenty-five years of jungle hardship. Worse is the burden of helping Indians when you, the curer, inevitably carry disease, when you, the protector, are by your *civilizado* nature bound to begin a process of disillusion and disintegration. After a quarter of a century of such self-imposed strain, the cracks will show.

*   *   *

[60]

A few weeks after the epidemic, we were filming in the jungle when a little boy ran up to Rauni, shouting. Rauni listened, his face grim.

"That Karinhoti," he muttered. "He wants to be savage with Txukahamei." He snatched a huge branch from a felled tree. "Now Txukahamei will be savage with him."

"Hey, the Caraiba are filming."

"Film Txukahamei fight," Rauni growled, as his shirt and trousers came off. He roared away with his club like a galleon about to loose a broadside. We panted along in his wake.

A band of Txukahamei rushed from one side of the village and swept into a hut. There is something about their aggressive, wide-footed, slamming stride that is like the mechanical movements of a pack of piranha. You know by instinct that they will hurl themselves quite blindly at their foes, smashing, tearing, clubbing in a way that no other tribe in Xingu will do.

The chiefs were in the square, shouting and gesturing. Groups of men milled in and out of the huts, long clubs and sword-sticks held on the right shoulder in a pre-strike position. They were black-faced with soot, flat-eyed with kill-glaze. Incredibly, it had begun—according to Rauni—when the daughter of Kumoy had hit the little daughter of Karinhoti. Karinhoti was the chief's son-in-law, but he was from the other village on the River Iriri. The respective mothers had immediately scratched and slapped each other, until Karinhoti grabbed a pestle and struck at Kumoy's wife. She ducked to protect her child, and was hit by two blows on her back. Kumoy leapt at Karinhoti, and they struggled out of the hut and into the village square. Then Karinhoti's two brothers ran up with clubs and beat at Kumoy until he was flat on the ground, coughing blood. Karinhoti jumped back into the hut, a line of Kumoy's relatives ran forward, and Karinhoti raised his gun.

It was a recurring moment in Txukahamei history. At the end of the nineteenth century most of the Kayapo bands had been grouped on the River Araguaia under the rough suzerainty of Pombo, the great chief of the Gorotire tribe. Quarrels frequently broke out, and some flared into civil war. The Txukahamei split from the Gorotire. A few years later the Gorotire lost the Kuben Kran Kegn, and Claudio was there when

[61]

Kretire's group ambushed five or six men of Kremuro's. Recently, Kremuro's faction had returned to the Kuben Kran Kegn, who killed a dozen of them because Kremuro had slaughtered several dozen of the Kuben Kran Kegn two decades before. And so on, through a host of Indian groups and hundreds of unpronounceable names. Thus the horde was scattered over the jungle, and thus it could happen in this Txukahamei village again.

But this time the chiefs were shouting, and no one was actually fighting.

"What do they say, Rauni?"

"They say it is not beautiful to fight at the head." (Clubbing between Txukahamei should be limited to the chest and arms, so only bones are broken.) "It is not beautiful to kill with guns. Now there are only a few Txukahamei. If we kill our brothers, then the *civilizados* will kill the rest. 'It is not beautiful to fight at the head,' the chiefs are saying."

The groups were still moving from hut to hut, shouting and holding their clubs. Then Karinhoti and his two brothers ran into the jungle. Some time later, Karinhoti's wife, baby on hip, pipe incongruously in mouth, went striding after them.

"She will bring them back," Rauni said, from the experience of three marriages. "Maybe after tomorrow."

"Will you kill them?"

"Once we kill," Rauni agreed. "Once we go to the Juruna tribe—kill. Once we go to the Suya—slaughter. Once the Txukahamei of Kretire kill the Txukahamei of Kremuro."

These were the two chiefs currently shouting in the square.

" 'But see,' Claudio said to us, 'the Indians are few. Look and you see they are dying.' So all the chiefs talk to all the chiefs. For a long time we talk, and afterwards we say, 'Claudio is right. We kill no more, not Txukahamei, not Juruna, not Suya.' "

The astonishing thing was that what was certainly the most feared tribe of Xingu, the slaughterers of entire villages in the past, had not touched a single Indian from another village since their settling in the Parque. They still killed invading prospectors and skin-hunters, but the Txukahamei had somehow widened and deepened their consciousness of the group to cover all the tribes in the Parque, and even the *civilizados* brought in by the Villas Boas brothers.

All night the chiefs shouted.

"Hear my talk. My talk is good talk."

They leant on staves and called out the "good talk" from the centre of the square to the huts around them in the dark. Rauni only called once, since he was not a chief by lineage, and had never learnt the ritual language of the strong talk.

"This land is our land," he called. "These people are our people. Before this time the Txukahamei fought each other. Now at this time the Txukahamei are few."

During most of the night Rauni moved from group to group, talking and arguing, and I could not help but be amazed by the change in the young man who, ten years before, had done little more than hunt and play practical jokes. ("Adriano, I have brought you a present of wild honey. Here it is—in your hat!") If our current visit to Xingu was exposing an ugly streak in tribal life, it was certainly also teaching me that there is no adaptation and no challenge which some Indian cannot meet.

A few weeks later Claudio arrived at the Txukahamei village, and Karinhoti, who had lifted the gun, sat beside his hammock, tears pouring from his eyes. Rauni sat behind and translated into Txukahamei.

"Tell him he's a fool, Rauni. Are there too many Txukahamei that he wants to kill them? Does he need no friends to hunt with? Tell him to fight no more, but when I call him, he can come and maybe we must fight together."

A year later Karinhoti joined our expedition, and he formed one of the party that entered the village of the Kreen-Akrore.

NOTE TO CHAPTER 4

1. A related tribe in the North.

5

THE FRONTIERS OF KILLING

During the months that followed, we went to the Kuikuro for the great festival of Javari, and flew to the river Jatoba, where Claudio rescued the Txikao from a horde of invading prospectors. We hunted with Pripuri's pack of eccentric dogs, and once we travelled to some rocks near the rapids of von Martius, where the Juruna said a black leopard lived under the water, coming out only to growl at anyone who passed. (It failed to growl at us.) Sometimes we hurried back to the Post with Indians who were sick, and once—when land-developers arrived close to the frontier of the Parque—we towed the whole Suya tribe away in their canoes. When we were in one of the more distant villages, a note would often arrive from Claudio:

Diauarum, 26th August.

Adriano,

Please distribute what I am sending in the boat. Nails. The small ones for Krumare. The big for Me-ure. Salt. A sack for each head of house. 16-bore cartridges. For Neitu. Tell the rest not to shoot at every little beast in the jungle. We have no more ammunition and there will be a delay 'til more arrives. 10 machetes. The chiefs know who have not got them already. The wire and fishing-line are for anyone who wants them.

Claudio.

During that year, as we travelled from one end of the Parque to the other, I gradually realised that my impressions were completely different from those of my first visit. In 1958, I had been almost hypnotised by the beauty of Indian life, and by the skill and freedom of their existence in the jungle. I heard little and asked nothing about war and murder. But during this visit I was beginning to learn that the Indian's attitude to killing is one of the central problems of the Parque, and the key to the blending of different tribes into a common society. Slowly this began to grow into something like a fixation or obsession in my mind.

*   *   *

About half a mile beyond the Txukahamei camp the men collected by the path in the jungle. It was a grey dawn and they carried guns and clubs and ammunition tied in little packets of banana leaf that hung down from cords around their naked waists.

"Follow my good example." The chief's voice sounded heavy. "Some go here. Some go there. Go, catching the paths made by the game. Run calling one another, following the track of the pig. Slaughter tapir. Bring back the tortoises. Kill, and look well to yourselves."

There was a roar, and the men scattered into the trees. Suddenly our group hurtled after pig, vanishing like a bullet; and it was only an hour or two later that we managed to find another group digging for armadillo. Red earth had vomited over the clearing like pus round a wound, and the shaft was, incredibly, four yards deep. A man with a stake was tunnelling in the hole, and the others were energetically hauling earth out with baskets they had made on the spot. It was amazing that so little meat could attract so much industry. As the digger got close, the armadillo tunnelled further into the earth, so the digger stabbed and stabbed at where he thought it should be. Eventually the stake penetrated, and the armadillo was hauled up in a basket. It had a friendly, inquisitive face, and its shell was like overlapping Japanese armour. They cut off the tail first, then delicately slit away the tissue joining its shell to the body, and gradually the armadillo recovered consciousness. Its legs waved, its body arched, and when the shell fell away, it stood up and staggered off, its flesh obscene and red.

The Txukahamei barely seemed to notice. One or two laughed, but there was no hint of pleasure in its pain. It was

[65]

just outside the limits of their comprehension that pain in anything else was a matter of concern to them.

*   *   *

"A terrible thing has happened, Adriano." Claudio was very upset. "It's a bad thing to tell about Indians, but it will help you understand. There was a boy in the Yawalapiti tribe called Pooyoo, twelve or fourteen years old. Perhaps he was a little unbalanced. He broke someone's pot and killed a pet. But that's never important. A strong and handsome boy like Kaluene could do much worse. But Pooyoo's parents were dead and people were complaining. So, when the men were away, the women put him in a grave, and painted him with *urucu*, with feathers on his arms and head. The boy didn't resist, but he said he didn't want to die. Then the woman who raised him said, 'Go and see your father. He is a long way away,' and she threw the first earth into the grave until they had covered the body, leaving his face open. 'I don't want to die,' the boy repeated, but the woman said again, 'Go to your father,' and filled the grave.

" 'How could you do it?' I said to the Yawalapiti who told me. Now he thinks about it, he weeps. He says all the men were out of the village, and maybe they would not have let it happen. But I know there were two men in the village, and when I asked them, they just said, 'What is it to do with us?' It's terrible, but can you accept that the motive was probably that the boy had no mother and father. Not because of the food they had to give him, or because he killed animals. That's not important for Indians. But to have no family is unnatural and ugly. Sometimes, when they come to kill a witch-doctor, he just calls, 'Come. I have no beautifulness. I have no brothers or children. You may kill me now.' And they do. Remember, Adriano, this is the jungle and to kill a deformed child—to abandon the man without family—can be essential for the survival of the tribe. It's only now that the jungle is vanishing, and its laws are losing their meaning, that we are shocked."

*   *   *

"Let us sing the song of one who has blackened himself for war. Let us shout Woooo, so the white man will fear."

[66]

Bemotire was a white man who had been captured as a boy by the Txukahamei. They had killed his Brazilian family, but had brought him up to be a war leader against the whites. Now he was standing in the centre of the village, chanting about the great raids of his youth.

"Over there, in the centre of the village, is a big Txukahamei." Bemotire pointed at an empty part of the village. He was obviously referring to the Txukahamei village of his youth. "There the Txukahamei is making great pictures of himself. He is bragging, just standing there. He will not smell the path. But I will go kicking down the grass, singing the song of war. So we go, and go sleeping [spending nights on the trail]. And when the sun is sitting on the low side, and our feet hurt, we arrive at the elbow of the Pgoro River. I put tobacco and fire in my pipe, and then I hear 'Tok', and 'Tok', 'Tok', 'Tok'.

" 'Is that them?'

" 'Yes, it is them.' And Moy-no comes running. 'Over there the forcigners are cutting wood for house.' So I go wrapping up [creeping round] the house, and already they are working the walls of the house. It is in the middle of a brightness [an open space in the jungle]. More men come along the path with palm branches for the roof. Then the white men hang themselves up in their hammocks, sleeping. So I say to the Txukahamei, 'Let's go and wait, sitting 'til tomorrow. Then when they go to the forest we will get their guns and kill them. Let us eat and be heavy-fleshed and strong.' So I go and kill a bird with an arrow, Moy-no gets sticks, Preure is making an oven, and Katokre cuts a vine and drinks the liquid. Then we sleep.

" 'Get up. Hurry. Let us wash ourselves in water, and paint ourselves with black. I will make myself fierce.' I go to the brightness and there stands the foreigner making something new. He isn't gathering rubber. He is making something new. 'Kruk' and the foreigner falls in the middle of the brightness. He rolls round his eyes and they do not see. 'Ko. Ko. Ko.' A chicken startles me. 'Wap. Wap,' a dog goes barking. Then I get a gun and put seed [ammunition] into it. Afterwards I take a wide-blade knife. Then Preure comes. He says, 'Always in vain I have wanted a little gun.' So I give him the revolver.

" 'With this flat seed weapon,' Preure says, 'I will kill one.'

[67]

Afterwards, when the sun is hanging high, Moy-no comes running. 'They are killing your uncle, Katokre.' So I run. I go shouting, 'Shall I kill the white man on the trail? Yes. Yes.' The white man, shooting off his gun. I shoot from the bushes, and he runs and falls. His blood is falling black. 'Get his leg there, Preure.' But the foreigner kicks it away and is free. So I go shouting. I go making myself wild. 'Tok. Tok.' He falls. His blood is falling black. He falls and his eyes do not see any more. Then I go walking, shaking the grass, and I see blood. Katokre is bleeding. Moy-no says, 'Look here. Look at Katokre. They have killed your uncle. He fell and lies there kicking, twisting like a cord on a bow.' I blow tobacco on the wound. I sit close to him with all my hearing and all my listening [in sympathy]. And he is kicking and then quiet. Quiet. He has died and is quiet. Then I cry in loving and longing.

" 'Let's bury my uncle in a clear spot before the white men come.' But Preure says, 'No, let us let him lie in the sun for the vultures. So they will eat him. Later we will come and take the bones to the village.' So I say, 'There lies my uncle in the clearing. Lies for the vultures to dry his bones.' "

*   *   *

"Look round this camp," Claudio said, "and you will see Indians are more loving than we are. But the expression of their love is confined to the limits of this society. They cut a hole in the wilderness to contain their family, but outside this camp is the jungle where they kill meat for food, bamboo for arrows, leaves for their beds. Killing is the essence of forest existence, and if you stopped it, the forest and the Indian would die. Within the Indian mind there is a complete division between the duties within the group, and the absence of duty in the land of killing outside."

In Claudio's opinion, what *civilizados* found hardest to accept was that just as the Txukahamei killed parrots for feathers, so they killed white men for guns. It was shocking that man, as man, had no greater right to life than an animal.

"But it was so for the Greeks and Trojans. In fact, the first to extend the love and duties from within the Jewish tribe to

[68]

all the world was Christ. And he was helped because the Romans had already extended citizenship from the Roman tribe to an empire, and thus widened the idea of society. How could Indians, who had never known strangers, who had not the remotest concept of an empire, be expected to have such ideas?

"Bringing civilisation is not teaching to read or write," Claudio went on. "It is widening the Indian's boundaries to include our own—books and tractors are merely by-products of this. You must have heard the missionaries saying that I tell Indians to kill white men coming into the Parque. And it is true that I do not say it is a sin to kill, because that is meaningless to an Indian. What I say is, 'Look how small your tribe is today. Isn't it stupid to kill a fellow tribesman just because he has beaten your child?' Then, a few years later, I say, 'Look how many white men there are. They surround you everywhere. Isn't it stupid to kill Indians from other tribes when you are so few and your enemies are so many? Who will you dance and marry with when the other tribes are finished?' Finally I try to protect the white man, but I have to do this cautiously. Every Indian knows the whites are shooting, raping their women, stealing their land and bringing disease. So when skin-hunters and prospectors invade, I say, 'Yes, they are invading your land. And yes, your law is to kill. But if you kill, then other white men will avenge, and their chiefs will make it difficult for me to help you. So it's better just to bring the invaders to me, and I will send them away.'

"In each case," Claudio ended, "we are widening the frontier of killing, extending the area of rights and duties. And you will see that is what our expedition to the Kreen-Akrore will be about."

6

THE SEARCH STARTS

On June 16, between seven and eight o'clock in the morning, we were in the main hut at Posto Leonardo at the time of the first radio link-up of the day. Orlando was sitting on his desk, waking up with a cigarette. He has an almost theatrical manner, and he sat there looking at his cigarette as if it had been dropped by a vulture.

The radio crackled. "Posto Leonardo. Posto Leonardo. Are you being attacked? Over."

"Leonardo receiving. Leonardo receiving. Attacked by what? Over."

"Posto Leonardo. Posto Leonardo. Request from the President of the Central Brazilian Foundation. Can you confirm you are not being attacked by Indians? Over."

"Posto Leonardo confirms to the President of the Foundation that it is not being attacked by Indians. What codfish is this? Over."

"The Kayapo have attacked the base of Cachimbo. Over." (Kayapo is a name commonly used in Mato Grosso for the Txukahamei tribe.)

"Leonardo calling. Leonardo calling. Not Kayapo. Not Kayapo. Repeat not Kayapo. They are here. Over."

"The Kayapo are besieging the base of Cachimbo. Over."

"Repeat not Kayapo. Repeat not Kayapo. Perhaps Kreen-Akrore. Over."

"Calling Leonardo. Calling Leonardo. Who? Over."

"Kreen-Akrore. K-R-E-E-N-A-K-R-O-R-E."

A few minutes later the Air Force station in Brasilia came sputtering through on the loud-speaker. They needed Indian scouts. Could they pick up Rauni, the Txukahamei, as they rushed reinforcements to Cachimbo?

Above The air-strip at Cachimbo, originally built by the Villas Boas brothers, which was 'attacked' by the Kreen-Akrore. Richard Mason set out from here the day he was murdered. (*Chris Menges*)

Below Brazilian parachutists recover Richard Mason's body after he had been ambushed by the Kreen-Akrore.

Above Mekrenoti family returning from the trek (p. 89). (*Chris Menges*)

Below Mekrenoti carrying tortoises tied in frames. The tortoises are collected for feasts. (*Chris Menges*)

Above Txukahamei hunting with club and bow. (*Chris Menges*)

Below Txukahamei on the hunting trail. (*Chris Menges*)

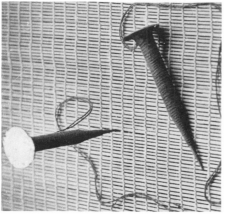

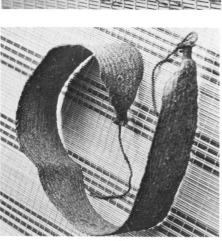

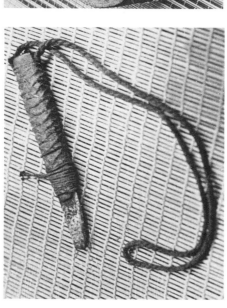

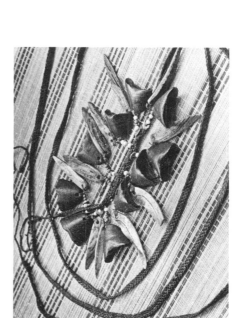

Artefacts taken from the Kreen-Akrore after the Mekrenoti had massacred them (p. 117). A knife must have been captured by the Kreen-Akrore and the metal blade splintered to make several knives like this. The coloured beads interspersed among the tapirs' toe-nails in the necklace were given by Claudio Villas Boas to a Txukahamei some time previously: the Kreen-Akrore, who made the necklace, must have killed the Txukahamei; to get the beads. A Kreen-Akrore belt and ear-rings. (*Chris Menges*)

Orlando was sitting on his desk in his blue sweater, with an old khaki cap on his large head, and as he sipped his second or third glass of black coffee, the contrast with Claudio looked like something from an early Hollywood farce. Where Claudio is thin, Orlando is fat. Claudio looks like a saint, Orlando a pirate. Where Claudio rarely stirs from his hammock, Orlando is usually at his desk. Claudio dislikes pets and reads philosophy. Orlando's comics and detective thrillers were being decorated that morning by two parakeets plodding up and down the bookshelf. Yet we all knew that the Parque's success was due to the brothers' unlikely combination of contradictory qualities. Claudio had the stamina to remain in the jungle and the gentleness to handle the Indians. It was his ideas which formed many of the Parque's policies. But Orlando shielded him from officialdom and the problems of administration, and Orlando was a leader of real flair with the instincts of a politician. It was he who had brought the Parque into existence, and without him it would have rapidly succumbed to the hostility of its enemies.

On that cool June morning, when the whole savannah to the River Kurisevo was covered with a low mist, we sat around with Orlando as he tried to cope with the situation. Cachimbo was the next base on the chain of air-strips the Villas Boas had built across the jungle to Manaos, and aeroplanes flying through touched down on our landing-ground. During that day and the next, Orlando asked the crews for news, piecing their fragments of information together with his own comments. He had been told that an Air Force sergeant was flown out of Cachimbo with arrow wounds received on the path to the plantation. He fired back at the Indians with a machine gun.

"Why was he carrying a machine gun to the plantation?" Orlando wondered, and we heard later that the story was untrue.

One 'plane left a copy of the Rio de Janeiro daily, *Correio da Manha*, which had the following stop-press item on its front page:

The Air Force has sent a squadron of TC fighters to Cachimbo with teams trained in jungle combat. Reason: the plane of the Commandant of the 1st Zone on landing there saw about a hundred Indians in a suspicious attitude.

[71]

"How do you use fighters against Indians?" Orlando asked. "However suspicious their attitudes?"

His questions were flippant, and people standing around laughed. But it didn't need much perception to realise that he was watching the situation with extreme caution, and was trying to isolate whatever truth lay beneath it.

The radio was blaring news. Aircraft and reinforcements seemed to be flying from all over the jungle; from Belem, Bananal, Manaos. Brasilia was issuing calming statements to the press.

"I have the impression that the Cachimbo crisis is turning," proclaimed Nilho Velloso of the Indian Protection Service at a press conference. "I don't believe that with so much military might, the Indians would dare another attack." (The Indians, it was learnt later, had not fired an arrow.)

Every now and again some department or organisation would come through on the radio requesting information on the crisis. Could Orlando launch an expedition next week? His replies were cautious, but when he put the switch down: "They are acting like cowboys—as if there are Indians riding round Cachimbo shooting arrows down the chimneys."

That night, what had seemed not much more than a glorious farce turned suddenly into tragedy. An aeroplane carrying over twenty military personnel, an official of the Indian Protection Service and an Indian guide, to the "relief" of Cachimbo, sent out a desperate message: "Total breakdown in radio compass. Petrol almost nil."

There was silence for a few minutes. Every radio operator listening in the black emptiness of Amazonia knew exactly what those words meant. Then there came the Brazilian S.O.S.

"Colleagues. S.V.H. S.V.H. I inform that 2068 is going to crash-land. We are flying without means . . ."

The ensuing air search over the forest between Manaos and Cachimbo went on for twelve days before a tiny fleck of white was located above the sea of jungle. It was a kite flown by one of the five survivors. In the panic to send reinforcements to Cachimbo, we learnt later, the 'plane had taken off with its spare radio compass out of order, and the other had broken down. The 'plane had flown hopelessly off-course until its petrol ran out. Twenty men and an aeroplane had been lost. At least £100,000 had been spent on an air search—and it was uncertain whether the Indians seen at the Post had even been hostile.

"Shout Indian and the whole world goes crazy," said Orlando. "The *civilizados* shoot. They fly aeroplanes all over the jungle. A brigadier is photographed crouched behind a machine gun. And it's just someone like Takuman looking from the trees."

Takuman was in the hut with several other Indians, and he grinned.

"We laugh, and the Indian dies," Orlando went on bitterly. "Only now that the government has lost men and money, perhaps something will happen. Perhaps they'll even grant money for a Kreen-Akrore expedition."

Another of the differences between Orlando and Claudio is that though their ideals are the same, Orlando has an acute sense of what is politically possible. He waits for the right situation, and times his moves with shrewdness.

Over the previous months we had made several attempts to reach some of the unknown tribes in the jungle round the Parque. The road that was approaching would not only give the land a commercial value, and therefore threaten the Parque's existence, but it would bring surveyors and prospectors into direct conflict with unknown Indians. To save them from bullets and disease, it was essential to make peace, and so we had circled and circled with Claudio in a 'plane over the smoke of what was probably a long-lost fragment of the Txukahamei tribe roaming the jungle to the north-east of the Parque. We had spent another few days searching an area further to the west for the Miahao[1] tribe (who steal from the Juruna's plantations nearly every year), and so to the south for the Agovotogueng (who may or may not exist outside the Kuikoro's fertile imagination). Finally, the problems were all brought home to Bruce, Jesco and me when we joined an emergency expedition to the Cabecas Peladas, who live not far from the mouth of the Amazon. A road like the one approaching the Parque had threatened the seclusion of the unknown Cabecas Peladas, and their arrows had killed one road-builder and wounded another.

[73]

The Villas Boas had rushed down to cope with the situation. We had marched down the Indians' trails and into their village, but during the brief two months of our expedition, there was nothing that could be done to lure them out of the trees. In jungle there is no power on earth that can force a hiding man to cease his hiding.

So when the Kreen-Akrore at Cachimbo suddenly became the focus of attention, we understood why Orlando said he would need a budget for a year or more. It was also easy to guess why—during the days of the search for the lost aeroplane —he doodled virtually all these known facts about the Kreen-Akrore on the back of a foolscap envelope which said *Ministry of the Interior. Confidential.*

Down the left-hand side he pencilled a line which became the River Teles Pires, which runs into the Tapajoz, and then, after about a thousand miles, into the Amazon. Orlando told us that parties sent out by the state government of Mato Grosso had canoed down this river as far back as 1746. Down the right-hand side of the envelope his other line grew into the River Kurisevo, which runs into the Xingu, and, again after a thousand miles, into the Amazon. The first descent of this river was made by von den Steinen in 1870. What we had were parallel rivers about three hundred miles apart, which had been travelled by various expeditions, but, except on the lower reaches, no-one had settled on either. And the important fact was that no-one had ever attempted to cross the vast jungle, about the size of Spain, which lay between.

In the 1940s, air supply had made it possible for the Villas Boas brothers to build the first permanent base in Xingu, and so they had also been able to cut across this heartland. Travelling from the Xingu up the River Manitsaua in 1949, they had marched over the watershed and down to the Teles Pires River. A short time before them, rubber-tappers pushing up the River Iriri to the north had also reached the junction with the tributary Bau. So on Orlando's envelope the block of unknown jungle had been reduced to a rectangle of roughly three hundred and fifty miles by two hundred miles, with the Cachimbo range at its centre. This was the territory of the Kreen-Akrore.

In 1951, Brazil's Chief of Staff had decided that it was

strategically important to have an air-strip in the middle of this rectangle, but because the jungle had been so dense, the Villas Boas had abandoned their usual expedition technique and crash-landed a 'plane on a bare plateau in the Cachimbo hills. This strip eventually grew into Posto Cachimbo, with half a dozen men manning a radio beacon for the Manaos–Rio de Janeiro air route. It was this base that the Kreen-Akrore had just "attacked".

From Posto Cachimbo Claudio had tried, in the 1950s, to continue the Xavantina—Roncador—Xingu—Tapajoz line by cutting a trail to the north-west. But after two years of incredible hardship on Claudio's part, the Central Brazilian Foundation changed its mind, and the trail was abandoned. It was during this period that Claudio frequently saw the smoke of unknown Indians.

In 1961, a young Englishman, Richard Mason, had led a private expedition from Cachimbo towards the headwaters of the Iriri, from where he hoped to descend by river. Two months later, his party were still making canoes only thirty miles from Posto Cachimbo, when Mason was found dead. He had been shot with eight arrows, and his skull and left thigh had been broken by clubs. This tragedy was the first definite evidence that the unknown Indians existed, and some months later the arrows from the body were shown to the Txukahamei tribe. From the distinctive binding and feathering they identified the arrows as belonging to the Kreen-Akrore. In Txukahamei, the name means "those men whose hair is short", and the Txukahamei said that a Kreen-Akrore bow was as thick as a man's wrist, a Kreen-Akrore bicep as thick as a Txukahamei thigh, and—to show their height—the Txukahamei put their hands above their heads and jumped. They said that the Kreen-Akrore regularly attacked them.

That was more or less the sum of Orlando's—and the world's —information. But there were some additional clues, or conjectures. To begin with, could this tribe of Kreen-Akrore, who raided across the hundred miles from Cachimbo to the Txukahamei villages on the Rivers Xingu and Iriri, be the same as an unknown tribe clashing with rubber-tappers on the River Teles Pires, a hundred miles to the west? The Kayabi who once lived

[75]

on the Teles Pires, called these raiders from Cachimbo "Ipewi"
—the men with clubs.

Cachimbo was also in the heart of one of Amazonia's richest
gold regions, and so it was bound to attract romantic rumours.
One was about African slaves, who, in Brazilian history, had
frequently escaped from gold-mines or plantations to form
African kingdoms in the jungle. One of these kingdoms, that of
Guaritze, had been on a tributary of the River Guapore, which
was not far from the river system of Cachimbo. The Kreen-
Akrore were always described as black and taller than most
Indians. Could this be the last of the African kingdoms, still
hiding from the slavers?

Finally, there was a theory from the parachutists who went in
to recover Richard Mason's body. Captain Sergio of PARASAR
thought the arrows had entered the body from below, which
implied that the Indians had been lying on their backs, bracing
the bows with their feet. This is hardly a normal position for
ambush, but in the early history of Brazil, the coastal tribes had
shot arrows exactly like that. Could the Kreen-Akrore, then,
have once lived on the coast, suffered the appalling cruelty of the
slavers, and then fled for refuge to the deepest and most inac-
cessible jungle? It could explain their ruthless killing of all
intruders.

There was no real evidence for any of these theories, and
much of Orlando's talk was speculation. But, as he said: "We are
about to search for a tribe that has killed *civilizados*, but has never
been seen by them. A group called Kreen-Akrore, who may or
may not be the same as Ipewi. A people who attack other
Indians, but have never spoken to them. What we can say
about the Kreen-Akrore is that we don't know about them."

With so little information, a slender clue could be helpful.
When we had arrived in the village of the unknown Cabecas
Peladas, we had found in their huts knives, pots, clothes, shoes
and guns. They obviously watched and stole from *civilizado*
settlements but avoided any contact with them. Amongst the
other debris, we also found an imitation wig made from palm
fibre to look like the eighteenth-century periwig a Portuguese
nobleman might have worn. Orlando's guess had been that the
tribe could have had peaceful relations with the Portuguese,

[76]

until driven away by some massacre or epidemic; this would explain their resistance to the road, and refusal to come out of hiding.

Such conjectures are vital to the understanding of unknown Indians, and from the time of the Cachimbo disaster, Orlando —and everyone else who was to be connected with the project —kept piecing and re-piecing together the few available clues about the Kreen-Akrore. For the contacting of a tribe is not just a question of finding and making peace with its members, but also of coming to understand the fears and motives which have, until then, made peace impossible.

NOTE TO CHAPTER 6

1. See Appendix II, the section on Uncontacted Tribes, p. 237.

7

CACHIMBO

The clouds of the rainy season were already making reconnaissance difficult when Claudio eventually flew to Cachimbo.
A Cessna aircraft picked us up, and just beyond the Juruna
village we turned to the west, flying up the line of the River
Huaia as it runs down from the Cachimbo plateau. It was here
that the unknown Miahao came every year to steal from the
Juruna, and Claudio suspected that they might be the same
people as the Kreen-Akrore. It was probably down the narrow
course of the Huaia that they moved.

For some time the land was perfectly flat, a green floor smooth
to the horizon. It lay completely still except for a white crescent
of egrets, drifting gracefully a thousand feet below. After ten
minutes, the ground crumpled into little formations of hills, and
gradually the whole area broke into a choppy turmoil, with
brown patches of rocks where the hills stabbed through. It
looked secretive. There were abrupt valleys, sudden cliffs, a
thousand hiding places, and the trees seemed to bend and
crouch over the rivers.

Somewhere in that empire of the Kreen-Akrore, we knew
trails would be criss-crossing from one end of the forest to the
other, and along the trails there would be hunting camps and
fishing places, sites for the cutting of arrows, places for the
special stones hard enough to make an axe. For the *civilizado*,
jungle never has "places"; it is an endless repetition of trees. To
the Indian, all the hundreds of square miles are divided according to their use and value. There are good locations to hunt
macaw—high jungle with plenty of Brazil nuts; good waters for
fish, where the river beds are not clear and sandy; bad places
for piumes and biting flies, near rapids. Sometimes Indians travel
for weeks to get the black wood for the strongest bow, or the

hard shell for the most beautiful necklace. We therefore knew
that the land would be full of secrets, and we peered down from
our 'plane trying to guess at anything that would help with the
search ahead.

A storm stretched across our route as we moved towards the
plateau, with arms reaching from one horizon to the other. It
moved slowly, like the phalanx of an army, and, under it, a
heavy black and purple shadow looked as threatening as poison
gas. The clouds rose in a solid rampart for ten or twenty
thousand feet above our little 'plane, and from behind, the sun
lit the top of the rampart with a yellow gleam.

Jungle is often described as malicious or evil, but when you
live in it, it is meaningless to talk in this way. Jungle is just
environment, a collection of trees. Flying into the plateau that
first time, however, we could almost see the forest rearing up
with the hills, and the storm crept towards us, visibly flexing
its muscles in little movements and eddies of the clouds. Suddenly it lashed out, caught our 'plane and flailed it about.
Amazonian storms can rip the wings off a light aircraft, or suck
it twenty thousand feet into the sky.

We were hurled about, but eventually came through to the
other side and saw below us the broken white of rapids, and the
first pure white of waterfalls. The rivers were falling off the
plateau. We were nearly there.

Claudio crouched by his window, peering out.

"Talk of demographic explosion," he muttered. "They have
never seen this. Hundreds of kilometres empty. Poof! Amazonia
can swallow an explosion or two and still have room for the
Indians."

He was making small, nervous gestures, and I found it hard
to understand why he should be so stirred; he had flown
thousands of times over undeveloped jungle. Then I remembered that Cachimbo had been one of the bitterest periods of
his life. He had spent two years cutting the trail from Cachimbo
to Cururu, on which a man and thirty mules had died. They
were frequently left without food, and several times most of his
men deserted. The Central Brazilian Foundation had lost interest, and the Air Force officer in charge of the supply route
had been a petty enemy. The expedition's supplies were

[79]

frequently off-loaded at Xavantina, and in desperation Claudio once had to arrange an air-drop.

"Even so," he grumbled, "Air Forces are not grocery services."

Finally, he flew back to report to the Central Brazilian Foundation that his two hundred miles of trail were finished.

"The President kept me waiting two hours outside his office," Claudio had told me. "When I went in at last he went on reading his paper. So I said to him, 'I have been two years in the jungle, and now you keep me two hours.' He said, 'I am the President of the Foundation. Is this how you talk to your President?' I said, 'Is this how a President treats his staff?' And I called him an imbecile and a crook and shouted many other things through the open door so all his staff should hear. I said that we knew he was surveying Indian land for himself on the Suya-Missu, that he was a swindler, and I was ashamed to work for him. The President became almost purple, and fumbled for his revolver in a drawer. But the Secretary of the Foundation—he was always our friend—he came and pulled me away. They called the Minister, and he said he understood, he would solve everything, and I must have a month's holiday. Ah, there were funny things in that Administration. We had already put one President of the Foundation into the street, and so they did not want a fuss."

The story was an obvious outlet for the bitterness of those Cachimbo years. As far as I knew, this was the first time Claudio had been back.

*   *   *

The 'plane taxied up to a grey stone building with a corrugated roof and a concrete path. Concrete pillars stood on either side, but surprisingly they did not support anything. They just stood on the grass in marshalled rows, giving an air of order and efficiency.

There was a little concrete pool at the side of the path and someone had roughly shaped an egret out of wire, painted it with whitewash, and popped it into the pool. Here, in the heart of Amazonia, for anyone who cared to come and look, was a wire

[80]

bird, drinking in a concrete pool. Behind the building were half a dozen grey, corrugated houses, with wire-mesh windows. A few stones and other objects had escaped the general clearing and levelling, but to complete the air of discipline someone had painted them with whitewash.

We walked into the building. From the radio-room to the left came squawks of static and the mechanical clatter of Morse. In there, too, was the purpose of the Cachimbo Post—the radio beacon emitting its beep, beep to the radio compasses in the air-route above. The room we entered was bare, except for a tall, narrow bar of an institutional type, used to serve coffee; there were white cups and a thermos on it. A sergeant, very neat in his uniform, with a narrow face and precise gestures, greeted us formally. Claudio told him that orders had come from the Ministry of the Interior that the National Park of Xingu should make peace with the Indians troubling Cachimbo. He had come for an aerial survey, and he needed petrol.

The sergeant said he had no authority. He repeated the word "authority" several times as he said he had heard about the project in general, but no orders had come through.

First Zone Headquarters at Belem, Claudio said, had radioed the Parque asking for the fuel requirements of the survey. These had been sent several days ago, with the number of our 'plane. It must all be in order.

The sergeant elaborated. Of course he would personally like to help, but it had to be realised that he was governed by regulations and could not depart from them. Without authority, not a single litre.

Claudio asked if he could send a message by radio to the General of the First Zone, who was a personal friend? But the sending of messages by unauthorised personnel proved to be strictly forbidden on Air Force wave-lengths. The sergeant offered to forward all relevant information through the normal channels. We must appreciate that maximum care was required in breaches of security. Claudio was an unauthorised person on a restricted military base.

Until then, Claudio had argued. There was even some bite in his replies. But this last statement depressed him. There was manifestly nothing to see at Cachimbo, and much of what there

[81]

was, he had built. Watching, I felt that of the many differences between Claudio and Orlando, perhaps the most striking was their different handling of officialdom. Orlando was almost a Czar by nature, and he moved into a situation with assurance. He would somehow have jolted this sergeant; a few hoary jokes to blur the issue, and soon the entire base would have been running round, brewing coffee and asking what Orlando wanted next. Claudio, by contrast, went for a little lonely walk on the air-strip he had built with so much trouble, many years before.

The sergeant sent Claudio's message to First Zone, and we had lunch with him as we waited for the reply. Before the meal, he bowed his head close to the oilcloth-covered table for nearly two minutes, then crossed himself with precise movements: head to chest, shoulder to shoulder, two vertical and horizontal lines.

"I am here," he told us, "working twenty-four hours a day for Brazil and the good of humanity."

Claudio could think of no reply to this. The sergeant's hands were clean, and his fingers kept brushing together to make sure that nothing dirtied them.

To me, Cachimbo seemed quite unbelievable after the Parque. Admittedly this was only the relief sergeant, as it turned out, known to his men—behind his back—as "His Excellency". But he said he had not once stepped off the air-field into the jungle, and there was, in the base, not one sign of the wilderness that surrounded it. No tree trunk. No parrot feather. Not a tortoise shell. Even the grass had formal paths laid between white-painted stones. If ever there was a human vacuum devoid of meaning, a place to question what civilisation does in the jungle, it was Cachimbo's platform of regulations emitting its beep in the world's largest unexplored forest, where pumas pawed the ground, anacondas coiled in the trees, where Indians and alligators, humming-birds and leaping spiders hunted and tortured and devoured each other with passion and joy.

"If the Indians come," said the sergeant, "I am going to shoot. I have nothing against Indians, but I know nothing about them. I cannot take the responsibility for the women and children who are here."

No authorisation came through on the radio, so we spent

[82]

the night at the Post. We noticed that there were loaded rifles in each house, and on the sergeant's orders no one went out unarmed.

"What can Indians do against stone houses with bolted doors?" Claudio asked. "Against wire-mesh windows and corrugated roofs, against buildings where no arrow can enter? Break down a door? Cut the wire-mesh? One loud bang from a gun and they will run to the Opera House at Manaos."

When Claudio asked about the "attack" on the Post, the sergeant said he had not been at Cachimbo at the time, so the other men took us out and showed us what had happened. A 'plane coming in for its approach had radioed that some animal was blocking the runway. As the base had no cattle, someone had been sent to look. An Indian! He ran back. The sergeant ran for a gun. It was fired into the air. To his understandable horror, three groups of about sixty Indians in all got up from the low scrub which surrounded the base and ran across the air-strip. The aeroplane, under the command of an Air Force brigadier, promptly dived and howled a few feet above the heads of the terrified runners, and then turned and swooped again. The Indians fled like deer and were not seen again.

For Claudio, this was tragedy. From all the signs, it was apparent that the Indians had been peaceful. If it was they who had ambushed and killed Richard Mason, it was because Mason had been cutting a trail into their territory. But in the fifteen years since Cachimbo had been built, they must have often been drawn to the Post by the sound of aeroplanes, but had not once made a menacing gesture.

From what Claudio could learn, everything indicated that the "attackers" had approached unarmed. When the area was searched after the "attack", arrows, clubs and bows had been found, left in bundles on the other side of the air-strip. Indians don't leave their weapons before they launch an attack. There were also footprints of women and children. No Indian takes his family to war.

The final clue was strips of parachute cord tied round some of the bundles of arrows. A few months before, PARASAR, the jungle rescue unit, had sent a training mission along the trail they had originally made when recovering Richard Mason's body. On their way back to Cachimbo, the mission had left machetes, parachute cord and other presents hanging up for any Indian who might find them. It looked as if the Kreen-Akrore had accepted the presents and had come to make friends.

"An irretrievable blunder," Claudio muttered. "Not so much the shot in the air, but a monster of a 'plane roaring and diving at them. They must have been terrified out of their minds."

Like many other incidents in Amazonia, it was not a case of criminals killing Indians for gain, Claudio said, but of well-meaning men who had become quite irrational on confrontation with unknown man. Indians! Bang!

*　　*　　*

We stayed at the Post until lunch on the following day. First Zone had still not come through with our "authority" for petrol. It was a public holiday.

Claudio seemed even more depressed than on the previous day, and said he would abandon Cachimbo as a possible avenue of approach. He would try the Txukahamei instead.

INDIANS MENTIONED IN CHAPTERS 4 TO 7

Bebcuche Relative of Rauni. Shot by a prospector.

Bemotire Brazilian captured as a boy by the Txukahamei. Became a minor war leader and, when the tribe was contacted, refused to return to his Brazilian relatives.

Karinhoti Txukahamei from the River Iriri village, outside the Parque. Son-in-law of the chief. Clubbed Kumoy.

Katokre Txukahamei on Bemotire's raid.

Kremuro A chief of the Txukahamei. Most of his group have died out.

Kretire Principal chief of the Txukahamei during this period.

Krumare A Txukahamei leader.

Kumoy Young Txukahamei.

Me-ure Txukahamei.

Moy-no Txukahamei on Bemotire's raid.

Neitu Txukahamei, son-in-law of Kremuro.
Pombo Famous chief of the Gorotire tribe at the turn of the century. The present chief is named after him.
Pooyoo Yawalapiti boy buried alive.
Preure Txukahamei on Bemotire's raid.
Pripuri A leader of the Kayabi tribe.
Rauni Claudio's right-hand man in the Txukahamei tribe.
Takuman Chief of the Kamayura tribe.

II
The Kreen-Akrore Expedition

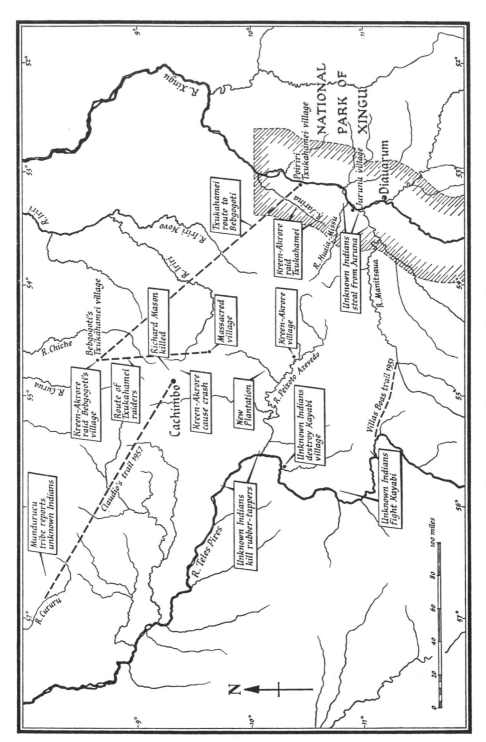

The Area of the Search for the Kreen-Akrore

8*

THE FIRST CLUES

Amongst Indians, the search for information should be a casual process. A direct question very seldom produces a reliable reply, and if Claudio had had to find out from the Txukahamei how many Kreen-Akrore had "besieged" Cachimbo it would have been a week before he could have got an answer. The Txukahamei only count up to twenty, and their word for twenty also means "so many it's not worth counting any more".

So when Claudio heard that the Txukahamei were about to leave on their great hunting trek before the feast of Biok, he said it was an opportunity not to be missed. They would move in the direction of the Kreen-Akrore, and without any prompting from him, the old men would shout out their triumphs in battle, and at night, in the circle of banana leaves, legends and stories would be told about the Kreen-Akrore. Eventually we would have to locate the village from the air, but the Txukahamei could tell us what to look for, and where to search.

*   *   *

The young boys broke the saplings ahead, scrambling through the forest, screaming like a pack of monkeys. Behind them the older boys widened the track into a broad ride. A generation before, they would have used sword-sticks instead of machetes, but otherwise the Txukahamei had broken their trail like this for thousands of years.

Ahead, lay the thin line of the path which crossed Kreen-Akrore territory on its 180-mile journey to the Txukahamei village on the River Iriri. But we were still in Parque territory, and a pile of women were striding down the track, pipes jutting

* The Indians mentioned in Chapters 8–12 are identified in the list on page 125.

[89]

out of their mouths as they screeched obscenities at the men blocking their way. Young babies and puppies were perched on top of their loads of potato and corn, and they moved with a fast, rhythmic pace. Children rushed about, dogs howled, and the women emitted piercing, and surprisingly feral, shrieks.

Above us, the great Amazonian trees were cutting off the sun, so the path was as gloomy as a dungeon. But a jungle outing is like a summer picnic for nomads, and everyone would soon be stealing honey, drinking from llianas and collecting nuts. Above, the macaws screamed and monkeys gibbered, but on the path the Txukahamei certainly outscreeched them all.

"Just so, the Kreen-Akrore walk," said an old man sitting by the trail. "Like us, they have no canoes."

Spoken casually, this comment was exactly the sort of information Claudio wanted. Most Indians can be divided into those who fish and live on the rivers, and those who mainly hunt and roam the hinterland. The canoe people are easier to find from the air because you search for their villages along the waterways. But nomad camps hidden by the trees are better located from inside the jungle where you find and follow their numerous trails.

Glad of a rest, Rauni sat down. His group of Txukahamei had not hunted the Kreen-Akrore for a long time, he said, but it would be easy to pick up their tracks.

"Follow this road to the Iriri, then half-way go looking in the direction of the rivers." (He meant follow the rivers towards the Cachimbo watershed.) "Kreen-Akrore roads are wide like this, and they have many camps. But the Kreen-Akrore can't swim, so their roads cross the rivers in the high places."

Claudio, who had come stumping up, muttered about this. Indians who couldn't swim? He had never heard of it.

"In water," Rauni insisted, "Kreen-Akrore sink."

*   *   *

The purpose of a nomad journey is to scavenge, not to arrive. And so the marches were from the previous night's camp-site to the next water—an hour, or even less. Then the men dropped their loads and fanned out to hunt the jungle ahead, while the camp rang like a building-site to the axes wielded by the boys. The women rushed out to the nearest patch of wild banana leaves[1] and returned looking like green haystacks, with only their feet showing beneath. Gradually the temporary village rose with roofs of banana leaf, walls of banana leaf, and beds of banana leaf. In the centre where the men would sing, the boys laid a banana leaf floor like green linoleum, and the whole camp began to resemble a green bowl dotted with coloured fruits. Brown baskets; yellow bananas; mounds of grey potatoes; and when the sun broke through, the smoke went up in blue and golden shafts.

"Do you see these houses?" An old man was sitting in a hut, too tired to hunt. "Kreen-Akrore houses are like these. Made of banana leaf and very small."

"Do the Kreen-Akrore have hammocks like the Juruna or Kayabi?" Bruce asked.

"No, they sleep like the Txukahamei—on the ground. But they have potatoes and corn, and roast them on stones like that. Roast only. Like us, they're ignorant of pots."

It was from fragments like these that our portrait of the Kreen-Akrore was to grow. And as the journey continued, their economy and life style gradually began to seem very like that of the Txukahamei. Perhaps they had, long ago, belonged to the same culture group.

*   *   *

"At last. At last, I know a site of the Kreen-Akrore."

It was late at night and Claudio had returned excited from a camp-fire across the clearing. "It was 1949. We were flying from the River Manitsaua—thinking of cutting across to the River Peixoto Azevedo—and suddenly on the left bank I saw a trail. Looking up, I saw a village about two kilometres from the river, and the huts of that village had sloping roofs and no walls, just like the huts in this camp. Now old Nhere has been talking, and in all this time he is the first Txukahamei to tell me that Kreen-Akrore houses had sloping roofs and no walls. It's obvious, the village I saw from the 'plane is a village of the Kreen-Akrore."

In Claudio's opinion that village was too far to the north to be the village that had "attacked" Cachimbo. But its position close to the River Manitsaua, which flowed into the Xingu not far from Diauarum, could be very useful to us.

*   *   *

"Now there are no more real killers. No more fighters of Kreen-Akrore."

Waving and gesturing with an 1870 .44 Winchester repeater, Nhere, the old man, was shouting in the centre of the camp.

"Now there are no killers, but your grandfathers looked well to themselves. They were not frightened to take their guns."

"Shut up!" Nhere turned to some children who were mimicking him. "Be quiet and sit listening. 'WWwwwoooooo,' we yelled when we ran firing at the enemy camp. Bang. Bang. I duck from side to side, but I run screaming at the Kreen-Akrore. I hear the long arrows shaking in the wind. 'Ku. Ku. Ku,' the Kreen-Akrore yell. 'Ku. Ku. Ku.' They sound like frogs in high-water season, tearing out after us, running as if behind a wild boar. They are great tall fellows, young wiry ones, fat ones, round-faced ones. They fall on us wildly. My two sons-in-law just throw their guns and flee. 'O, ari. O, ari. Here they come.' My sons-in-law are killed. They are so many we don't even shoot. They just kill us and I am seeing it all, holding a tree, my tummy [sic] shrunken with lying there, hiding like this."

Nhere's disjointed account went on for nearly an hour, and night after night we heard scores of stories about dozens of skirmishes. One thing we noticed was that the Kreen-Akrore did not use the Txukahamei technique of surrounding a village in the dark to charge in the dawn. They just ambushed parties in the jungle or plantation and stole what they were carrying.

On the other hand, we heard one story about an enemy child captured during a Txukahamei raid. The Kreen-Akrore counter-attacked, and though the Txukahamei were shooting with .44s across an open clearing, the Kreen-Akrore charged straight into their guns. A huge Kreen-Akrore knocked aside the gun of a Txukahamei called More, and snatched back the child.

"Except for Txukahamei, Indians seldom charge," Claudio whispered to me. Rauni heard us.

[92]

"The Kreen-Akrore are hard," he said with feeling. "Truly hard." And he went on to describe their attitude to prisoners.

In the jungle, women are the deciding factor in war. If you capture the wives, you not only eliminate your enemies' battalions of the future, but, with a little application, can double your own force in a generation. And so most Indian raids are for women, and this serves the—unconscious—purpose of bringing new genes into an isolated group. For instance, when Orlando and Claudio contacted the Txukahamei, they had found half a dozen white captives, and roughly a dozen children taken from other tribes. The white women had taught the Txukahamei to load and repair their captured guns, and thus, for tribes isolated in the jungle, captives represent a vital window on the outside world. That window the Kreen-Akrore had closed.

They killed all women and children at the site of an ambush, and the Txukahamei said this was why they had never learnt to use guns taken from Txukahamei bodies. In addition, Kreen-Akrore adults refused captivity. On their last successful raid, the Txukahamei had caught four Kreen-Akrore women in a plantation. Two had struggled so much that they were clubbed on the spot, and the other two were virtually carried back to the village. There, they lay down on their mats and killed themselves by starvation. Amongst Amazonian Indians this was a quite exceptional demonstration of self-will, and as the stories of the Txukahamei continued, our portrait of the Kreen-Akrore began to acquire something of an unusual, even a twisted, cast.

Claudio reminded us that centuries of inbreeding had already produced a remarkable feature amongst the Kreen-Akrore. One of the prisoners he had discovered in the newly contacted Txukahamei tribe had been a Kreen-Akrore captured as a boy. This man, Mengrire, had at that time been about thirty years old, and was six feet three inches tall. Few Amazonian Indians are more than five feet eight inches, but the Txukahamei insisted that many Kreen-Akrore were taller than Mengrire. What Claudio wondered was whether the inbreeding which had produced the tallest Indians in Amazonia could have also produced a people who were more introverted than other Indians.

As the Txukahamei screamed the falsetto screech of their

[93]

war dance, and pounded, shook their clubs and fired their guns, raising the fury of the pack to bloodlust, it was hard not to think about the people against whom all this enmity was directed. A people who had crouched for centuries in the self-made dungeon of Cachimbo, lashing out at anyone who came near, a people with an inward-looking eye. For the first time we began to wonder whether it would take more than a year to meet them.

*   *   *

When the trek reached the River Jarina, the Txukahamei camped by some rapids with a small island of stone in the middle. There was a fallen tree running out from our side, and every now and again a green mossy rock stuck out of the foaming water. It was here the nomads forded on their way to the River Iriri, or on their raids against the Kreen-Akrore. This time, the Txukahamei turned back for the feast of Biok. But it was across these rapids that a party of half a dozen came hurrying from the Iriri some weeks later. Bebgogoti and the group of Txukahamei outside the Parque had just attacked a Kreen-Akrore village. They had killed twenty and captured three girls and a boy.

The news got out, and eventually the following press cutting was flown into Diauarum:

MISSIONARY SAYS
WAR AMONGST INDIANS IN CACHIMBO

Folha de Goiaz. 19/12/'67

The director of the defunct Indian Protection Service, Colonel Heleno Dias Nunes, received part of a letter written to his chief in Belem by a foreign missionary on the River Iriri—about the war between the Indian tribes Kreen-Akrore and Mekrenoti (another name for Txuka-hamei) . . . The missionary says that more than twenty Kreen-Akrore were killed in combat, including men, women and children, according to the attacking Mekre-noti. "The Indians affirm that there is no danger for us," writes the missionary, with the same ingenuousness that carried the Englishman Richard Mason to his death at the

[94]

hands of the same Kreen-Akrore Indians. The Director of the Indian Protection Service, who had only just received the letter, asked if he was going to prepare an expedition to attract and pacify the Indians of the Serra do Cachimbo, declared that it did not form part of his plans to pacify any Indians whatsoever, since he did not have the resources to do so. It was known, however, that the brothers Villas Boas were disposed to carry out the work without cost to the Indian Protection Service.

NOTE TO CHAPTER 8

1. The Pakova leaf looks like a banana leaf and is called "wild banana" in Xingu.

9

THE CAPTURED CHILDREN

Rauni lumbered into the film-hut at Diauarum, and stuck his great bear face close to Chris Menges, the new cameraman out from England.

"Shall we go to Bebgogoti's?" he asked in a high-pitched, enquiring voice, and then laughed at Chris's surprise.

Rauni stalked into our store-shed, rummaged among the boxes, and emerged dressed for his ambassadorial role in a grey shirt, brand new jeans and two hats, one inside the other. When somebody pointed out that this was more hats than usual, he took them off, stumbled about the hut shaking with laughter, and then replaced both firmly on his head.

Claudio sat beside the pilot, and Rauni, Chris and I squeezed on to the floor in the back. We were off to the Txukahamei village on the River Iriri, which had become separated from the group in the Parque during a minor civil war in 1958. Both villages belonged to the same tribe, but the group by the Iriri is known by its correct name, Mekrenoti, whilst the group inside the Parque is called "Txukahamei", which means "the men without a bow". Bebgogoti was the chief of the Mekrenoti, and he had led the recent raid on the Kreen-Akrore.

The 'plane flew down the great silver plate of the Xingu River to the Txukahamei village, and there Genario, the pilot, looked at Rauni. Very carefully Rauni raised his arm and lined up on a point in the distant jungle. The pilot set his compass: 350 degrees. There had been no previous flight from the Parque to the village we were bound for, and it was not marked on any map. Rauni, who had travelled there once as a boy, was our only means of navigation.

The River Jarina was narrow and twisting where we crossed, but we could still see the Xingu gleaming a long way to the east. Then we were over a few patches of grassland.

"This was Capoto, the Txukahamei place," Rauni said. "That was the time of my father, before the people of Kretire fought the people of Kremuro."

We looked down on a bald patch of savannah that had passed into frontier legend as a sort of Assassins' Valley. From here the Txukahamei had set out to attack the rubber camps of the Lower Iriri and Xingu, and such terror did their raids produce, that a hundred miles of river-front would be deserted at the first hint of an attack.

Almost immediately the savannah began to change to jungle, and the flat Xingu plain folded up into the Cachimbo hills. Rauni was checking each river as we crossed, and his eyes had become beady with concentration, his lipdisc almost touching the window. The only landmarks were the streams, and they could just be identified as creases in the carpet of foliage below.

Then we saw the first real river, probably the Iriri Novo.

"Other water," Rauni directed.

We crossed another fifty miles of jungle and came to what must be the Iriri itself.

"Other water," Rauni said, and we crossed the Iriri, and after about another forty miles came to the River Chiche.

"More!" Rauni seemed confident, and we flew further into the jungle. But it was now over an hour and a half since we had left Diauarum, and there had been no sign of anything remotely connected with human existence. I began to wonder whether an Indian, trained to find his direction in the forest, was the best guide for an aeroplane.

Suddenly there was a patch of white in the dark jungle ahead, and it had the long, geometric outline of an air-strip. Soon we saw a circle of yellow huts, and ring after ring of emerald plantations. Rauni had brought us, without deviation, across two hundred miles of jungle.

When we landed there were fifty Mekrenoti standing by the strip, and their eyes had that completely flat, impassive expression which is possibly the most frightening thing about Indians. They register your movements without recognition that you are human, and therefore have a right to life. Claudio had not visited the Mekrenoti for ten years, and they must have guessed that his visit was connected with their murder of the Kreen-Akrore.

Claudio got out and walked down the long path to the village, and eventually our file of black-painted warriors from the air-strip snaked across the yellow dust of the square. It was a large square, with a great circle of huts, and in it the fighting men seemed even more daunting than before. There was also no sign of the chief, Bebgogoti. He had not met Claudio at the air-strip, he had not welcomed us at the entrance to the village, and Claudio had to walk around the square, asking where he was. Eventually we found him sitting on a stool in the centre of the men's hut.

Bebgogoti had a striking imperial face, and a silver chain with a heavy medal hung round his neck. He must have been very tall and powerful in his youth; now in his fifties, he appeared as authoritarian as a Roman general. He did not look up as Claudio entered. Claudio said something to him and sat down. Bebgogoti barely acknowledged the greeting, and went on pulling some eagle and macaw feathers from one of the long tubes of bamboo that are used by Indians to protect their headdresses. His expression was stern, and as the line of black-painted men pressed in after us, the hut began to grow hot and oppressive.

There was an awkward silence. We could hear Rauni outside the hut, greeting friends, joking and laughing. The silence continued. One of Bebgogoti's men offered to interpret. Claudio refused. Then a white man who was in the hut offered to interpret; it was a missionary we had heard of, a Canadian called Dale, who was establishing himself in Bebgogoti's village. Again Claudio refused—and he was unexpectedly curt.

To the Txukahamei, interpreting is an important ritual, so we waited for the Parque's official interpreter, Rauni. Bebgogoti, his heavy face sullen, went on fiddling with his headdresses, and in the crowd pressed round the door I could see a pathetic little group which I guessed were the captured Kreen-Akrore children, each with a foster-parent. The oldest girl seemed to be about five years of age, and there were two girls of about two years old, and a boy of the same age. Their hair was smooth, their skin brown, and they obviously had no African blood. The

story about the "slave kingdom" in the jungle was nothing but
rumour.

These children would be Claudio's first concern. They had
been kidnapped as their parents were slaughtered before their
eyes, brutal strangers had carried them through the jungle,
then dumped them amongst an alien people. The little boy was
still nervous, and trembled violently whenever I turned my face
towards him. ("It's your beard," Rauni consoled me later.)

The agonising question for Claudio was what would be best
for the children. If he made contact with the Kreen-Akrore, he
could restore them to their relatives; it would be a valuable
factor in the contacting process, a tangible demonstration to the
Kreen-Akrore of his sympathy and power. It might also prevent
reprisals against the Mekrenoti. But if contact should be de-
layed for a year or more, would it be fair to wrench the children
out of their environment a second time, reviving the old fears
and dislocation? And if he did not return them, would not the
Kreen-Akrore, even if contacted, try to recapture them?

Claudio looked at the children only once or twice. As the
unease in the hut grew, he just sat there, hunched and shabby,
a little figure on a small stool, surrounded by a sea of Mekrenoti
faces.

Then Rauni came in. He dropped on to his knees and bent
until he was crouched right forward. Bebgogoti did the same.
When they meet, Txukahamei relatives mourn the friends and
relatives who have died since their last meeting. Txukahamei
from the Parque, Mekrenoti outside it, they were the same
tribe, and the high-pitched words of the ritual weeping echoed
about the hut.

Rauni turned to Claudio. "What do you wish to say?"

"Tell Bebgogoti I have come because the Mekrenoti have
attacked the Kreen-Akrore and killed many men." He paused.
"I have come to say I am very sad. You are brothers. It is not
good that one Indian should kill another." Claudio turned towards Bebgogoti. "Ask Bebgogoti if he will kill any more?"

Bebgogoti was sitting with a face as hard as iron, still pushing
the red and blue macaw headdress into the bamboo tube. He
flung out one arm, whilst the elbow of the other struck his side
with a sharp thwack.

[99]

"My anger has gone."

"Ask if he will come to the Parque and help make a good land for the Indians." Claudio spoke very quietly, but I saw Dale, the missionary, turn to look at Bebgogoti before Rauni translated.

"Ka—ti." The Mekrenoti "No" was spoken in two vicious staccato syllables.

"Ask if he will give me the oldest of the Kreen-Akrore children to raise?"

Bebgogoti lifted his head for the first time. He looked at the eldest captive, held by one of the women in the doorway, and he threw a question at the faces around him. There were so many sharp answers of "Ka—ti!" that it was like a salvo of gunfire.

There was little more to discuss. The pilot said that the airstrip was too short to take all four of us back together, so he would return for Chris and myself the following day. It would give us time to film, and perhaps—since we had no official position and no need to reproach Bebgogoti—perhaps we could find something out. Bebgogoti could solve most of the problems of our search, if he chose. To begin with, he knew the site of the Kreen-Akrore village.

And so, as the 'plane with Claudio and Rauni flew back to Diauarum, Chris and I stayed behind with a very precise objective, besides our filming. And we were to learn that just as the whole business of contact is the approach of one group of people towards another through an intervening barrier of jungle, so the whole process of extracting information from Indians depends not on your questions and the Indians' reply, but on the mental, cultural and political barriers that lie between.

*　　　*　　　*

Dale, the missionary, asked us to dinner. He was an earnest man, and belonged to the Unevangelised Fields Mission, which had first tried to contact the Kayapo group of tribes (which includes the Txukahamei) in 1935, when the "Three Freds", young missionaries from Britain, had approached the Kuben Kran Kegn. Unfortunately for them, a Roman Catholic priest had for some time been exchanging presents with the tribe at the Smoke Falls, on the boundary of their territory, and so the Three Freds went beyond the Falls and into the heart of the country.

Their bodies were never found, but their boat was discovered, battered with clubs. Fred Wright, the leader of the trio, wrote in one of his last letters to his Mission: "Should the result be that which I suppose we least want, pray, and send others out to continue what the Lord has commenced."

The Mission accepted the challenge, and now missionaries were with most of the groups outside the Parque. The Iriri was the most recent extension of their net.

We went over to Dale's house, and he introduced us to his Scottish wife, who cooked a magnificent meal of game, corn and potatoes, all from the jungle and plantations. It was only a year since Dale had walked into the village on the three-day trip from the nearest navigable river, and extended the airstrip to take their 'plane. He had built the house himself, and made beds, tables and chairs from skins and wood. Outside the house there was a shower, and a plastic sheet to catch the rain.

As we ate, about a dozen Mekrenoti watched, fenced off from us by a half-rail that kept the Indians in an area by the door. Dale talked, and it was obvious that Claudio's brusque manner in Bebgogoti's hut had left its mark.

"They say that man [Claudio] tells the Indians to kill the white people that come into the Parque," he said. "They say he gets drunk on alcohol. But I judge a man on what he is. The previous inspector from the Indian Protection Service at Bau didn't even say 'Good morning' when he was here. He just ignored me and then wrote a report against us. He said we were giving clothes and no soap, and it was bad for Indians to walk around in dirty clothes. But we had brought in caustic soda, and all the Indians had to do was to mix it with fat as we showed them. It was the Indians themselves who do not want to make the soap."

Dale was bitter about the sometimes overbearing control of the Brazilian authorities.

"I admit missionaries have made mistakes in the past. I admit the Mekrenoti at Bau are dispirited and depressed, and missionaries can interfere too much. But there is a good part and a bad part in the Indian's culture. It is a virtue for a Mekrenoti to be angry. It is a virtue for them to have many women. It is a virtue for a chief to have concubines—he is keeping the little Kreen-Akrore girl to become a concubine. It is, or used to be, a virtue to kill. And some of the names are impossible, so I just can't mention them. I just say, 'What were you called before this name?' 'Oh, such and such,' they say. I say, 'I will call you by that.' " (Dale didn't specify the names, but a Txukahamei who worked for the film-unit was called Stone Penis, and Txukahamei humour can rise to Fish-hook Penis.)

The excellent dinner made the daily rice and beans of Diauarum seem like sawdust.

"What we try to keep is the good part of their culture," Dale went on. "Look at their dances. It's not body dancing—there's nothing unclean about it. It's good healthy exercise."

We saw something of Dale's methods of dealing with the Indians during the meal. Once or twice a woman came to the window and handed in some bananas or potatoes, and these were noted in a book, according to their value. On one day a week, Dale told us, the Mekrenoti could use this credit to buy a knife, or any other article they wanted, and medical treatment was also debited against it. Dale believed that Indians valued medicines more if they had to be paid for, and he said the whole system helped to prepare primitive people for a money economy.

The contrast with Diauarum was striking. There the Indians sat all over Claudio's hut, and everything—medicines, bullets, fishing-line—was without charge. Sometimes the Indians brought presents of corn or game, but there was no obligation to pay, even in kind, and there was no grading according to value. The whole purpose of Diauarum was exactly contrary to Dale's system; the Villas Boas tried to protect the Indian from the eroding effects of the money economy.

Yet, from what Dale said, his methods were based on as long and as wide an experience as Claudio's, and he had the whole mission organisation behind him. He and his family would fly in for three months at a time, and these flights were arranged by the Missionary Air Fellowship, a specialised transport service. He was already teaching the Indians through a primer evolved with other groups of the Kayapo, and Dale's linguistic pro-

Typical unexplored jungle. It took days of flying to locate
the Kreen-Akrore in this area. (*Jesco von Puttkamer*)

Above Bebgogoti, chief of the Mekrenoti and leader of the incursion against the Kreen-Akrore, with the captured Kreen-Akrore child 'Little Spin Around' (pp. 98, 115).
(*Adrian Cowell*)

Below A Kreen-Akrore plantation laid out in a remarkable pattern of circles and crosses —usually Indians make ragged plantations, sowing among felled trees (p. 122).
(*Chris Menges*)

Above A Kreen-Akrore village. Many of the men are painted with black dye (p. 123). (*Chris Menges*)

Below A Kreen-Akrore hut. (*Richard Stanley*)

Above left Antonio, the Mekrenoti interpreter. (*Chris Menges*)
Above right Pripuri, one of the expedition leaders. (*Adrian Cowell*)
Below The expedition travels up the R. Manitsaua (p. 128). (*Jesco von Puttkamer*)

gramme was co-ordinated by the seminars and study groups of the Wycliffe Bible network, who had their own teams of linguists, aeroplanes and interlocking chain of radio transmitters. It was a carefully thought out and co-ordinated plan, the ultimate aim being to teach the Indians to read, and then "give them the Bible in their own language".

"They are good people," Claudio often said of the missionaries. "Send an underpaid Indian Protection official to a tribe, and you can never be sure he is not seducing the women or cheating the Indians. With missionaries, it's different."

But Claudio objected strongly to the unconscious criticism in such phrases as "concubines", "body dancing" and "good and bad part of their culture".

"It is up to the Indian to decide what is good or bad for him," he would say. "The Indian must not be pushed as fast as possible into the money economy and the life of the salaried rubber-man, just because that's the quickest way to produce a Christian. In their own way, at their own speed, if they want to become a Catholic or a Protestant, then I am happy for them. Religion is a valuable guide and support for life in civilisation. But only when they have learnt enough about civilisation to understand what our religion means. And particularly not soon after contact, when missionising destroys their culture. It's like an operation on their minds—a lobectomy. You force them to change all the unconscious data through which they view the world."

Thus missionaries were banned from the Parque. Thus Claudio had been rude to Dale in Bebgogoti's hut. And hence Dale would resent any attempt by Claudio to move Bebgogoti into the Parque. I guessed that anything we attempted to find out from Dale about the Kreen-Akrore would be hindered, or at least complicated, by this conflict. Perhaps we should try Bebgogoti instead.

10

PARLIAMENTATING

We had been invited to spend the night in the chief's hut, and when we got back from Dale's house, Bebgogoti came over to where Chris and I had slung our hammocks. He sat beside us on a stool, and the Portuguese-speaking Mekrenoti, Antonio, translated.

"Bebgogoti is sad that Claudio did not stay. He is sad that they could not talk in the night. He is sad that they are not friends like they were long ago at Capoto."

In the firelight, Bebgogoti's expression seemed friendlier, and I began to suspect that his previous surliness had simply been a negotiating position. He knew Claudio would have to be angry first—then compromise later. Claudio's sudden departure must have disconcerted him, and now he was hoping we would carry back a more accommodating impression.

The conversation went on through Antonio.

"Bebgogoti says he went to Xingu before. But he got much sickness. There was sickness and sickness, and many Mekrenoti die. So Bebgogoti takes his people away from Xingu to Bau, and then he comes here. Here he has big plantations. We hunt deer and tapir and monkey and jacubim. Now he has medicines from the Americano [Dale], and the people are not sick. Why does Claudio want him to come back to Xingu?"

Chris and I made no attempt to answer the question. We knew there was more to Bebgogoti's reluctance than sickness, for Rauni had told us that Bebgogoti was not the son of a chief, and therefore he could not speak the ritual "strong talk" which a chief must use in the village square, calling to the houses in the dark. Bebgogoti had won his authority as a fighter and a leader, and if he went to Poiriri, he would be overshadowed by Kretire and Kremuro, whose lineage gave them a stronger claim to be chiefs.

"Is it true that the white men will come and kill us?" Antonio was translating glibly, but Bebgogoti seemed to be watching him carefully. "Does Rauni speak truth when he says the soldiers will burn this village? I say this is lies, I say that Christians will never come here to kill. A long time ago they killed. But now, hunters. They come. They come from the river to the village. When it is time for them to go, they give their due—bullets, beads and knives. They do not kill. They never kill us. We do not kill Christians."

Antonio had learnt his Portuguese from rubber-tappers who call themselves Christians and the Indians pagans.

"We do not kill Christians," Antonio proclaimed. "Only Rauni! There arrives news here. Rauni has killed one Christian. Rauni has killed two. Rauni has killed three. Rauni kills! We do not kill. The Christians will not kill us. So why is Rauni making our people frightened? Do you hear that baby crying?" A sly look came into Antonio's rubbery face, and the lie obviously did not come from Bebgogoti. "The baby is frightened by Rauni. So why does Rauni say we must come to Poiriri? And where is the road? When I was a boy they said the road of the white man was coming. Now I have children, and there is still no road. The Americano says the road will not come."

This road, we knew, was planned to pass close to Bebgogoti's village some time around 1972, but Claudio had said there was no need to move until it arrived. So I replied for Claudio—and his clearly enthusiastic ambassador, Rauni.

"This land is not Indian land. So when the road comes, the Christians will live here. They will take your land and give you sickness. Claudio does not like the Christians coming, but there are many who are unlike Claudio. They kill. So then you can go to the Parque. The Parque is Indian land. The government says so. Everybody knows it. Even Claudio cannot own it. When he is old, he will have to go away from Diauarum. That is why he is trying to buy a ranch near Goiania. Then the people of Bebgogoti can always have as much land as they want in the Parque."

I then gave the presents Claudio had brought, and Bebgogoti looked friendly and pleased. When he eventually left us, Antonio remained behind, and it seemed, at last, as if the opportunity had arrived to find out about the raid against the Kreen-Akrore. Antonio had been one of the raiders. But his expression should have warned us. This was an ideal opportunity for Antonio, too. His manner became unctuous and patronising, and he told us that the people in the village were a crowd of savages. Then he launched—for lack of any better word—into the history of his "civilising".

"In 1910 my godfather took me to Minas Gerais." This first sentence was untrue. The tribe was not contacted until 1954.

"At that time no aeroplanes had been invented. So I, a gentleman in my privacy, walked in the ways of nautical navigation. And with all your goodwill you will see that at that time motors were inboard and outboard."

He threw a shrewd sideways flick of his eyes at us, as if revealing a little-known piece of information. And I began to realise that here was one of those tragic cases of an Indian living in the intolerant society of the frontier, who had become a parrot, mimicking the words and the postures of the rubber-tappers without relevance to any meaning at all. It meant that any information passing through Antonio as interpreter would be distorted and quite valueless, unless someone like Bebgogoti was watching closely.

"With your goodwill you will know that I returned to instruct our personnel in the just usage of merchandise . . ."

Antonio's eyes were blank, his face blubbery. Eventually I fell asleep in my hammock, but every now and again some phrase would jolt me awake.

" 'You, sire, we must Parliamentate! I am a gentleman in my privacy watching you steal from the sweat of the poor.' Then he liberated my credit so that I should depart from the middle of the Christians . . ."

I awoke next morning with Antonio's "Parliamentating" still going round in my head. Bebgogoti and the men of the hut lay on their mats; the little Kreen-Akrore girl played by the fire. She had a sweet face and was playing very seriously by herself, like any child who plays alone. From the little I had seen of her she did not, at least on the surface, appear to be very disturbed by her kidnapping.

Dale and his wife and little daughter came in, found stools, and began a service—it was Sunday. A dozen young boys and girls had come in with them, and stood around. Dale sat with his fair, plump little daughter on his knee, and you only had to watch him to know that he was a good man—without any undertones to that adjective. His pale face was intent and sincere; the light glinted on his spectacles. His wife sat with a book on her lap, looking up every now and then and raising her hands, palms upwards, to encourage the young Mekrenoti. A hymn rose; it had Mekrenoti words, and the boys and girls sang with startling gusto. Bebgogoti and the men reclining on mats watched without much interest, coughing and spitting, as their children roared away.

When the singing stopped, Dale switched on the tape-recorder that he had brought with him. His voice came out with a carefully prepared sermon in the Mekrenoti language, which he explained to me later.

"It's a story from *Acts*, Book 5. Ananias and his wife sell some land and say they will give all the money to the church. But they decide to keep some of the money. First Ananias goes to the church and says to Peter, who was head of the church at the time, that he is giving all the money to God. Immediately he is struck dead for his terrible sin of a lie to God. Then his wife comes in and tells the same lie."

As the recorder preached, Antonio very ostentatiously detached himself from the bystanders and came over to our corner of the hut.

"Do you think these singers have the sight of God?" he asked, not bothering to lower his voice. "They say they sing to know Him. They say the body is interred and the spirit goes to the sky."

His words were less pretentious than last night, but his eyes were sly as he continued:

"I don't believe they see Him. To my mind, no. On the contrary, to my mind, God is one. And now the American is saying to us in the night we must move the village away to Bau or Curua. Move further from our brothers in the Parque. Bebgogoti says, no. Bebgogoti says moving is not to our convenience. No matter nothing, no. Have you strolled in the plantations? No? Well, our domain is fertile. So Bebgogoti says, no. He says, no—in Bau the travelling salesmen steal."

I listened as another hymn rose energetically towards the roof. So now it was not only Claudio trying to move the tribe into the Parque, but Dale trying to move the tribe away from Claudio. And Bebgogoti, the brave and shrewd warrior who had shot the last of the Kuben Kran Kegn as he swam the river, who had fired beside Kremuro into the Kreen-Akrore onslaught, who had launched the recent massacre of an entire village, Bebgogoti was also the wily diplomat balancing between two factions of civilisation.

Dale came over to us after the service.

"You know, when I was preaching a sermon on Cain and Abel a few months ago, Bebgogoti looked very angry. He got up and walked out. And it's only now I've realised he must have been planning the massacre. That's why he didn't like what I said about Cain."

A few hours later, the 'plane flew in from Diauarum with Rauni grinning through the window.

"I have come back to pass time with the people of Bebgogoti," he told us as he got out. "Then I will walk the jungle to Xingu."

"You've come for politics, Rauni. Your soldier stories have got the Mekrenoti climbing the trees."

Rauni grinned again. The only soldiers who come to Xingu are with the rescue unit, PARASAR, and they invariably ask for Rauni as a guide. He wears their uniform and boots; he has his own pack and canteen. And it was quite obvious he felt he could twist any mere 'plane-load of soldiers to his own ends.

"Don't worry, Adriano, it will happen like this," he said, scratching himself thoughtfully. "Bebgogoti is old and he will not move from here, and all these people are his relatives. They will not move too. But one old one will die, and then his family will come to Xingu. Another old one will die, and then more will come to Xingu. And when Bebgogoti dies, they will fight, and some will go to Bau, and many will come to Xingu. I know, I am Bebgogoti's relative. Bebgogoti likes me."

"When the chief in Xingu dies, will you be chief, Rauni?"

"The people say they want me. Maybe I will be one chief."

I suspected that perhaps Rauni's importance increased with every group tempted from the Iriri. So the pale, sincere face of Dale, the imperial countenance of Bebgogoti, the rubbery

visage of Antonio were all to be confronted by Rauni, with his
honeyed and mischievous tongue.

It seemed to Chris and me that if we had ever had a chance
to ask some straight questions about the Kreen-Akrore, that
chance had passed. After twenty-four hours in the village, not
only had we failed to pick up a single shred of useful information, but Chris said that we had never even approached the
position in which a question could be asked. What we had learnt,
if anything, was that an Indian village on the brink of civilisation is not as simple as it might seem.

"This Americano," Rauni said, as we were getting into the
'plane. "Is he a good man?"

"Yes, Rauni. He wants to help the Indian. But he and
Claudio want different things. The Mekrenoti have always had
plenty of women, three or four if they want. So Claudio says,
what the Mekrenoti want, that is good. But the God of the
Americano says Mekrenoti must have only one woman. He will
tell the Mekrenoti it is bad to have more. Also the Americano
wants to teach you the songs of his God. But Claudio says, no,
you should have only your own songs and dances."

So unconvincing was this answer that I could see disbelief
registered all over Rauni's face. He always had many women,
and he could see no reason why the Americano should not
rant and shout against this—just as Rauni's wife did. Rauni
would listen to him, as he did to her—and have his women.
And why should anyone withhold those enjoyable God-songs?

"Tell Kretire to send Txukahamei," he called casually into
the cabin. "Send six with guns to wait for me in the middle of
the trail. The Kreen-Akrore are there."

When we were airborne, the pilot confirmed that they had
seen smoke rising from the jungle half-way from Xingu. It
looked like a hunting party, and since all the Txukahamei were
in their village, it must be the Kreen-Akrore.

[109]

THE MASSACRE

Rauni turned up in Diauarum a few weeks later, and with him came Eketi, Bebgogoti's son. They had walked the two hundred miles from the Iriri, and had then paddled up-river from the Txukahamei village.

Rauni was off-hand about the Kreen-Akrore hunters. They had moved on elsewhere, and were no longer of importance. On the other hand, he and Eketi had come as an official mission of good will, and they bore with them the following proposals from Bebgogoti:

1. Cessation of raids.
2. Help for our expedition.
3. Information about the Kreen-Akrore—from Eketi.
4. One of the Kreen-Akrore children—to be given later.
5. A Kreen-Akrore youth to be captured, "tamed", and returned to the Kreen-Akrore as truce bearer.

Article 5 did not impress Claudio as much as Rauni had hoped, but his visit to Bebgogoti's village had undoubtedly swung things in our favour. Bebgogoti was now anxious not to antagonise Claudio, and he had agreed that it was to his advantage that the Kreen-Akrore should be pacified before their inevitable raid of reprisal.

Claudio questioned Eketi for several days; he had taken part in both the massacre and the preliminary reconnaissance. But there were many discrepancies at the end, and like all information from a single Indian informant, his version needed cross-checking against the accounts of other Mekrenoti.

As Claudio had to stay to run the Parque, it was Rauni, Chris and I who stepped out of the 'plane one afternoon at the

Mekrenoti air-strip, to find the village deserted. Dale had finished his usual three months' tour of duty and returned to his base on the River Araguaia, and a few old women who had stayed behind told us that the rest of the Mekrenoti had left on a nomadic journey. Later that evening, however, a party came rushing back from the jungle—they had heard the sound of the 'plane—and by noon next day we had caught up with the nomads and were moving through the forest.

AAaayyyeeee! The shrieks were shrill. AAAAaaaayyyyyyyy-eeeeee! The trek was part of the women's festival, and both the yells and the chanting at night were those of wives and mothers.

It was the rainy season, and day after day the rain fell, grey sheets cascading through the trees, turning the trail into a brown morass of mud. Chris and I sloshed up the path, very wet and muddy. Our camera and tape-recorder were wrapped in two plastic bags, but they were streaked in mud, the lenses swam in condensation, and the machinery wheezed. After our last visit to the Mekrenoti, the sound camera, a 16mm Arriflex BL, had been sent to São Paulo, where half a tea-cup of chewed-up cockroaches had been taken out of the motor. But now the camera was safe. "Rain", Rauni explained, "is not the travelling time for cockroaches."

Night after night we shivered in soggy camps under a flimsy shelter of banana leaves, and often my hammock rope would be tied to the same branch as Rauni's. I therefore felt the sag of the branch as he climbed into the hammock, and then the second sag as another, lighter, weight climbed in on top. Every night the giggling came from a different voice.

"Oh-ho, Adriano, are you asleep?" "No, Rauni."

Laughter. "So-ho, Adriano. Would you like a Txukahamei girl?"

Unlike cockroaches, the Mekrenoti will travel through a hurricane. No matter how thick the mud and how determined the downpour, their whole nature seems to change with the journey. They chatted and gossiped, they joked and sang. And as we were following the trail they had taken on their raid against the Kreen-Akrore, everyone was also talking about the attack. Chris and I listened; Rauni interpreted. We checked everything again and again, one fragment against another, and

[111]

sometimes we would tape whole speeches, and go over them laboriously in the hut at night. Eventually we had it all more or less summarised in a rough sequence of events.

*   *   *

Antonio insisted on beginning:

"With your goodwill you will understand that it was on the eve of my return to our homeland that they attacked, sir. Those Kreen-Akrore immigrants attacked us. Here we were, living quietly within our property, and they came making a disturbance. It was a good half-dozen of us they killed, and before that, several pairs. So we were only taking our right. We avenged ourselves. But we are not killers, thanks be to God. We don't want to molest them in their occupations."

We knew that Claudio would be sceptical about any information from Antonio, but listening to the accounts of the raid from other Mekrenoti we caught the names Kukrore, Atorote and Babure—the victims of the Kreen-Akrore raid—so many times that we felt it must be true. They had been ambushed by the Kreen-Akrore as they came into the plantation just across from the air-strip, and after killing them the raiders stole their machetes and clothes. The raid had been four years before, but it was as fresh to Mekrenoti minds as if it had happened a month ago. They insisted that their raid on the Kreen-Akrore had been a justified reprisal for that attack.

Bebgogoti had waited for several years, then he had sent his son to find the Kreen-Akrore village. Eketi followed the trails to the village, watched for some time, and then returned to tell what he had learnt. Finally a Mekrenoti war-party set out, led by Bebgogoti and some of the older warriors.

Their route was easy to establish. Every time a soaked Mekrenoti scrambled in from the rain and huddled, shivering, under our plastic sheet, he would raise an arm and point.

"That was the way," he would observe conversationally, "that we went to kill."

Checking my compass, we confirmed that different men in different places, over a number of days, had all pointed in the same direction; 190 degrees, with a margin of error of about ten degrees. The question was, how far? Indians have no measure for distance beyond the time of a journey, and this can vary with the traveller's enthusiasm. We hoped that Antonio, who had been a boatman for the Indian Protection Service, would be able to help. He must have measured the petrol for each official journey, and would have learnt to calculate distances.

"The village is just over the hill, by the Iriri," he said. "You can't miss it."

I looked doubtful. Antonio tried again.

"What is the hour?"

"Ten past ten."

His brow furrowed. "You could be there by half-past four on Tuesday."

Several days later, after stumbling in and out of three muddy streams, one after the other, I thought of finding out the names of the rivers. With a river name for all the camp-sites, we could discuss what was hunted and eaten at each place. Mekrenoti remember this sort of detail with wistful clarity; and this would help us to isolate each camp.

The idea worked. But it revealed that half the Mekrenoti had slept in ten different camp-sites, and the other half in five—though both had been travelling together. It was only a day later that the obvious explanation dawned on Chris: some were describing the outward journey, laden with bananas and potatoes, and the others the much faster return.

Our summary for the return journey was as follows:

1st day Attack early in the morning. Return to sleep in Kreen-Akrore plantation some way along the route.
2nd day Early departure. Arrive at mid-day at River Bi-quieri—a small stream, probably a tributary of the Iriri.
3rd day Arrive at River Burti with the sun in the lower branches. Roughly four p.m. The Burti was a bigger river (probably the Iriri).
4th day Arrive at mid-day at a stream called the Pakreti—probably a tributary of the Iriri.
5th day Camped at River Capremti-Nyojer—the Chiche.
6th day Slept in village.

[113]

Route: 190 degrees.
Travel time: five days and part of a day. Probably no day
totalled less than twenty miles. (The Mekrenoti do the 180–
200 miles to the Xingu in nine days.)
Distance: one hundred miles or more.

*   *   *

Now that we had an idea of the direction and distance, the
next problem was what to look for. The Mekrenoti talked at
first of several villages, but these gradually resolved themselves
into camp-sites along the trail from the Kreen-Akrore village
to their fishing place.

Eventually we were able to establish that as it was a long
journey for the Kreen-Akrore to fish, then the village must lie
inland between the larger rivers. We also knew that it was a
single village with a number of plantations, and a larger number
of abandoned plantations further away. But in spite of all our
questioning, we never discovered a single feature that would
distinguish the particular village we were looking for from any
others we might see from the air.

As the meat roasted on the scarlet fires at night, as the men
peeled and ate the purple potatoes, one of them would glance
at the camp around us.

"The Kreen-Akrore village is like this," he would say, munch-
ing away at a little pile of Brazil nuts. Next evening, another
man in a similar camp would be sociably gnawing the fat from
an armadillo shell.

"The Kreen-Akrore village is not like this," he would observe
between gnaws. "It's like our village by the air-strip."

We never reconciled these discrepancies. It was only much
later, when we entered the Kreen-Akrore village, that we
realised what both men had meant, but what we had been
unable to understand. The Kreen-Akrore village was like the
Mekrenoti's because it was out in the open, not under the
trees; but its huts were made of banana leaves, and in this it
resembled a nomad camp. That day of recognition, however,
was still more than eight months ahead.

*   *   *

[114]

The most vital clue to any contact with Indians is some hint of the language. The tribe you cannot speak to is obviously the one that is hardest to reach, and sometimes it only needs two or three words for the professional linguist to discover the language group to which your tribe belongs. Then an expedition takes Indians of that group with them, and they shout "Friend!" "Peace!" or some equally basic word into the trees. The unknown tribe may have doubts about whether you really are friends, but the fact that they have a doubt implies that they have accepted you as similar humans, communicating by the use of language. That single word transforms the whole nature of the relationship.

The Summer Institute of Linguistics had sent one of their girl linguists, Micky Stout, to spend a week with the Kreen-Akrore girl in Bebgogoti's hut. Micky could speak the Mekrenoti language, and the idea was that she should try to catch any words the child said that were different from Mekrenoti. The little girl liked Micky, and continued to play quite normally; but though Micky listened whenever she spoke, not a word other than Mekrenoti came out. From this it was possible to make two deductions: either that the Mekrenoti and Kreen-Akrore languages were so similar as to be indistinguishable in the mouth of a five-year-old, or that the kidnapping was such a cathartic experience that the little girl's memory had been obliterated. During the massacre, she had run round and round in terrified circles, and the name they gave her meant, in the Mekrenoti language, Little Girl that Spins Around. Perhaps "Little Spin Around" was making her captivity less frightening by pretending she was a Mekrenoti.

Chris and I also heard several of the raiders imply that they understood the Kreen-Akrore language.

"When I run at him, this old man kneels down and holds up his arms. 'Don't shoot!' he shouts."

"Did he speak Mekrenoti?"

"No. But I understand."

How did he understand? Was it because the old man spoke a similar language, or because it was obvious what any victim would say? It is hard to state anything precisely in Mekrenoti. Two or three questions would get us no further, and we knew that if we really pressed, they would say anything to please us.

We never got any nearer to an answer about language. And despite the hours Micky spent with the little Kreen-Akrore girl, she got no further, either.

* * *

Chris and I now went on to find out what we could about the actual massacre.

It seemed that Bebgogoti and some of the older men had planned the operation, but then waited in a plantation while the young men carried out the attack. When we asked these warriors what happened, they became incoherent, leaping and shouting with excitement.

"Why not shout all at once?" I said one day, in frustration. "Why not run about shooting? It would be no harder to understand."

Their faces lit. To be invited, no matter how unthinkingly, to re-live the feat, to act out the whole glorious enterprise a second time! Everyone started talking to everyone else, and we added our encouragement—naturally.

It was in this way that a mock attack was planned, and eventually launched against one of our nomadic camps early one morning. Twenty "attackers" with guns, naked and smeared with paint, gathered in the jungle outside the camp. Antonio, among them, looked rubbery and a little sheepish in his war paint. To our surprise, the warriors crept together—not spread out—through the undergrowth. Suddenly they leapt up and rushed at the camp, screaming and firing into the air, battering through the hut walls and "shooting" in every direction. Children screamed, dogs howled, pandemonium reigned. It was obvious that many Kreen-Akrore must have been shot down in their huts, and that only one or two would have had time to fire back with their bows. It must have been sheer butchery.

The young men took it in turn to shout their exploits.

"We were near each other, running together in battle. My uncle and nephew found an enemy on the edge of the path. He was standing there, weaving buriti palms. My brother-in-law

[116]

shot him down. Then we were on them, coming down on them in the houses. I shot and missed, hitting only a gourd. The enemy ran after me. I dodged an arrow I saw coming—twisting and falling aside. So I threw the enemy down with a shot. He sits there and my older brother, Kayti, shot him right down. Ha! Kreen-Akrore. I just killed one of you. Be!"

We counted what seemed to be eighteen separate killings, but there were probably more. Besides the four captured children there had been two women prisoners, one old and the other young and beautiful.

"But they bite very much, so, club, club!"

Each man waved his booty. "From the body I took this."

"Look, this I took from the body."

There were stone axes, rush baskets, and a fascinating knife made of a Kreen-Akrore wooden handle and a tiny fractured piece of steel. The Kreen-Akrore must have captured a knife in an ambush, and then fractured the blade to provide as many "knives" as possible. The Mekrenoti laughed and said they had never done that; it was simpler to get more knives by killing more *civilizados*. And the obvious deduction from this was that the Kreen-Akrore did not make regular raids against the pioneer frontier.

There was, too, a curious "necklace" made out of shells and tapirs' toe-nails, that clattered when worn round the waist. Woven into its centre were some blue and red Czechoslovakian beads that had been brought into Xingu by Claudio. A Kreen-Akrore had killed a Txukahamei for those beads. Now a Mekrenoti had killed a Kreen-Akrore to get them back. Beb-gogoti gave it to us, and I still have it—a reminder of the empty futility of most tribal wars.

Finally, the most revealing detail was that many of the Mekrenoti had been lamed by splinters of bamboo as they chased the survivors fleeing to the south. Hundreds of splinters had been embedded in the trail, and we knew this was a trick of the Ipewi Indians who raid into the River Teles Pires area. It was yet another indication that the Ipewi and Kreen-Akrore could be the same people.

*　　　*　　　*

As the Genghis Khan-like faces moved past us in the jungle, as we watched the excited men shouting in the camp, we wondered if any hint of the Kreen-Akrore attitude to war would come from the Mekrenoti.

"See my game," Boti shouted in the mock attack. "See lying there in the house what my brother and I killed."

Were the killings just for trophies—an exciting extension of the hunter's life?

"I killed this enemy and he lay." This was Ayo. "I killed this enemy and beat him. There was one that I shot with his child, and he fell so. The child there sat."

Then Kanga. "The enemy made me an orphan. And I, Kanga, have now in revenge killed one of them. The enemy made my younger brother and uncle orphans. Now that I've become a man, my uncle and I took our guns and shot two of them dead. Be! There they lie. And there one tried to hide in the grass. Be! I got my gun and killed him. There. Did I kill these two with help? No."

It is easy to explain Indian killing as part of their savage nature—until you know the Indians themselves. But on that trek the Mekrenoti were courteous and gentle. We saw husbands, wives and children all sleeping curled up in a tight ball of animal love. And the expressions and gestures of the men could be so affectionate that they would look homosexual to a *civilizado*. They are a very generous, loving people.

And yet during the mock attack, one of those friendly, loving men picked up a captured two-year-old boy and ran out shouting into the yelling turmoil. The child sobbed in terror, thinking it was another massacre, re-living the slaughter of his parents. The man waved the child, then dumped him on the ground in the centre of the raiders. The child seemed frozen with fright, holding up his arms, begging for his captor—the only known thing in this wilderness of savagery.

If the Indian attitude to killing was the central problem of the Parque, was it perhaps the key to the process of jungle contact? Did the Kreen-Akrore kill as thoughtlessly? And since the Mekrenoti were the only strangers they knew, would they expect us to behave and kill like the Mekrenoti?

12

WE FIND THE VILLAGE

The 'plane had to twist and weave between the clouds as we searched for the Kreen-Akrore. The rainy season had reached the stage when the clouds parade across the sky, trailing long tentacles of rain, and these tentacles would flick out to lash the windscreen of our Cessna, or sometimes whipped the fuselage so that we could feel it shudder and groan. On other days there was so much water on the ground that the 'plane would come tearing down the runway with a bow-wave like that from a speed-boat. We could feel the wings struggling to lift the wheels out of the water, and then, with spray hurtling right over the cabin, the pilot would shout "Hard over", and we would go back to try again.

For our first flight in search of the Kreen-Akrore village, Claudio had decided not to follow the route of the Mekrenoti attack, the 190 degrees from Bebgogoti's village. Instead, he had marked this course on the map, and had drawn another line to represent Richard Mason's route to the River Iriri. Where the two lines met was roughly where Mason was killed, and where the parachutists who recovered his body had found Indian trails. The region was about a hundred miles from Bebgogoti's village—the distance we ourselves had calculated from the Mekrenoti accounts. Claudio therefore shaded in a wide area round this point—it was to the south and east of Cachimbo—and we began to scour it methodically one morning, eliminating patch after patch in a series of matching boxes.

The pilot was Genario, Claudio sat beside him, and Chris and I were in the back of the 'plane. The first few minutes of flight located the shelter where the Indian Protection Service had left presents for the Kreen-Akrore after the C47 crash. But then there was nothing for a couple of hours. The jungle was broken with hills, and the valleys and ravines formed dark shadows that confused the clean outline of the forest. There were open hill-tops that appeared deceptively like village squares, and occasionally a series of trees had blown down in a storm, so that from a distance they looked like clearings for a plantation.

We strained our eyes to see, dodging the storms, tossed on air currents, peering through windows opaque with rain; the beep that tied us to the radio beacon at Cachimbo buzzed incessantly in our heads. After some time, Genario pointed at a series of lighter patches that looked like scrub on top of a plateau. Dropping down in spirals, we realised they were areas of secondary forest formed in a pattern of circles.

"Bananas," shouted Claudio. "Old, but true bananas."

It was the yellower leaves of the banana trees that were making the outlines of the circles.

From this first sign of man, Genario flew in concentric boxes, and we began to find more and more dents in the jungle. Every year, Indians cut a new plantation, so an inhabited region is soon covered with patches of secondary forest where plantations have been abandoned and then overgrown. From what we could see, cultivation had been going on for at least thirty years.

Suddenly we saw the distinct outline of a relatively new plantation. Then the bare earth of a village square. We swept back for a second run.

"Not huts. Not a single building," said Claudio.

But several naked posts were sticking out of the ground, and there were one or two blackened patches of thatch.

"It's the village!" Claudio clutched at the window. "The one the Mekrenoti burnt."

The 'plane stood on one wing, circling. Not a sign of life. No hint of survivors. Not even shelters under the trees. In all the descriptions we had heard of the massacre, the survivors had fled in a direction away from Bebgogoti's village; so now we, too, turned to the south, following the line of a stream until it dropped off the plateau. There, beyond, we could see the mysterious lowlands of the River Peixoto Azavedo, stretching away to the horizon.

"The petrol's almost gone," Genario warned, and we turned back to Cachimbo.

On that first flight we had found the village of the massacre and confirmed that it was no longer used. But this information was, of course, negative and brought us back to our starting point. The vast unknown of the Cachimbo range was all around, and the Kreen-Akrore could be in any of its seventy thousand square miles. We did, however, have one clue. If he were a Kreen-Akrore, Claudio said, he would keep as far from Bebgogoti as possible.

Our next flight was therefore planned to search the Rio Peixoto, where Claudio had seen his unknown village twenty years before. This was nearly eighty miles south of the village of the massacre, but Claudio reminded us that the huts had had the single-roof characteristic of the Kreen-Akrore.

We flew out of Cachimbo down the southern line of the Rio Braco Norte as the river plunged into a series of rapids, frothing and foaming over slabs of red and brown rock. This northern arm of the Peixoto eventually arrived at the flood plain leading to the main river, and there it corkscrewed round and round, meandering through glutinous, swampy jungle. Claudio remembered—somewhat absent-mindedly—a village here, too, but there were no signs, not even secondary forest.

At the Peixoto, we turned up-river, flying east.

"The site is on the next northern tributary," Claudio said. "Perhaps the one after."

Thirty miles on, there was the tributary. We turned and followed it to the north, climbing up over rapids, flying into the hills towards the massacre site. The river would have been the logical route from the village of the massacre to the village Claudio had seen, but there was not a sign of life. The jungle looked blank and meaningless.

We turned and flew back down the other bank of the river, Claudio hunched by his window. Once he thought he saw smoke, but it turned out to be rain. Then, suddenly, Genario heeled the 'plane in from the river and turned towards a distant hill. The rest of us could see nothing, but he had had twenty years' experience in the Central Brazilian Foundation. Gradually we began to make out a faint crease in the jungle. Then, with agonising slowness, it grew into a wall of trees. There was a sudden flash of emerald. In the dark green of the jungle, this light green shone almost like neon.

"Fantastic!" Claudio shouted. "An astonishing thing."

The 'plane veered round, and we piled on top of each other, staring out of the window.

"Never, never has there been anything like this. The anthropologists will run to see it."

We were looking down on a smooth, ordered pattern of geometric gardening. There were circles and ellipses, bisected and sub-divided. Even the Parque's relatively sophisticated Indians, using steel axes and steel machetes, leave ragged holes in the jungle when they cut plantations. It is too much trouble to move the trees from where they fall; they scatter their crops between the stumps, and so their plantations look disorganised and shabby.

What we were looking at now was—for Amazonia—indeed fantastic, as Claudio had said. We flew backwards and forwards, staring at the sight below. The outer rings consisted of single rows of banana trees, in beautiful curves and circles. The crosses and double avenues were straight lines of maize, looking like paths over lawns of grass. It was as if we had stumbled on a Versailles.

"It can't be grass," said Claudio. "They must be potatoes."

But what purpose could the patterns serve? And why had they bothered to remove the fallen trunks and cut the stumps? With stone axes it would have been a Homeric task.

We began to search the immediate area round the plantation. There was no sign of a village, not even old plantations. Our discovery was like a genie's garden in the desert, and the industrious geometric genie had vanished.

The rain had worsened. In almost every direction we were now blocked by moving pillars and walls of water, and we had to creep away with our tantalising discovery still the subject of speculation. Had the survivors fled here from the plateau? Was it a site for a new village? Could it be a ritual plantation? Did it provide the food for a festival?

"There is only one matter of certainty," said Claudio. "The crops are untouched and the Indians will be back."

Next morning we took off from Cachimbo and cut across the triangle of our previous flight, direct to the plantation. Having established that there was nothing between it and Cachimbo, we took a line to the east, and flew away to strike the Peixoto. In a few minutes we saw a plantation, an old one. Almost immediately there was another, and then another, all in the same pattern as the first we had seen, and each newer and more clearly defined. Finally we saw one with three abandoned huts in the centre, and then we were over and past. Concealed by a high black ridge of trees, we had flown straight across a village without realising it.

The 'plane heeled. We swept back. There was the village. A long double path, a ring of half a dozen huts. Some of the figures standing in the square were brown, but most were black. Arrow after arrow rose towards us, and at the summit of their flight, turned over gracefully, catching the sun in a golden flicker of light—messages of resistance from the Indian world below, glinting and shimmering just beneath the 'plane.

The huts were very small and shabby, which was surprising for a people with such ambitious plantations.

"They have to be Kreen-Akrore. The roofs are single."

We felt as if we had been prospecting for years, and had then come upon the largest gem ever found in Amazonia. This tiny circle of life was pure to itself, unadulterated by an idea from our civilisation, by a seed from Europe, a wheel from Sumeria.

From the surrounding plantations we could see that this area had been cultivated for over thirty years. It was, therefore, a separate, long-established village, and not one built by the survivors of the massacre.

Claudio said there was no point in searching any further. The survivors of the massacre had fled south; four or five days would have brought them here. The single-roofed huts, the ringed plantations belonged to the same culture, and the two villages would have spoken the same language. Claudio believed that there were half a dozen other villages in the Cachimbo jungle, but for us, this one had all the advantages. The Mekrenoti had attacked from the north and east; the harassing aeroplanes had always come from Cachimbo in the north-west. Claudio intended to approach from the south—the opposite direction. And when we eventually contacted this village, it could lead us to the others.

Our next series of flights was therefore up the Peixoto, looking for a stretch of river that would be navigable by canoe. Then we flew inland across the hinterland of jungle to the River Manitsaua that flows almost parallel to the Peixoto but into the Xingu. The Parque's boats could use the Manitsaua to bring up supplies and men. We flew a series of courses, trying to find the best route between the Manitsaua and what would be our canoe base on the Peixoto, but everywhere looked depressingly lumpy and broken with hills, and there was no stretch shorter than fifty miles.

"It's nothing," said Claudio. "We cut four hundred kilometres to Cururu."

During most of these flights we dropped presents on the unknown village—knives, aluminium bowls, small rolls of cloth, rubber balls. These were tied to "parachutes" of coloured balloons. On our final flight, the Kreen-Akrore responded. Two large fires sent up a double pillar of black smoke as our string of brightly coloured presents plummeted down.

"They like our presents," someone said.

"Wouldn't you make smoke if it was raining pots?" someone replied.

That double pillar of smoke was the first formal communication between the village below and civilisation, and we all looked at it with some kind of awe. We knew that for the Kreen-Akrore it was the beginning of the end. Of course, if we did not get there first, another Mekrenoti attack,[1] or disease picked up when the road arrived, would finish them in a decade. But the rain of presents and the answering smoke was the beginning of an interchange which could now only develop, until this vast, unknown area of Cachimbo would be chained by roads and padlocked by farms.

"Walking naked, sleeping on the ground, cutting with stone, roaming the wilderness, they are happier down there," Claudio said, "happier than they will be for the next hundred years—even if the contact does go well."

NOTE TO CHAPTER 12

1. For the subsequent Txukahamei raid, see Appendix IV.

INDIANS MENTIONED IN CHAPTERS 8 TO 12

Antonio Mekrenoti who once worked as a boatman for the Indian Protection Service. Bebgogoti's interpreter.

Atorote Mekrenoti killed in a plantation by the Kreen-Akrore.

Ayo Mekrenoti who took part in the massacre of the Kreen-Akrore.

Babure Mekrenoti killed in a plantation by the Kreen-Akrore.

Boti Mekrenoti who took part in the massacre.

Bebgogoti Chief of the "Mekrenoti" section of the Txukahamei tribe living by the River Iriri. He led the raid against the Kreen-Akrore.

Eketi Bebgogoti's son who led the reconnaissance before the raid.

Kanga Mekrenoti who took part in the massacre.

Kayti Mekrenoti who took part in the massacre.

Kremuro A chief of the Txukahamei—most of his group have died out.

Kretire Main chief of the Txukahamei.

Kukrore Mekrenoti killed in a plantation by the Kreen-Akrore.

Mengrire A Kreen-Akrore captured as a boy and brought up by the Txukahamei. Killed by Neitu in 1960.

More Txukahamei who had fought the Kreen-Akrore.

Nhere An old Txukahamei who had fought the Kreen-Akrore in the past.

Rauni Claudio's right-hand man in the Txukahamei tribe—he later became one of the chiefs.

13*

THE TRAIL

Pripuri swung the leading machete, and every twenty or thirty yards he would pull out the compass that hung round his neck on a nylon cord. His long black hair was topped by a railway-man's red cap, and he flourished the compass like a station-master's whistle: 340 degrees. Pripuri lined up dramatically on a tree and cut towards it.

Claudio followed, hunched and less impressive, in a floppy hat and dirty shirt, checking Pripuri's bearings and holding a sack on his shoulder. It contained knives, beads, aluminium pans and other presents in case we ran into the Kreen-Akrore. After him came the second Kayabi leader, Cuyabano, who cut and widened the trace. The small satchel swinging by his side usually held a cooked snack of two or three monkeys' heads.

The cutting party was strengthened by the film unit; Erno, the new cameraman (who came for three months and stayed eight), myself, and our two assistants, Bejai the Txukahamei and Cagrire the Suya. A mile or two behind was another party of a dozen men, widening and cleaning the trail into a broad ride along which the supplies of the expedition would flow. Finally, there was a group of four or five who guarded the camp, and formed the small convoys that carried lunch and water to the cutters.

It was several months since our discovery of the Kreen-Akrore village. Food and petrol had had to be transported a thousand miles by truck from São Paulo to the headwaters of the River Kuluene, and then ferried down-river by motorised raft. Indians had gradually come into the Post to join the expedition, and towards the time of our departure night fires had flickered

* The Indians mentioned in Chapters 13-19 are identified in the list on page 188.

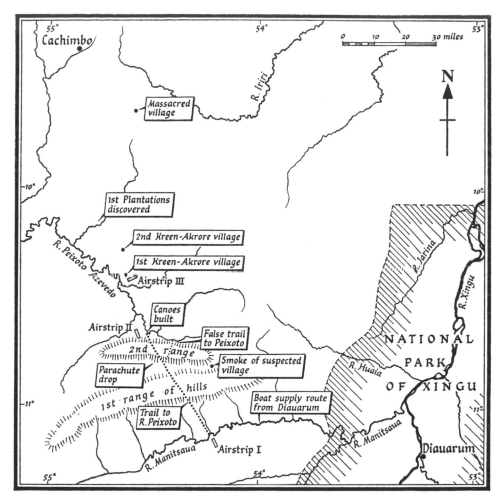

The Expedition to Contact the Kreen-Akrore

under many of the palm trees round Diauarum. A boat was
sent for the feckless Suya.

"Cocumba, are you sure you have finished your plantation?
Are you certain you won't have to come back to plant?"

Claudio had complex negotiations with heavy-nosed Juruna
wives about which husband should be released by which woman.

"The wife of Soriri does not wish him travelling about,"
Claudio explained after a two-hour conference.

So-and-so could come because his brother promised to look

after his plantation; so-and-so would have to join the expedition later, or return to plant his mandioca. It all seemed like a feudal levy, except that Claudio was an absent-minded "baron" and the vassals just came for the adventure. They received clothes, hammocks and bullets for the journey, but no money or salary.

It took five days for the heavily-laden boats to travel up the River Manitsaua; another month was spent cutting an air-strip for supplies. Then the trek began.

* * *

Almost immediately, we were in "black jungle". This is the name given by the Txukahamei to forest which is so high that humans seem to live in an underworld of semi-darkness; we were not to see the sun for months, and our skin was to become so pale that it was almost green. In this new world, every sound we made produced an echo, every movement disturbed a life. Jaguars stalked through our camps; coati scampered beside us as we walked; angry spider monkeys rained dead wood on our heads. Oblivious of our existence, all the game of the forest seemed to parade to and fro across our trail.

Since war parties in the jungle usually attack naked and painted with *jenipapo*, our Indians wore coloured shirts and blue jeans. They were from ten tribes, and between them they had long hair, rounded hair, parted hair, cropped hair covered by Air Force hats, straw hats, officers' caps, cloth caps, slouched hats and Pripuri's red railwayman's cap. They were always laughing across the language barriers that lay between them—usually over some obvious joke. One night a Juruna told a story about rapids, and instead of saying "A rock broke my paddle", he said "The paddle broke my rock". As they marched out next morning, someone called: "Adriano, did the rock break the paddle?" "No," was the expected reply, "the paddle broke the rock." They moved off, holding each other up as they shuddered with laughter, and we heard them calling out the same question and the same reply for the rest of the day.

"What a marvel the Indian is," Claudio said, as we moved behind them on the trail. "On the Roncador and Cururu expeditions we had frontiersmen—violent men, each with his re-

[128]

volver. But the *caboclo* is terrified of wild Indians, and to prove he still has courage, he fights with the others. Several had killed two or three men before, and one kicked a boiling pot of coffee over our cook, just because he had forgotten his food. The cook crouched there, trembling from the scalds. I was so angry I filled the pot with water and said, 'You kick it again'. If he had, I would have put three bullets in his stomach. There's the difference. With Indians, you don't wear a revolver for your own men."

Our expedition was following a *civilizado* plan—air-strips linked by trails—but it was the skill of the Indians that made the plan possible. The nature of jungle dominates the game of contact with an unknown tribe, and wherever we were, whatever was happening, an Indian would pause every few minutes to pick a strange sound out of the maze of animal noises around. Every track, every broken twig, was examined and assessed, and the safety of our party depended on their jungle skill. They were our radar in the forest.

Once, when Erno and I came to the cutting head, Pripuri waved us to stop.

"The monkeys are going down," he whispered. "The monkeys are running on the ground."

Pripuri loved announcements of this sort. Apparently, Cuyabano had left the trail to shoot some Capuchin monkeys, and the pack had dropped off the trees and escaped through the undergrowth.

"When the monkeys only know the puma, they stay in the trees. But when the monkeys know Indians, they understand his arrows." Pripuri paused dramatically. "Then they drop."

Next day, Pripuri halted a swing of his machete. In front of us, at knee height, there was a hole cut in a rotten tree. He pointed at thick, blunt cuts which must have been made with a stone axe, but said that from the dried-up state of the comb, the Indians who took the honey had done so four or five years before.

A day or two later, Pripuri paused at a small sapling bent at waist height. Like most Indian leaders, he is a teacher almost by instinct, and was always trying to improve our jungle education. He showed us the definite break in the sapling, and how the top was dropping to the ground. We already knew that no animal except the tapir breaks at this height; but every hunting Indian does, as a matter of course, to mark his trail. Pripuri looked carefully for a tapir's tell-tale tooth marks under the break, and ran his finger up and down to show us that they were not there.

With Cuyabano he cast around and discovered a whole line of these broken stems and twigs, moving at right angles across our trail.

"One man and one boy," he said, indicating that some of the saplings were broken lower down, at the height of a boy's hand. "Maybe a month ago." They could tell by the degree the saplings had dried.

"How do you know it wasn't a Kayabi?" I asked.

"*Civilizados* and Kayabi mark with a knife. Truly, Adriano, the men who walked here were wild Indians."

And so, from the journey's start, at sixty miles from their village, the Kreen-Akrore had begun to feel for us in the jungle. Like wrestlers in the dark, their scouting parties reached towards us through the camouflage; and at the speed of half a mile a day, our trace advanced steadily towards them.

All around us was a whole continent of vegetation undisturbed except for animal tracks that twisted through the gaps between the bushes. Through it our trail advanced, gaping at every yard with the yellow wounds of branches, the mauves of sliced llianas, the white sap of the rubber tree which bleeds for hours. Indian paths are much less of an intrusion in the jungle because they beat the bushes aside with clubs; our machetes sliced so clean that the track was studded with shoe-high stakes, half-concealed by the debris. Canvas shoes were stabbed to pieces in a fortnight, and most leather boots were finished in a month.

Perhaps in the film unit we were more aware of the trail because our equipment required five cargo journeys compared with everyone else's single stage. We hung up the game we shot —to be carried back later—and some stretches of the trail were as gaudy as a butcher's shop with brown and red jacus, blue macaws, silver macacu, and great pools of blood dripping from spider monkeys. Old camp-sites were littered with plucked feathers and coloured labels, and stank with unburied entrails. It did not need much imagination to think of our line of 340 degrees as something cruel and revolutionary in the jungle.

Any forest Indians, striking our path, would, as hunters, sit and wait for the animal that used it. If the animal were alone, then the Kreen-Akrore would probably kill him, as they had killed Richard Mason, for what they could take from the body. If it was a large party, they would probably remain for several days, watching. They must have seen our line creeping in the direction of their home, and when they arrived back at their village, and described what they saw, it would have seemed to the tribe like some giant centipede feeling for its prey in the dark. We were nervous of the unseen Indian watching from the undergrowth, but they must have been a hundred times more frightened of us.

* * *

At the end of the first week, we struck a wide stream with the clear, amber water of deep forest. Claudio chopped down a tree trunk to serve as a bridge, and on the other side we came to dark slabs of rock and trees that began climbing up, row after row. We realised, as we struggled between boulders and llianas, that we had stumbled on to the steep face of a range of hills.

The trail went up and down a series of switchback humps. Strung out, we would have been easy to ambush, but we always travelled in convoy, and kept together as much as possible.

"Indians are hunters who kill by surprise," Claudio said. "Even when we were outnumbered by two hundred Xavantes on the Serra do Roncador, they never charged an alert, well-armed party."

Claudio left presents strung across the cutting head every night; four saucepans, twelve knives, eighteen strings of mauve beads, two strips of cloth.

"Certainly they will refuse them. But presents jolt the mind," Claudio argued. "All strangers, according to Kreen-Akrore experience, are enemies. Can a present-giver be an enemy, too? It will disturb their psychology, dislocate the reflex to kill."

It was a similar theory that prevented any attempt to reach the Kreen-Akrore. Pripuri and Bejai said several times that they would follow the Kreen-Akrore's tracks back to their hunting camp, but Claudio always refused.

[131]

"That was the stupidest mistake I ever made—to walk into a Txikao camp. They were all lying in their hammocks under the trees, and not one of them saw me. I was almost up to the hammock of an old man when he opened his eyes. I offered him a red-handled machete as a present. And suddenly what screaming, what running, mothers grabbing children, arrows flying everywhere. I would be dead if Cerilo the Kayabi had not been following behind. He fired in the air, and with just that one shot, they were gone."

Claudio laid down the expedition's policy for what must have been the hundredth time.

"It put the Txikao contact back for eight years. It is, therefore, a disaster to come upon Indians in the jungle. First, they must watch from safety. Then they must have time to understand. Finally, they must take presents without pressure. And in the end, the contact must be in an open place, where they are safe and can see. The Juruna would never have held their ground the first time if they had not watched us drop our revolvers in the river."

As Claudio talked, during those first few weeks on the trail, Erno and I began to sense that we were not manoeuvring with the Kreen-Akrore at all, but with an imaginary Indian who lived in Claudio's head—a composite Xavante, Juruna, Suya, Txikao—who had somehow materialised on the screen of iungle around us. Once, when we were carrying equipment up the trail, we found an excuse to rest a little longer—the loads were very heavy—by analysing the forest we could see. We were faced not by a wall of vegetation, but by an infinite variety of leaves in a limitless number of planes, and looking closely we realised that what made vision difficult was less the mass of vegetation than the variation of light. The sun was striking through the canopy of branches down into the jungle and occasionally a brilliant shaft hit a leaf facing in our direction, so that it was like a mirror aimed at the eyes. An elephant could have stood behind that leaf and remained invisible. Over the whole scene, however, the sunlight was ricochetting from one leaf to another, one plane to the next—a million variations of brilliance and darkness. Every few minutes the sun moved, so that light pierced the canopy in different places, altering the values beneath. The dew dripped from leaf to leaf, and the tree-tops moving in the wind opened new channels for the sun, making everything dance and shiver. We realised that the jungle is not so much a wall, but a shimmering, winking screen before the eyes.

In the long run, its effect on every man is to reflect his gaze back into his own mind. You do not search for your enemy in the jungle, you play chess with him in your brain.

As we cut our way up a hump in the first range of hills, Pripuri thought he heard axe blows. But later that night he came to talk to me as I lay in my hammock.

"Adriano, you know that axe noise?"

"Yes."

"I think it was two monkeys banging nuts together."

Next day, however, he saw a definite column of smoke, and several Kayabi who climbed nearby trees saw it, too.

"It's a big smoke," said Pripuri. "Maybe a plantation."

"But who could have a village so close to our trail, and only fifty miles from the Kreen-Akrore?"

Claudio, renowned for his forgetfulness over minor matters, often mislaid both his spectacles and the date. Sunday usually had to be found for him by the two or three Indians who had transistor radios and who could catch up with the date by listening to the news. So the Tuesday after Pripuri saw the smoke was declared a Sunday, and in the morning everyone washed their clothes, sewed up their boots, and talked.

"For me these smoke-makers are not Kreen-Akrore. No." Pripuri was probably the only Indian who really understood the idea of the expedition, who helped in order to add the Kreen-Akrore to the Parque's strength. He enjoyed making speeches.

"For me these are those Indians who came to the Manitsaua and messed with the rubber-tappers. That is why the rubber-tappers have gone away. But the Kreen-Akrore do not frighten, they finish everyone. So I am thinking these are the peaceful Indians who messed me when I lived down the Manitsaua. Those broke my corn and ate my melons, but they did not kill. They made smoke behind the Juruna village, and one ran out in the plantation to catch Bimbina's daughter, but they messed only."

Claudio did not agree. "We know the Kreen-Akrore travel hundreds of miles to the Txukahamei on the Xingu, so why not to the Juruna? Bimbina's daughter says the men who chased her had short hair—just like the Kreen-Akrore. Perhaps to the north the Kreen-Akrore kill the Txukahamei because they are attacked. But to the south they do not kill because the Indians here are more peaceful."

If Claudio was right, the contact would be easier. If Pripuri was right, then the whole operation would become a more complicated triangular process.

"For me," Pripuri insisted, "these Indians are of the family of the Apiaka.[1] Once the chief of the Apiaka said to me, 'A gang of my people have gone up there, up the Peixoto. They went a long, long time ago.' Now I am thinking those Apiaka are still here. Adriano, who do you think taught us to put whiskers on our face?"

Surprised, I said I didn't know, though I knew Pripuri was talking about the blue "cat's-whiskers" tattooed across Kayabi cheeks.

"It was the Apiaka," Pripuri said triumphantly. "The Apiaka speak the same language as us. You will see, I will call them, and they will come and live in my village."

Pripuri obviously saw himself adding to his already Moses-like reputation.

Next day the trail dropped into the lowlands below the range, and there Pripuri found an Indian trail—only two or three days old. This was followed by more fresh signs of Indians in the vicinity.

Claudio's plan had originally been to go on until our food ran out, and then to re-stock at the Manitsaua base, hoping to reach the Peixoto on our second thrust. But the Indian signs made everyone nervous, and Claudio began to talk of racing back to Diauarum to get a 'plane to fly over the mysterious village on our flank. If there really was a village, it probably dominated the valley ahead, and he would find it helpful to know how large a group we had to deal with. Perhaps at the same time he could plan to divert our trail to the best place for an air-strip.

Next day we strung up a large bunch of presents, and buried

Above Cutting the trail in Kreen-Akrore territory (p. 126). (*Jesco von Puttkamer*)

Below Claudio checks the trail by compass. (*Jesco von Puttkamer*)

The Kayabi dance after killing a rubber-tapper in 1961 (p. 152). Claudio insisted that the actual body be replaced by a dummy. (*Louis Wolfers*)

Above left Claudio with hundreds of sweat bees on his hat. In untouched jungle they swarm round intruders (p. 137). (*Adrian Cowell*)

Above right Claudio holds up presents at night to invisible watchers—the Kreen-Akrore (p. 156). (*Adrian Cowell*)

Below Claudio crossing a river in Kreen-Akrore territory. (*Adrian Cowell*)

Above Building a bark canoe for the expedition. The fire makes the bark curl inwards. (*Erno Vincze*)

Below Building a canoe out of a solid tree-trunk. (*Adrian Cowell*)

the remains of the food, and much of the film equipment. As the cameras were worth £4,000, every shovelful of earth drew a wince from Erno and myself. Then we marched back for a whole day to our air-strip on the Manitsaua.

NOTE TO CHAPTER 13

1. The Apiaka are a semi-unknown tribe that fled from the rubber-tappers and have been seen by no-one since but the Kayabi. An account of why the Apiaka fled is in Captain Manuel Theophilo da Costa Pinheiro's report to Colonel Rondon in 1912. "Once he [Sr. Fabio Freire] invited all the Apiaka for coffee; they accepted in good faith; and when they were in the hut drinking, Sr. Freire commanded the contingent of the Collectorate, who were already waiting, to open fire, killing almost everyone. Only one woman escaped. And today whoever goes to the Collectorate can still see in front of the shed that was the barracks the place where all were buried in a common grave. After this deed, Sr. Freire gathered together about a hundred men amongst rubber-tappers and personnel of the Collectorate to attack the village that used to be on the rapids of S. Florencia. The assault was made very early, when the Apiaka were still within the village, and the Indians, terrified by the fire, came out of the huts making gestures and exclamations, and were received with bullets. Few escaped ... As it is easy to understand—persecuted and molested by the *civilizados*—the Apiaka buried themselves in the forest and abandoned the banks of the Juruena."

14

THE TRAIL HALTS

Three weeks later we moved up the trail, and when we heard the sound of Claudio's 'plane, Pripuri piled branches on the fire. Smoke rose up the tree trunks. The white cloud seeping through the canopy pin-pointed the head of the trail, and though we felt like mice peering up through the floor-boards, we knew everything must be revealed to Claudio above. For the face of the land that you have only felt in the darkness of the jungle acquires features and character from the air. Those two streams moving in opposite directions were, in fact, different stretches of the same river; that apparently limitless range of hills was just a peak you had the bad luck to strike.

A week later Claudio came stumping up the trail with two Brazilians, Maprim and Muniz, and half a dozen Indians.

"We are in a throat of the hills," Claudio said. "To our left there is a range. To our right there is a range. And in front there is a monster of a range. But I marked a gorge, and we will deviate and go through it."

"What about the village to the right?"

"Oh," said Claudio, "there is no village. Whoever made smoke makes smoke no more."

It was as simple as that. For weeks we had worried about that smoke, and now from the Olympian viewpoint of the aeroplane, the worry was just flicked aside. Claudio added that they had flown over the Kreen-Akrore village and had dropped presents tied to balloons. The Indians had rushed after the falling gifts, and one man had actually danced.

For the next few days we advanced at a steady mile and a quarter a day. But we were moving into a deeper valley, and soon progress became slow and trying. There were so many biting flies in that valley that a hundred bite marks could be counted on every hand; and in the evenings, if you tried to pull away the crab-like ticks, the flies pounced on every exposed inch of skin. The mosquitoes hunted in clouds, a foot-insect laid its eggs beneath our toe-nails, and the horse-flies had such long bloodsuckers that just when you thought you were protected by three layers of hammock, blanket and jeans, they would stab you neatly in the behind.

At the cutting-head, Pripuri had to be careful of the small hornets' nests which hung in the bushes. We ran when we heard his shout, and once, when I was stung four times on the lips, I was delirious most of the night. In one camp, about fifty red ants scrambled on to our shoes and up our legs at every step, and in another, the whole ground seemed to be black and moving. One Indian was stung by a scorpion, and several Kayabi were bitten by the inch-long "formigao" ant, whose bite can bring a fever.

But it was the sweat bees that won the title of plague of plagues. As soon as we stopped moving they swarmed up our nostrils, down our ear-holes, under our eyelids, crawling over every centimetre of body, sucking for salt. Someone had once told me about the "Geneva Convention" of the jungle; if the flies bite by day, then the mosquitoes fold their wings at night. But in that soggy forest between the two ranges of hills we were breakfast, lunch and dinner for everything that was hungry, and there was one novelty which even Claudio had not met before. Hard, marble-sized boils appeared on exposed areas of skin, obviously caused by bites; but though we watched, we never discovered who did the biting.

Erno and I passed a group of Kayabi slumped on the ground, lying by their machetes.

"Today we are weak," they said. "We think it was the monkey we ate yesterday."

As day succeeded day, the Indians seemed to be nearing a standstill. Food was dwindling, and the slower we went, the greater was our need to make the long supply-haul back to the Manitsaua. Claudio reduced rations, and the cutting slowed even more. Almost fifty miles of trail lay behind us, and almost hourly Claudio expected to strike the Peixoto. It would mean clear water, fish, a permanent camp, an air-drop, rest. But suddenly, to the despair of everyone, the trail began to climb right up into a range of hills. That evening we were back at the foot of the range for the night. Bitterly Claudio called it the Camp of Disappointment.

"I diverted the trail five degrees, just as we calculated in the 'plane. But where is the gorge?" he complained. "We have no luck in this jungle. The mountain just follows us round, pushing itself up in front of our noses."

Next day we cut from one shoulder of the hill to the next, higher and higher, until the trail flattened and began to drop again. It went down steeply for several hundred yards. An hour later, Pripuri parted the bushes and called out in excitement. Before us was a golden river. Bars of yellow light played on the surface, and a school of fish flicked their tails casually against the current. The sand was warm and yellow, and the water was a soothing green. Perhaps it is not strictly true that the only beauty in the jungle is to be found beside a river, but it seemed so to us. We washed in our first deep water since the Manitsaua, and stood on a rock where the sun actually touched our skin.

Next morning, Claudio searched up and down both sides of the river looking for an area suitable for an air-strip. By the afternoon the air-strip had become as elusive as the vanishing gorge. High jungle was all around, with huge tree trunks and many outcrops of rock. There was no possible site. Claudio decided that his only alternative was to build the air-strip by Disappointment Camp at the other side of the range, and we all trudged back down the trail. That night several Kayabi announced that they were going to leave, and Claudio was caustic as we marked out the air-strip next morning.

"They aren't any good any more," he said. "They sit. They don't want to work. They've lost their enthusiasm and only think of going away. Maybe, after all, frontiersmen would have been better. In three days the knives are out, but at least they stay for their salaries."

I reminded Claudio that he had been right and that the Indians had not had a single quarrel.

"Look at Cuyusi," Claudio interrupted. "He wants to go because he has toothache. Ipoh thinks someone is seducing his wife. Aru decided to get married—now, at this time! Cuyabano suddenly feels he should cut another plantation. One gets the idea, and the rest are like sheep."

It was against Claudio's principles to influence them to stay, and later that day he measured out food for their return journey. In the end, group after group, including Pripuri and Cuyabano, drifted back along the trail, and our strength was halved. We now numbered a total of fifteen, including the film unit, and Claudio's strategy had always been built on the security of a large party. Now that we were only twenty-five miles from the Kreen-Akrore village, and we knew that they were coming to within a few yards of our camp, it was more necessary than ever to show that we were strong.

Without any doubt, we were being watched. The cook heard voices in the jungle one morning, and called out: "Who's there?" There was no reply, only the sound of footsteps stealing away. Then came a more welcome sound.

"Aeroplane!" The forest echoed with Indian yells. "Aeroplane—aeroplane! AAAaaaayyyyeeee!"

Within a few minutes we could see the silver cross of the Helio-Courier 'plane which had been lent us by the University of Brasilia because it is specially designed to land on short airstrips. It came circling round our rising smoke. Claudio pulled out his miniature walkie-talkie and talked to the pilot.

"Tell Orlando the personnel are leaving. We need ten to fifteen more men." But the pilot's reply could only be heard when the 'plane was directly above; after two sentences he would pass out of range, until he came back on the return run.

"Tell Orlando the personnel are leaving! We need ten to fifteen more men!" There was a pause until the 'plane returned.

"We only have six days' food."

"How many?"

"Six! Half a dozen. Six. When can you parachute supplies?"

Pause—an anxious one.

"Wednesday. Wednesday. Wednesday."

"How far are we from the air-strip we chose?" Claudio shouted.

The 'plane flew off and came back ten minutes later. "Ten kilometres at 320 degrees."

It was obvious what had happened. In the fog of jungle,

Claudio had diverted a little too far to the east, and we had missed both the gorge and the site for the air-strip. As soon as the 'plane left, we started cutting again, this time on 320 degrees.

The river bent in a great curve, and three days later we struck it lower down. Claudio came back from examining the site for the air-strip that evening in great excitement. On the previous day, he had tied presents up at the head of the trail near the site.

"The beads are gone. Not the knives—they are still there. But all the beads—gone completely. And I tied carefully, so the monkeys couldn't steal them."

"Why," Erno wondered, "did they leave the knives?"

"The Txukahamei say we interrupted him. It was only one man."

It was not an entirely convincing explanation, but at this stage we believed the Kreen-Akrore were still deliberately refusing our presents. It was conceivable, however, that one, possibly a younger man with a particularly pressing mistress, was unable to resist the shimmering necklaces. When he had slipped back for the beads, perhaps he had felt the knives would have been too difficult to hide from his companions.

There were more signs.

"We were cutting through banana," Claudio said. "We were making a great noise when Bejai came running. 'Listen,' he said, 'an axe.' 'It's only Cupionim cutting in the jungle,' I said. Then I turned and there was Cupionim just standing behind me. Bang, bang, bang. It was like that. Quick blows on a tree. And only five minutes before we had shot a bush turkey. They were signalling—calling our attention—from just fifty yards."

The news ran round the camp.

"Are they coming up the trail?"

"Certainly. Didn't Tacara [the cook] hear them talking? I am sure they have been all around."

So the Kreen-Akrore were near, and in the blind language of the jungle they were letting us know that they were coming closer. Presumably they understood our intentions were peaceful, and a contact was possible.

This did not make our weakness any less dangerous. Most

massacres occur while Indians are visiting the camp of an expedition. They make friends, watch where every person and every gun is placed, and then start the clubbing. Or they are suddenly frightened by something the *civilizados* do, and the result is the same. At the critical stage, when both sides doubt the intentions of the other, it is essential to have a party of such strength that even a surprise attack has no chance of success.

*   *   *

Hour after hour passed on Wednesday, but no 'plane. Claudio again decided that he would cut the air-strip close to Disappointment Camp. This would have the advantage of concentrating our strength, since the air-strip, the air-drop site and the camp would all be within two hundred yards.

Next day, the 'plane came—but the pilot only shouted a message by walkie-talkie. The parachutes had not arrived: could we last till Monday?

Then, on Monday, when packages began to drop from the 'plane, they plummeted down without parachutes. They only contained unbreakables—hammocks, rubber balls and plastic toys—all presents for the Kreen-Akrore. Orlando was in the 'plane, shouting down the walkie talkie. The fuel in the Parque was almost exhausted, he said; the aeroplane had to be returned to Brasilia, the parachutes hadn't arrived. But there would soon be a food drop, this he promised. And twelve men had set off up the Manitsaua and were travelling towards us. The 'plane flew off.

Claudio continued working on the air-strip for another day, then all work stopped when the rice and beans gave out.

"You'll see. You'll never starve with Indians," Claudio said optimistically.

Already our diet included wild honey, monkey, jungle fowl, roots and the tips of palm trees. But we were only able to collect enough food for the whole party when everyone was hunting. For instance, to dig up ten pounds of the delicious potato-like tuber called *cara*, it took three of us several hours of work.

For the first time on the expedition we began to live and hunt as Indians—for subsistence only. And this brought home to us how different was an Indian trail from that of a *civilizado*. An Indian transports only his body, but he finds his food and other requirements in the jungle. A *civilizado* transports all the supplies of an expedition, and his trail is a channel for the stored energy and accumulated power of the cities. How dependent we were on that distant energy was confirmed when the 'plane dropped, not supplies, but a letter from Orlando.

Posto Leonardo.

Claudio,

This comes with the little 'plane. Affairs are so confused that one almost comes to despair. I have made a great effort and cried without limit. When the Minister was here, he liked everything very much, so much that he commanded a decree should be drawn up right here, bringing the area of Itavanunu into the Parque. Of him, I made only two requests. His personal intercession with the University of Brasilia for the loan of the 'plane and a request direct to the Air Force for fuel for the expedition. Of course, the Minister said he would deal with it personally, and he would have, if it were not for the mosquitoes at the back-side of every Minister. Immediately one came up and said, you can leave it to me, Mr Minister, I will handle it all in your name. The Minister commanded urgency. Fine. I kept quiet. But two days later I began to agitate by radio and telephone to ascertain the result. And there the tangle began.

I sent at least nineteen messages on this matter to Rio and Brasilia. I agitated God and the whole world. Our

situation was becoming difficult. Alvaro [the youngest
Villas Boas brother] was making a tremendous effort in
Brasilia. But the request went by bureaucratic channels.
The Air Force refused the gasoline and the University
withdrew its 'plane. On the day after the drop, the 'plane
was officially withdrawn and its extension has not been confirmed till this day. The under-developed—principally
those that clothe themselves as intellectuals—are domestic
animals, submissive, fawning, nauseating, in front of any
foreigner that turns up. The Rector is interested in pushing
the 'plane into a large botanical research programme—in
a collaboration of the highest degree, he intends to lend it
to an English group, the Royal Society, which is in the
Serra do Roncador, with a road at their tail and in shouting distance of everything they need. Even better, the
English—six are here at present—are not making any particular request for the 'plane. But the Rector surely thinks
that, poor devil, he will gain international projection by
this. I don't know if I already said in a previous letter—or
if I left it to say personally—that on the first occasion when
the Rector refused the 'plane, I was abrupt, almost rude,
at a "round table" formed to discuss the matter. I even
arrived at the point of saying that we were poor unfor-
tunates, occupying an immense country. Poor, unhappy,
humble and humiliated, where the truth is such that in a
problem like this—humanitarian, national, involving the
saving of life—there are still men who judge it more important to divert a 'plane to transport leaves and grass to
decorate the little saucers of a Department of Botany. The
Rector left somewhat annoyed, but the next day ordered
that if I made an official request he would concede the
'plane for thirty days. Olimpio who is diplomatic—a
student, though ceremonious in front of the Magnificent
—requested permission to speak and said remember, Sir
Rector, that this aeroplane was given to the University by
the Summer Institute of Linguistics and the people of
Philadelphia to provide assistance for the Indian, and it
would not be good in this hour of need to divert it to other
ends.

[143]

We are arriving at, we are already, in a difficult situation. Look:

Plane tied up in Brasília.
Air Force refusing gasoline.
Health Service Unit team of doctors marooned in Poirıri
from lack of gasoline.
Our truck in Xavantina awaiting orders to go to Garapu
but this depends on the raft going up river to meet it.
I despatched it today to fetch four drums of gasoline
that I bought in Xavantina for the Health Unit doctors.
The Post—as always. With six English from the scientific group, six journalists sent us by the Minister's office
—foreign journalists.
The budget runs out in June, with no prospect at present
of a new budget.

Still, I don't despair. Nor Alvaro. I sent a note to Gollen
for Reporter Esso of Channel 4, giving a brief history of the
expedition, but saying that it was necessary and urgent to
have better collaboration—from the Ministry of Aviation
and the University of Brasilia, to FUNAI and the Parque
expedition in the attraction of the Kreen-Akrore Indians.
On Saturday this went. Today we hear that it has been
launched on three different T.V. programmes, several radio
stations and newspapers.

Later. The news today is better. Alvaro has radioed that
Custodio the pilot of the University aeroplane—who was
in Rio—has arrived in Brasilia and will probably reach us
tomorrow, since the University, it appears, will cede the
'plane again tomorrow. But only for twenty days. From the
Ministry of Aviation—nothing. I told our São Paulo office
to make two phone calls to Rio about it. Alvaro also made
two as well. We learnt that Dr Queiroz head of FUNAI is
incensed about the matter. The Ministry of Aviation wants
payment for the gasoline. Our Minister says to pay what-

[144]

ever they want, but they have still not resolved the point. How magnificent if the Kreen-Akrore could make a little raid up to Cachimbo.

There followed several paragraphs on minor details, and it was signed "Orlando".

15

WAITING FOR THE AIR-DROP

The dark spaces between the trees were just growing opaque when we set out in the dawn. Claudio's orders were that no-one should travel without a companion and no hunting party should move in the direction of the Kreen-Akrore. Erno and I therefore followed the first abortive trail to the Peixoto.

We padded along the beaten track, listening for the jungle fowl that call in the hour after sunrise. We had brought back coati, monkey, ant-bear, peccary and tortoise in the last few days. But the greatest prize, a deer or tapir, would almost certainly elude us. They stand invisible in the undergrowth, and only crash away when you are within ten yards. Then their flight is so sudden that in the tangle of jungle, there is no possibility of a shot. But like roulette, camouflage is unpredictable. On one morning a tapir walked down a narrow stream-bed towards me, completely unsuspecting, strolling into my sights. I even had time to creep along the bank and change the cartridge for a solid slug. As the slug sank precisely behind the neck and between the shoulder blades, the tapir probably died without even being aware of my existence.

Today we did not expect the same kind of luck. The forest sounded hollow from the click-clack of the heavy dew, and there were patches of mist in the little valleys as we climbed. We presently came out into a summit area of bare rock and white skeleton trees, and there we caught a hum—so faint a vibration that you almost doubted that it came from a living being. It was down the shoulder of the hill to our right. As we crept forward, the hum swelled to a snore, rising and falling, rich and self-assured. It was the summons of male to female, the great Amazonian bush turkey calling to its mate.

Two men had taught me to hunt bush turkeys: Kaluana who

died of measles, and Bebcuche, who was shot in Mato Verdi. I always thought of it as a memorial to them that the *civilizado* now knew that the turkey would be high in a tree, standing on a branch, twisting his head and huge beak from side to side, watching for every movement. At the first hint of danger, he would shrill and bend his legs, and almost instantly launch into space.

We tried to make each step as balanced as Kaluana would have liked, to feel for the leaf or twig beneath. I bent and twisted to prevent my clothes catching on the leaves; I held my breath, waiting for the next snore. If the turkey heard us, the snore would stop, and we would be without our guide in a featureless sea of jungle.

A flock of parrots rocketed across the sky, and we took ten quick paces under cover of their screaming. The snore was ahead. I crouched and peered through screens of leaves, trying to penetrate the variations of light so that I could focus. There —suddenly a shiver across the light. As each snore came, so something twitched, and bending and twisting as soundlessly as possible, I at last saw a black tail-feather tipped with white. Moving slightly, I found a gap in the foliage, and through the leaves glimpsed the powerful neck and swelling breast. I fired, the turkey thumped to the ground, and we moved back to the trail.

Ten minutes later there was a clatter above, and a black face peered down at us. Boom. A second spider monkey came shrieking through the branches, shouting in fury, shaking every branch in a shower of falling debris. A second shot, and a second rain of scarlet drops. We had to sit for ten minutes more before either corpse relaxed its grip on the branches and fell to the ground.

The silent avenue of the trail had worked to our advantage. But now, as we carried the food back to the camp, we knew that just as the snore gave the turkey away, so the trail and the sound of gunfire would tell the Kreen-Akrore where to find us.

As Erno and I made our way to the camp, we knew that we should not search the undergrowth with our eyes, since straining to see makes them tired and less receptive. Indians move casually, watching the ground for obstacles and signs; it is their ears that are alert to catch the hundreds of signals which form their radar-like image of the surrounding world. The harsh scream of a hawk, the golden bell of a ricongo, the whoosh-whoosh of humming-bird wings—the range is infinite and difficult to interpret. Even a sound as simple as a whistle can come from a tapir, a monkey, a resonant frog or a pheasant-like *macucu*, depending on its tone. Your interpretation of these sounds is vital, and the rustle of a companion is like static on a radar screen. Erno, walking behind me, made me feel "blind" and therefore nervous.

We stopped and listened every few hundred yards, and were almost half-way back to the camp when there was a crash about fifty yards ahead. In a bound of flowing beauty, a deer leapt across the trail. Half a minute later, a *macucu* rocketed up through the branches. We listened carefully. If a pig had disturbed the deer, that meant a herd; and when attacked, herds can rush hysterically round in circles. I once saw a Txukahamei shoot nine in twenty minutes; with a break of luck we might get two or three. Two hundred yards on, I caught a sound of movement parallel to our own. When we stopped, the movement stopped, too. We started again and the sounds started, too. They seemed more furtive than any pig.

In the jungle, a turkey moving on dead leaves makes as much noise as a man, a pack of coati even more than a tapir; the sounds of movement are deceptive. But thirty yards away in the undergrowth I was sure a large animal was moving parallel to us. A monkey cheeped at him; the birds were flustered and giving alarm calls. Something low and black slunk across the path twenty yards ahead—a small ant-eater. Something unseen slithered off a tree and padded away. The tap-tap of a woodpecker sounded to the left, and in the distance a rotten tree fell with a moaning crash.

All this time, the crunch and rustle of our fellow-traveller moved parallel to the left of the trail. He was about thirty yards away, no closer and no further than before, and his course seemed too regular and too controlled to be that of an animal. Erno dropped back forty yards so that we could hear better without the distraction of the other's movements.

If it was a Kreen-Akrore, there was no question of attack. He could not approach through the undergrowth without our

[148]

knowledge, and if he had wished to kill us, he would have waited by the trail, and we would have heard nothing until the first bow-shot. We padded on; there was nothing else to do. But my legs had become stiff and therefore clumsier and noisier, and my nervousness grew to a climax of quite irrational fear when we approached the camp and found it completely silent. Not a pan rattled, not a voice spoke, not a throat coughed. I almost fled. Then some unseen hand switched on a radio, and the whole edifice of fear was toppled by reason. Imagination had got the better of commonsense, and I felt guilty enough not to mention what had happened to Claudio. Erno and I never discovered whether we had been followed by a Kreen-Akrore or by a puma, but it did teach us that it is not really danger which raises the tension over months in the jungle. It is the fact that you can seldom prove that your imagination has played you false.

As we entered the camp, the tinny sound of the radio added to the welcoming feeling of return. The mauves and scarlets of the hammocks were a cheerful sight, and it would have been a pleasant camp except for the foetid smell. A week before, we had killed eight wild boar, and so many people were sick from over-eating that four of the carcasses had been left behind when we moved camp to our present site fifty yards from the last. Those carcasses were now decaying, and every few minutes vultures passed overhead, circling the trees. Other vultures, too bloated to fly, sat in the higher branches and watched us with bilious eyes.

Claudio waved a book excitedly at us as we came in.

"How can he be such a pessimist, Adriano?" he demanded, as if we had been arguing together for the last hour. "Of course Marx was a great man. The means of production and the fruits of labour should be controlled by the people. But how can you say production is all? How can that justify the death of one child, one-tenth of Vietnam?"

I could see that the book was Huxley's *Brave New World*, and I wondered how long it had taken Claudio to get from Huxley to Marx, and why at present he should be interested in either. But there he was, sitting on the edge of his hammock, immensely excited, waving the book away from me and in the direction of

Maprim, one of the two Brazilians who had come up the trail with him. He talked on and on for the rest of the afternoon.

"Take the humanity of Christ, for instance . . ."

Claudio has an academic mind and responds eagerly to ideas in books, but it was a bizarre moment to express those ideas. Here we were, locked in some sort of classical dance with the Kreen-Akrore, our finger-tips almost touching their finger-tips through the screen of jungle. Our expedition machine had run down, while the very elusiveness of the Kreen-Akrore was beginning to play on our nerves. Every footprint, every broken twig the Indians found could have been caused by something else. And only when Bejai found a monkey shot by the Kreen-Akrore did it seem that, at last, we had something concrete.

"Was the arrow in the monkey?" Claudio had asked.

"No. He bites and pulls it out."

"Then how do you know it was shot by a Kreen-Akrore?"

"The hole."

That seemed definite enough. No predator other than human can make a clean hole straight through a monkey's stomach. But when Bejai took us next day to see the carcass, it had been picked clean by vultures. The evidence, as always, was inconclusive, and we seemed to be moving through a jungle of fantasy.

I lay in my hammock that night asking and answering the questions that troubled us. Our fires were making red caves in the night, and the jungle near me danced and shivered as the flames rose and fell. A frog was ticking every second regularly away, and another frog, of a different kind, was starting to croak slowly, winding himself up to a frantic crescendo. Together— the monotonous and the hysterical—they seemed to be practising for a Hitchcock soundtrack.

Why, I wondered, hadn't Claudio built a palisade round our camp, as he had when he had been approaching the Xavantes? The answer was obvious. Not a single stone or arrow had come in our direction. Why didn't he build a fence of brushwood to slow down a charge? Again, simple. Because a charge is seldom the kind of attack made by Indians. Why had the Kayabi left us so suddenly, knowing we would be outnumbered? This time the answer was more complex, and I began to think back several weeks. When we had returned to the Manitsaua, and Claudio

Above Claudio and Pripuri examine a sapling broken by the Kreen-Akrore to mark a hunting trail (p. 129). (*Adrian Cowell*)

Below Cutting through driftwood blocking an unused river. (*Adrian Cowell*)

Above Hauling the canoes overland. (*Adrian Cowell*)

Below Hauling the canoes through rapids near the Kreen-Akrore village. Expeditions were normally attacked when helpless in rapids. (*Adrian Cowell*)

Above Jungle on the river's edge; the Kreen-Akrore followed the expedition along the bank. (*Adrian Cowell*)

Below Orlando and Claudio lead the expedition descending the unknown R. Peixoto Azevedo—unknown because the Kreen-Akrore had killed all previous intruders (p. 163). (*Adrian Cowell*)

Above Orlando measures a Kreen-Akrore footprint. (*Adrian Cowell*)

Below Orlando examines a twig broken a few moments earlier by one of the Kreen-Akrore shadowing the expedition. (*Adrian Cowell*)

had gone to get the 'plane at Diauarum, the rest of us were camped by the river. One night a rubber-tapper's boat came gliding across the water. A swarthy, melodramatic figure stepped out, wearing two revolvers. He turned out to be the overseer of the rubber group which had been pushing down the Manit-saua for the last few years.[1]

Over coffee, he asked after a missing rubber-tapper whose name sounded like Ervilho de Luque.

"A *pretinho*—a little black man—with a wife and four children. He ran away owing me one million two hundred thousand." This was roughly £200.

Pripuri said he had not been seen in the Parque, and the overseer left. But later, several Kayabi began to talk. They had seen Ervilho de Luque, for when his debt grew too big to pay, he had avoided the company's gunmen waiting up-river, and had canoed down to the Parque with his wife and children. The children, the Kayabi showed me by indicating the height, were about seven, five, three and a babe in arms.

The first village in the Parque, turning south at the mouth of the Manitsaua, was Cuyabano's.

"The man is tired," the Kayabi explained. "He says to Cuyabano, 'You help me to paddle to the Post and I will reward you.' So Cuyabano agrees, and they go paddling. Cuyabano behind. Then in the middle of the way they land, and the woman gets out with the child in her arms, and the man bends over the food. Cuyabano avails himself. He gives a paddle to the head. The man falls in the water. Splash. Cuyabano hits him. Pah. On the neck with the axe. Pah."

"Did the children run?"

"No, they cry. They wave their hands. Then Cuyabano puts the axe to their heads."

"Did the woman run?"

"No. She just waves her hands."

"Did the man insult Cuyabano?"

"No. He thanks and rewards him."

"Why did Cuyabano do it?"

"We don't know."

On Claudio's return, the murders[2] had seemed too serious to discuss. If he didn't know, he would certainly find out through his own channels. And a few days later, we were all cutting the trail, when Cuyabano imitated the call of a group of zoggi-zoggi monkeys. They answered and he replied, and this went on for several minutes until the monkeys were directly above—beautiful small creatures with grey, fluffy fur, like Persian cats. Their faces were inquisitive and mischievous, and we laughed and talked to them as they chattered to us. They seemed to be our only friends in the indifferent forest until Cuyabano, smiling his Japanese smile, swung his gun and killed two with a single shot.

That night I heard Claudio talking across the camp.

"A monkey, yes. All right, you must eat, Cuyabano. But man is not a monkey. The more gentle we are, the stronger the Parque will be. If a rubber-tapper comes to your house, then you say, 'You cannot stay here. This is our land. I will take you to Claudio.' But never kill him."

I lay in my hammock in that camp called by Claudio the Camp of Disappointment, remembering that the "man is not a monkey" theme had gone on for hours, and that it had seemed to me that Claudio might have a chance of changing Cuyabano's son but he was unlikely ever to change Cuyabano himself.

But I also remembered something I had not previously connected with these murders. While we were preparing for our expedition, a Kayabi boy had danced up and down in our hut; and I worked it out that it must have been a week or two after the killings. The boy was one who was mentally retarded, but he often visited us for sweets or coffee. During those days he had picked up a pole and danced up and down, chanting. No-one had paid any attention, but the dance was the one the Kayabi perform after a killing, and it suddenly seemed obvious to me that the retarded boy was dancing because it was fresh in his mind. The ceremony must have been going on in one of the villages at the time.

It was inevitable that I should jump to the next conclusion. The Kayabi had gone back to their villages for the festival of the necklace; that was why they had left. The festival takes place after the first ceremony—when the teeth have loosened in the skull.[3]

By this stage in our search for the Kreen-Akrore, I had ceased to be surprised by the Indians' matter-of-fact attitude to killing.

For him it was a functional act, without guilt. And as I co-operated in our daily destruction of life as we ran and fired and hunted, and felt the blood dripping from our shoulders, I knew that the hunter's eyes watch an animal with one quite practical goal—eating it. An Indian is aware that an animal may kill and eat him one day, so he kills and eats it today. The killing of a human being outside the tribe is just an extension of this facet of his life.

I could feel a hundred thousand square miles of forest pressing into the hollow red space above my fire, and as my nervousness increased, I remembered that this had been Claudio's life for nearly thirty years. It was not just a life surrounded and stalked by unknown Indians, but one dependent on unpredictable Indian associates. And the last time some of the hot-headed Txukahamei lost their temper at Diauarum and threatened to kill Claudio, it was Cuyabano who—to Claudio's great annoyance—had quickly organised a dozen armed Kayabi in his defence. Cuyabano had now killed four pathetically small children, and in doing so had virtually hamstrung our expedition.

Perhaps his brutal act was hard to understand. But it did illustrate the years of tension behind the argumentative academic, who—as our expedition lay paralysed and surrounded by Kreen-Akrore—had talked all afternoon about Aldous Huxley.

NOTES TO CHAPTER 15

1. Their supplies come from Cuyaba, and most of their rubber-tappers are men who once worked on the River Teles Pires. For six years or more they had been gradually pushing down the river towards the Parque.
2. Under Brazilian law, Indians from recently contacted tribes are regarded as children and not punished for their crimes.
3. Months later, when Pripuri and some of the Kayabi had returned to the expedition, I asked if they had made a necklace from the children, too. "No. Just the father and mother. One old man made a hole. Another threaded the line. Another made the knot. Another supervised. Then all the Kayabi sang."

[153]

16

THE STONES

A coloured parachute came swinging out of the sky next morning. Rice. Beans. Coffee. Salt. It seemed like Christmas.

A second parachute failed to open, and split like a ripe tomato on the jagged stumps of the air-strip. Tins of oil and condensed milk lay shattered across the ground, and we all stuck twigs in the pool and sucked at the mess.

"Like honey with turtles' eggs," Bejai suggested.

In the afternoon, two more parachutes dropped supplies, bringing our total to 150 kilos of rice, together with enough beans, oil, coffee, salt and sugar to last three weeks. Two days later, fourteen of the Parque's more ebullient Indians came whooping up the trail with even more food.

"Where are those Kreen-Akrore?" said the Txukahamei, striding into the camp.

On that day the first heavy rain of the wet season fell, and with it all our nervousness seemed to vanish. Claudio even said he would abandon his concealed air-strip by Disappointment Camp and cut a more exposed but more convenient one on the Peixoto, where our canoes would be built.

Soon a new camp stood on a ten-foot bank above the River Peixoto Azevedo, with its kitchen and eating place on a beautiful sandbank jutting into the water. It offered a perfect site for a contact with an unknown tribe. The kitchen area was clearly visible across the water, and the audience on the other bank would feel safe, hidden behind a thick screen of jungle.

On our second night in that camp, Claudio came hurrying back in the dark.

"I was just going out of the camp," he said, "when he ran. I know the sound of a tapir or paca. With certainty it was a man. Six or seven steps, then he crouched."

Our audience was arriving.

Next day a message came from the air-strip.

"There is smoke down-river. You must keep at least five in the camp."

On the third evening, the cooks came running from their spit of sand to say that two or three sticks had been thrown at them from across the water.

"Maluware, that's cigarette and whisky soft talk," Maprim called out to one of the cooks. Maluware was a very *civilizado* Karaja from the River Araguaia, who, instead of being jailed for a crime, had been exiled to the Parque. He had come up with the relief party, and spoke in the dialect of the Brazilian frontier.

"Sirrah, are you not believing that I am receiving sticks in the night?" he replied.

Suddenly we heard club blows coming from across the river, and we all leapt from our hammocks. Dark bird shapes, disturbed by the banging, flashed over the water.

"They are approximating," Maluware whispered.

"We are approaching the moment," Claudio said. "It is a classic opportunity."

Nothing more happened that night. Next morning we crossed to the far bank and looked at the freshly broken branches and the marks where a club had been beaten on a fallen log. Though Claudio's plan had always been to enter the Kreen-Akrore village, the technique of the Indian Protection Service was to make a contact at a distance from a village, sometimes as far as sixty miles or more. We were now about twenty-five miles from the Kreen-Akrore village, and the summons of the clubs could be the opening move.

If it was, then the passage down-river would no longer be necessary, and no-one knew the weakness of a canoe expedition better than the Kayabi. The River Peixoto flows into the River Teles Pires in the heartland of the Kayabi tribe, and here the Teles Pires is broken by rapids for over a hundred miles of seething water. Expeditions in the past had often reported[1] how the "catmen" dogged them, sniping from the trees and then, when they were caught in the rapids, attacked or launched a hail of arrows. As Claudio put it: "A contact would be more comfortable here."

[155]

That evening, Erno, Maprim and I sat by the river, which was slowly turning black in the fading light. The fallen trees in the water stood out as white as skeletons. A frog started croaking like a rusty hinge, another joined him with a whining hum, rather like a cricket. Several of the Txukahamei were sitting around, talking.

Plop. A stick fell in the water.

"What was that?"

"Just a stick," said Bejai.

"Where did the stick come from?"

"Maybe the other side."

Plop. Plop. Two stones dropped into the water. Someone dashed up the bank for Claudio, and we kicked the fires down to a dull glow. Then we all sat on the warm sand, looking across the water at the blank line of the river bank. On this stretch the channel was about six feet deep, but in spite of the fact that the rains had begun, there were shallow patches lower down which were still impassable by canoe. A large dead tree reached across the water towards us. There was no moon, and we could only see dimly.

Plop. Plop. Ping. A stone clattered on the pebbles close to me. There were thirty of us, but there was no sound until—rattle. Plop. A stone crashed through the branches of the dead tree into the water.

"Don't shine your torches," said Claudio. "It may frighten them."

The stones began to come in a spasmodic hail from only twenty yards away. But we all knew that we were watching something almost like a mime or ritual, and there was no question of arrows.

"Don't be careless," Claudio warned. "Sometimes a younger one or a 'mule' will shoot on his own."

Eventually Maprim shone a torch on Claudio. Cave-chested and entirely undramatic, he stood up holding an aluminium pan in his hand, and shouted across the water in the Kamayura language.

"Friend," he called. "We are not savage. Come here."

To this there was no reply. Several of the Kayabi now stood up and shouted in their language; Dudiga called in Juruna, and then Claudio whispered for Caraiwa, the Txikao.

"Txikao is a Carib-group language. Maybe they are re-lated."

The Txikao tribe had been contacted four years before, and had only come to live in the Parque during the last few months. They had never talked to other Indians before, and so they found it difficult to learn both the Indian languages and Portuguese. When Caraiwa joined the expedition he had wandered vacantly about, bemused by our activity, unable to speak to anyone.

Claudio took Caraiwa gently by the arm.

"Shout to the Cumari," he whispered. Cumari was the Txikao name for their principal enemies; the Kreen-Akrore and the Cumari might conceivably be the same people. "Shout to them, *'Bonito. Amigo',*" Claudio suggested.

Caraiwa stepped forward. "Bonito. Bonito. Amigo. Amigo," he called in Portuguese.

"No, no," Claudio whispered. "Txikao. Txikao!"

"Txikao. Txikao," shouted Caraiwa obediently.

"No," Claudio said.

"No." Caraiwa warmed to his task. "No. No."

Only gradually did it occur to us that since all Indians known to the Txikao spoke Portuguese, Caraiwa assumed that Portuguese was an inborn *lingua franca* of all Indians except Txikao.

"Try and see where the stones come from," Claudio said.

Plop.

"There!" Torches flashed on to the other bank, but there was nothing visible but branches and cluttered patches of leaves. In general, the stones seemed to come from three or four different locations; there were no sticks any more, only stones.

"Bejai, turn on your wireless."

A voice suddenly emerged from the air. "The Pope will be leaving Rome on Thursday . . . Cardinal . . . and Cardinal . . . will accompany him by 'plane to . . ."

The names were indistinguishable, and not particularly relevant to us or to the Kreen-Akrore, and when Bejai switched off the news, we found that the pebble-throwers on the other side had lost interest. The throwing had stopped, and there we were, sitting on a sandbank, wondering what it had all been about.

"Perhaps they want us to know that they're not going to attack," Claudio suggested.

If he was right, it was an odd, revealing way of expressing their intentions. Like children lobbing stones at other children on a beach, they seemed to be saying:

"Look, we are shy, but want to be friends."

That was a remarkably timid act for Indians bred to the internecine warfare of the jungle. They could have shouted. It would have been no more dangerous in the dark. We went back to the kitchen, where someone lit the lamp, and for the next hour we discussed why the Kreen-Akrore had crouched behind their defences in Cachimbo for more than a century.

It is probable that most of the unknown tribes in Amazonia today are deliberately hiding from civilisation. Like the Suya, some may have retreated after an attack by the other tribes, but most will have fled from a *civilizado* massacre, like the Apiaka.[2] This memory can so dominate the thinking of a tribe that its members will change their way of life, the pattern of their society. For instance, the Urubu, according to Francis Huxley, who studied them, ceased to be a highly developed agricultural society during the slave-raiding epoch of the Portuguese, and degenerated into a scavenging group, living off game and what they could find in the jungle. It was only some generations later that they felt secure enough to settle down again and cease to be nomads.

But the greatest terror in the collective memory of most tribes is probably an epidemic. When we arrived with Orlando and Claudio in 1967 at the village of the Kararao outside the Parque, we discovered only eight survivors of a 'flu epidemic. These lay paralysed in their hammocks, shivering and sweating, hypnotised by fear, gazing like rabbits at a spectre quite beyond their understanding. If those eight had fled into the jungle, they would have carried with them a story of the creeping death that came with the *civilizados*. And then on, from generation to generation, passed from mouth to mouth, distorted in the isolation of the jungle, this would become a nameless, haunting evil associated with all strangers.

Something of this sort, we felt, might explain why the Kreen-Akrore killed their captives. It could also explain their reluctance to approach us. But why, then, the stones, and why the banging on the trees?

One of the strangest features in the stories of the Txukahamei tribe is that though most of their civil wars end with the flight of the losing faction, five or ten years later the refugees usually return—often to be clubbed to death by their victorious enemies. The Indian can comfortably exist anywhere in the jungle. Why does he come back to such a predictable fate?

The answer seems to be that many Indians prefer death to life outside the tribe. From the edge of the jungle they watch the gorgeous dances, listen to the magic songs, and one day they can bear it no longer. They step out of the darkness into the light of the village square—to their probable death. Man is a magnet in the loneliness of the jungle, and now we were probably a magnet to the Kreen-Akrore. They had lived for centuries without speaking to anyone, and here we were, bright in coloured shirts, magnificent with wonderful tools, gay with music, bearing presents. As our steel-cut trail stabbed at their village, the inhabitants would have swung from fear to fascination, and back again. Like Diauarum a year before, when the Kamayura hypnotised the Trumai with their dancing, their tiny clearing in the jungle must have become a cockpit of hope, fear and rumour.

Two weeks later, the pendulum of excitement and terror would have swung even further. As we fired the air-strip, our great pall of black smoke must have been clearly visible from the Kreen-Akrore village.

NOTES TO CHAPTER 16

1. My favourite account is Lieutenant Pyrineus de Souza's report to Colonel Rondon in 1914:

"At first the Kayabi received me well; but when the axes and machetes were finished, they started to attack at the rapids and other places where passage was difficult. However, it was enough to shoot off the guns for them to run and leave us in peace.

"After the rapids, they tried a night attack against our camp, probably with clubs. However, I avoided it, transporting all the baggage and personnel to the other side of the river at night.

"There were four attacks which I avoided with prudence so as not to do any harm; and I tried to make them understand that I would return bringing more axes and machetes.

"On the night in which I moved camp, passing from one side to the other without being seen, I avoided the fight which one of their chiefs wanted to provoke, entering the water with bow and arrow, and threatening us in a high voice. While he was performing this act of bravado, from the interior of the jungle rose the war cries of many other men that we did not see. Arriving at the other bank, we tied up the canoes, and remained in them awaiting whatever would happen. By morning we saw that they had penetrated our abandoned camp, and were beating everything with clubs, which perhaps served more to encourage them than to frighten their adversaries."

2. The related tribe Pripuri hoped to discover. See footnote on page 135.

17

THE KREEN-AKRORE VILLAGE

As soon as a hundred yards of strip emerged from the blackened chaos of our landing-ground, the Parque 'plane began to fly in supplies and more experienced Indians for the contact. Kretire, chief of the Txukahamei, came with Pripuri, and some of the Indians from up-river. Then, like a chieftain descending on his clan, Orlando arrived to organise the final phase.

"Oh-ho, so you're here." He embraced the Kayabi who helped him out. "How do you spare the time from love-making?"

With his great belly bared to the air, Orlando took over the camp and kitchen.

"Most beasts are made for us to eat," he said, sharpening his knife. "Shoot a turkey and it falls to the ground with its plump breast sticking up. All you do is pluck the feathers. Just look at a jacubim and in three months it is fat enough for the pot. But a tortoise—" There was one on the table and Orlando prodded it with the point of his blade. "A tortoise comes out of an egg and takes twenty-five years to grow. Its shell is designed to discourage anyone eating it, and the meat is hard to extract. What a shame to swallow twenty-five years of creation. But," he added in a theatrical whisper, "what a delight."

A radio and small generator arrived in the same 'plane, so two or three times a day the quiet atmosphere of what had been Claudio's jungle retreat echoed to the complexities of Brazilian politics and the details of the Parque's administration. Alvaro Villas Boas had recently taken over as head of the Assistance Department of the Indian Foundation, and almost every day Orlando shouted advice and criticism to him down the radio.

Claudio watched from his hammock, and, during this period, it seemed to me that the partnership meant more to Claudio than it did to Orlando. Anyone could see that Claudio did not enjoy the planning and administration of an expedition, and he often appeared to need shelter from criticism and his own self-doubts. Of course, Orlando relied on Claudio, particularly on his bull-dog capacity to sit it out in the jungle. But now that his elder brother had arrived, Claudio almost visibly leaned back and sighed with relief. It was to become clearer in the months ahead, however, that this dependence was mutual. In most of the critical moments of our approach to the Kreen-Akrore, it was Claudio's opinion that usually determined Orlando's decision.

* * *

By the end of the month, seven trees we had felled were floating on the water, axed, burnt and shaped into canoes. The first rains of the wet season had been falling for some time, and the river was rising inch by inch. The *civilizado* party had all arrived; besides Orlando and Claudio there were Murilo, the doctor, Agnello, Orlando's nephew, Maprim, the Brazilian photographer, Muniz, who worked for the Parque, Erno and myself. And there were twenty-eight Indian volunteers from the Txukahamei, Kayabi, Juruna, Trumai, Txikao, Waura and Mehinako tribes. Quite a few of these tribes had been contacted by a similar Villas Boas expedition, and thus many of the Indians knew already what a "contact" was about.

On October 8th, we stumbled about early in the morning loading cargo in the mist. A jacubim flew up, and was shot by a Kayabi; it fell—like a good omen—into our canoe, and soon after we were paddling down the grey-green surface of the River Peixoto Azevedo, with dark banks of jungle forming a narrow gorge around us. The sky was cut off by a roof of branches, and occasionally we would pass a huge, fortress-like mass of black basalt—the bedrock of the hills behind.

The punt-poles dripped and groaned as they bit into the sand. Whole graveyards of dead trees lay rotting in the water, so that we frequently had to axe our way through. Deer moved in the shallows, and a tapir scrambled up a bank. Huge schools of a type of fish called matrincha filed under our hulls, and bacuda shot like torpedoes across the surface, slashing into their victims. We knew that intruders from the Teles Pires had always been ambushed at the mouth of the Peixoto, and that the Kreen-Akrore themselves never used canoes. It was possible that no boat had disturbed this secret waterway since the beginning of time.

"This is the river of savage Indians," Orlando called back to a straggling canoe. "If they were Kayabi you'd be in the mixed grill already."

The Kayabi grinned, and stared at the wall of jungle on either side. They knew that rapids were our chief danger, when our hands would be full carrying baggage or hauling on ropes. Because of this, a shore party under Claudio moved on both sides of the river, "beating" the banks ahead, but in Orlando's opinion it was not worth the trouble. At worst, a shower of arrows would wound a few men, but why should the Kreen-Akrore take the risk? Attack invites reprisal, and to Indians armed with bows, our thirty-six men with guns would seem like an armoured division in the jungle.

"We must look strong," Orlando had said, when he planned the expedition. "Our job is not to win a fight but to forestall it."

By the second day, the river was widening, and a Waura found a camp on the northern bank. It was a small hut bound with bark and covered with banana leaves, like those in a Txukahamei camp; on the ground there was a broken arrow and a stone half-formed into an axe-head. Kretire said it was a fishing camp, about a year old, on a long-established trail running back to the Kreen-Akrore village.

After that, Pripuri and Kretire searched for clues every time we stopped, and you could see his history of a hundred raids in the way Kretire almost sniffed at the tracks. He found the embers of a recent fire, some timbo llianas that had been used for poison-fishing, and a trail that was only a few days old. But soon everyone was discovering bits of basket, broken arrows caught in driftwood, and little platforms that stood out in the centre of the current so that the Kreen-Akrore could shoot at the fish swimming below.

At night we usually camped in a site protected by a dense

thicket of bamboo, and three times a day—at dawn, mid-day and dusk—there were radio links with Posto Leonardo, to assure them that everything was all right. By the fourth day, several tributaries had joined the river, and it was broad and studded with sandbanks. Time after time there were footprints on the thick golden sand, and from the marks of rain Pripuri calculated how long it was since each print was made.

Apparently a large party of Kreen-Akrore was moving down the northern bank, about half a mile ahead of us. At convenient spits or sandbanks some would come out to watch for our canoes as we rounded a bend. Then they slipped back into the jungle.

"They eat bananas, and women bring them." Kretire showed me some fresh banana-skin and a footprint which was smaller, and turned inwards.

The wall of jungle crept by, web after web of creeper, loop after loop of llianas. We were paddling up the "front drive" of the Kreen-Akrore, and as our advance made them increasingly nervous, we knew they would come to peer from behind that screen, holding and fingering their bows. It is a measure of the *civilizado*'s irrational fear of jungle that I felt safer on the river than I had on the trail. In the jungle we shared the same advantage with the Kreen-Akrore—camouflage. In the sunlight, with the river only thirty yards wide, it was the lack of shelter that was our greatest weakness.

"This time we have not come to take." Kretire was haranguing some of his more belligerent Txukahamei. "Remember that. This time it is not beautiful to kill."

I looked at Karinhoti, who had started the clubbing months ago, when we were in the Txukahamei village. He had steady eyes and a hard face, and he watched the passing wall of Kreen-Akrore jungle with total unconcern.

"Just call them," Kretire advised Karinhoti, "and then take the Kreen-Akrore by the hand." Even Kretire seemed a little doubtful about this, but, according to Orlando, expeditions were a proven method of teaching Indians about peace between tribes.

On the fifth day out, there were so many signs of the Kreen-Akrore that it was obvious we were close. We stared at every

gap, trying to find the mouth of a trail. A Kayabi pointed—
but it was only a monkey. Something rustled in the bushes—it
was only a capivara. A little before ten a.m. we rounded a bend,
and saw a flowering tree bent over the water; its branches
pointed like curved fingers at a line of rocks.

"The village is due east." Claudio stood up in the canoe.
"That's the tree I marked from the 'plane."

"Are you sure?" Orlando asked.

"Precisely four kilometres."

It was one of the contradictions in Claudio that though he
had an unreliable memory for many things, he had an amazing
grasp of aerial reconnaissance. Anything seen from the air is,
for most people, hard to recognise from the ground. But Claudio
could do it, and he was seldom wrong.

To the east, four kilometres away, the Kreen-Akrore village
awaited us.

A sandbank backed with a tangle of bamboo made a safe
camp-site on the southern shore. The box of presents was un-
packed. Mirrors, beads, knives, pans and one symbolic link
with the almost weekly gifts which rained down from the sky,
a toy aeroplane. Half the party were left to guard the camp, and
the rest of us crossed the river and climbed the steep bank.
Shotguns and rifles had been left behind, in case Karinhoti or
anyone else got carried away, but there were half a dozen
revolvers between us, should a warning shot be necessary.

After five dreary months, this was probably the moment.

Cupionim was in front, cutting the trail, and Claudio followed
with the compass. Orlando, shirtless, occasionally flicked with
a machete to widen the trail, and the rest of us came behind in
a long file. It was dark because of the clouds, and the sounds of
our movement were muffled by the recent rain. As we advanced,
several Kreen-Akrore paths cut across our route, but instead of
following them to the village, Claudio went straight over. By
arriving from an unexpected direction, he may have hoped for
some sort of tactical surprise.

"A cry," Pripuri halted, pointing to the left. "First a little
cry. It is a boy. Then a big cry. It is his father."

No other sound followed, and we moved on through a patch
of high jungle which was unexpectedly open. Then we came to

[165]

a stream of clear, amber water running over black leaves, and climbed down and up two steep ravines, arriving in an area of lower forest. A tree rose above the surrounding jungle, and one of the Kayabi climbed into its highest branches.

"I see no village," he called softly, "but the jungle drops."

Two hours after leaving the river we moved into an area of old plantation. A tree had been chopped with a stone axe; nuts had been gathered into a pile; some bark was already kneaded into cord. Soon we were passing new mandioca plants and clumps of unripe banana. We were in the garden of the village.

"Give me a pot," Orlando whispered. "Pass the mirrors to the front."

Down the broad Indian trail we advanced, each man holding a present in his hands. Half a dozen logs had been set out as seats under some tall trees, and from here we could just make out a patch of brown banana leaves at the end of the trail.

"The huts."

A macaw flew off, screaming, and then came back to screech at us, again and again.

"It's tame," one of the Indians whispered. "It belongs to the village."

Orlando's bare belly led the way, forming the spearhead of what must have looked a very odd procession. In his hand he swung an aluminium pot like a thurible, Kretire came next waving a mirror, and Claudio made benedictions with his saucepan, as if we were some religious order about to exorcise the devil.

We came closer, and entered the village. The doors of the huts faced away from us; it was impossible to tell whether anyone was inside. There were thirty seconds of incredible tension, and then we were crunching over dead leaves that had fallen off the huts. If there had been anyone inside, he would have heard already.

"Look for trails," Orlando ordered. "Those without shoes stay where you are." Bare feet could be confused with Kreen-Akrore footprints.

Kretire moved forward. We were on the edge of a rough circle formed by half a dozen huts, and when he reached the centre, he looked round.

Above Marching into the Kreen-Akrore village waving presents (p. 166). (*Adrian Cowell*)

Below Hanging up presents in a Kreen-Akrore hut. (*Adrian Cowell*)

Above Claudio hangs up presents for the Kreen-Akrore in the jungle. (*Adrian Cowell*)

Below Examining one of the 'present sites'. The Kreen-Akrore have taken all the presents except for the toy aeroplanes, and have left war clubs in return (p. 168). (*Adrian Cowell*)

Above Kretire, chief of the Mekrenoti, and other Indians examine baggage left by the Kreen-Akrore when they fled from their village (p. 169). (*Adrian Cowell*)

Below Kretire demonstrates the bones of a victim of the Kreen-Akrore. The Kreen-Akrore do not eat the bodies of their enemies but burn them close to their village (p. 176). (*Adrian Cowell*)

Above Kreen-Akrore tree carvings of a tortoise and a snake (p. 169). (*Adrian Cowell*)
Below Kreen-Akrore stone axe (p. 174). (*Adrian Cowell*)

"They left running," he called in a half-whisper. "But they did not sleep here."

He pointed to a hole in the ground where a bunch of green bananas had been buried to ripen quickly. The bunch had been freshly dug up, and the lining of green banana leaves had not even begun to dry in the sun.

"With bananas, they run," Kretire explained succinctly.

"They must have seen us," Orlando whispered. "Let's shout in Txikao." He pointed at the green leaves in the hole and turned to Caraiwa, the Txikao who had shouted when the Kreen-Akrore were lobbing stones into the Peixoto.

"Look, Caraiwa. Look, it was just now. Shout 'Venca. Presentes[1]'."

"Venca. Presentes," Caraiwa shouted in Portuguese.

"Puta merde, you mule," Orlando gasped. "I know how to shout Portuguese. Quick, Pripuri, shout Kayabi."

Pripuri's words rolled away through the jungle. Silence. The words echoed through the trees again. Silence. Later, Kretire showed us the trail down which the bananas had been carried, and Claudio drove two stakes into the ground and hung up a string of gifts on a nylon cord. On another trail, he hung up some more, then we returned to camp.

Next day, work began on a new air-strip, and a party stayed behind to protect the camp. About the middle of the afternoon this group suddenly saw three black figures moving across the sand down-river. The Kreen-Akrore walked calmly out of the jungle and stood on the sandbank, six hundred yards away. It was an unexpected, and, therefore, frightening confrontation.

Dudiga advanced to the waterline, and shouted in Juruna, waving an axe. There was no response. The Kreen-Akrore stood motionless. Quatara, one of the youngest Kayabi, tried in his language, but his words came out in a nervous whisper.

Across the water on the yellow sandbank, the three black figures stood like a line of Toltec statues. They did not call. They made no gesture. And after a few minutes of tension, they just turned and vanished into the jungle.

Kretire sat on the beach looking after them.

"Now they are watching from the jungle," he said. "To-morrow they will come with many men."

[167]

They returned, in fact, two nights later, though unseen by us. The party that checked the village was electrified to find the presents gone.

"Forty-eight knives," Claudio shouted to those behind. "And all the little pots."

Kretire and Pripuri began picking up burnt faggots of wood. "They came using these as torches," was Orlando's explanation, but he decided they must have stayed until daylight. "See the pan they dropped on the path. They ran when they heard us coming."

All the plastic dolls and most of the mirrors had been broken, and Pripuri suggested that the Kreen-Akrore connected them with witchcraft. The few unbroken mirrors were turned face downwards on the ground, so a passing Kreen-Akrore could not see himself in the glass. But nearly everything else had gone, and, most important of all, the Kreen-Akrore had left four of their clubs for us. They had accepted our gifts, and then had left presents of friendship in return. It was a momentous act. Between their tribe and the rest of the world, it was the first diplomatic exchange.

"This is the beginning," said Orlando, examining the clubs. "A contact in three days. That's not impossible."

He picked up one of the clubs, which was beautifully carved with a blade-like shape at the end. But the other three were just rough staves, with a heavy root forming a kind of hitting knobble like Xavante clubs.

Next morning, Orlando decided to press our advantage. We crossed a log bridge over a small stream and then followed the well-beaten route down which the Kreen-Akrore had fled with the presents. The forest was sodden after a night of rain, and when we glimpsed the dark brown banana leaves ahead, we moved forward gingerly. Four huts. But they were deserted.

The trail crossed the tangled thorn scrub of an old plantation, and on a bough jutting out like a dead finger above our heads we could see the black silhouette of a bird.

"It's a gralha," Orlando whispered. "It will cry."

It did, despite our efforts to tread softly; its harsh, cackling voice carried for miles across the forest. In the next patch of high trees, Pripuri smelt the embers of a fire. Yesterday, he said.

Then we found another village of several huts under the trees, and we began to realise that the Kreen-Akrore did not have a permanent village, but a number of temporary ones. Their huts were so simple that they could be put up in an hour.

"Every plantation, every hunting place, will have its village," Orlando said. "They must move from one to the other."

The path cut across an overgrown plantation, and we seemed to be on the edge of a major clearing. It was an area of tall, almost park-like trees, and they were decorated with a whole series of animal carvings. In the thick bark, a stone axe had cut the blunt outlines of a tortoise, a deer, a snake, a monkey, a man. We were staring at them, fascinated, when Pripuri pulled Orlando's arm.

"A cry," he said softly. "A cry across the village."

"What will they do?"

Kretire, near by, mimed a club falling, but after whispering together, Claudio and Orlando moved forward. The bushes parted on to an open space about a hundred yards in diameter. We advanced into the circle of huts, waving our presents as we had done before, but this time it was like arriving at a cartoon picnic after the bull had chased the picnickers away. We saw huge baskets of mandioca, banana, potato. Clubs, bows and stone axes were strewn around. Sleeping mats on the ground still held the dents made by human forms, and there was cotton woven round a woman's spindle. It looked as if the tribe had jumped to its feet and fled.

Checking the fires, Pripuri said that they had been out for some time, certainly since dawn. The Kreen-Akrore were probably moving deeper into the jungle, and had carried out their first loads in the early hours. We had interrupted as they had come back for second loads, and the cry we had heard was probably a scout warning those behind.

We strung up the presents, and left some aluminium pots in the huts. But as we left the village and returned to camp, we knew that the situation had changed. It was only too obvious that now we had stood in the warm and living home of the Kreen-Akrore, there was no further goal to seek. If they had not welcomed or fought us in their village, they were unlikely to confront us anywhere else. It was obvious that for every step

[169]

we were taking forward, the Kreen-Akrore had begun to take an equal step back.

Two months before, when the stones were thrown into the Peixoto, we had been able to argue that the shyness of the Kreen-Akrore was nothing more than caution. But during our five days' journey on the river, they had been safe and within shouting distance, yet no call had come. Three Kreen-Akrore had stood on a sandbank only six hundred yards from our camp; not a word or gesture. Finally, when we had advanced to their first village, they had retreated to the second. And when we advanced to the second, they had retreated again.

The pattern could no longer be ignored, and Claudio said that any further pressure might drive them to the other end of the jungle.

We walked back to camp knowing that our positive approach had failed, and that there was now no alternative to the more passive technique practised by the Indian Protection Service. If we could not go to the Kreen-Akrore, then we must attract them to us. And that meant sitting in a place where the Indians could watch us, month in, month out. Only gradually, as they saw that we meant no harm, would their fears subside.

*　　　*　　　*

Next day the camp was moved to a stream close to the first Kreen-Akrore village. Soon after, the air-strip was finished, and the Helio-Courier flew in with supplies and a bundle of press cuttings. The first thing we read in *O Globo* of October 2nd was that Alvaro Villas Boas had resigned as Director of the Welfare Department.

DIRECTOR CRITICISES INDIAN FOUNDATION

IT WILL BE ANOTHER INDIAN PROTECTION SERVICE

The National Foundation for Indians is rapidly becoming a second Indian Protection Service. Lack of adequate personnel and means of transport, together with excessive centralisation of administration and of transport: and the arguable basis on which Inspectorships are assigned, throws its whole future effectiveness on behalf of the forest people into doubt. The Department of Welfare has only two officials besides the Director, but the Department of research—which carries out anthropological studies—has thirty, and the office of the Director of the Foundation, Sr. Jose de Queiroz Campos, has that again.

For the Department of Welfare to get a typist, it has to go to the Minister of the Interior, but when Inspectors are nominated for a post, the Department of Welfare is ignored. With this, a new injustice is being committed against the Indians, compromising their whole future. The Inspectorate of Campo Grande in Mato Grosso controlling some of the most cultured Indians of Brazil—some with academic qualifications—has been handed over to a man of the old Indian Protection Service whose previous job was a driver. This shows not the least respect for the forest dwellers.

This information was given to *Globo* by Sr. Alvaro Villas Boas, Director of the Department of Welfare of the National Foundation for Indians.

In other cuttings and in letters there were rumours that there would be a new Minister of the Interior, who would insist on a new policy for the Indian Foundation. Riots had broken out in São Paulo, and a thousand students were in gaol. An article in *O Popular* on October 3rd mentioned an attempted rebellion in the Air Force:

AIR FORCE INVESTIGATES MOVEMENT OF
REBELLION AMONGST ITS OFFICERS

Air Force officers are forecasting the outbreak of a crisis in the Air Force because of the involvement of PARASAR in repressive operations, and also because of the punishment and transfer of Major-Doctor Rubens Marques Santos and of Captain Sergio de Carvalho, who refused to kill student leaders and politicians, as ordered.

Major Santos and Captain Sergio were the officers who had retrieved Richard Mason's body when he was killed by the Kreen-Akrore, who had rescued the survivors of the C47 that crashed on its way to Cachimbo, and who had mounted the expedition to rescue some Kayabi from the River Tatuim. They were friends of the Parque, and had agreed to rescue us by helicopter if we ran into trouble.

Orlando read the cuttings with despair.

"Just leave for a moment, and pouf! everything goes up in smoke," he groaned.

When the aeroplane left next day, Orlando was in it. The rest of us settled down to a long siege.

NOTE TO CHAPTER 17

1. "Come here. Presents."

18

THE UNKNOWN MAN

Several weeks later, Claudio called us early one morning for a reconnaissance trip. It had been raining on and off for days, and we set out through dripping jungle. There were twenty Indians, Richard Stanley (who had replaced Erno Vincze), myself and Claudio. The jungle was black with rain that had soaked into the trees, and the clouds made everything gloomy and hard to see. We followed the trail to the second village.

"Of course, it's outside the limits of their imagination," Claudio said over his shoulder, as we walked. "We are asking them to meet a stranger, and that is outside all their history, a revolutionary idea beyond their comprehension. They are nervous. Clearly they must hesitate."

Claudio had to speak and gesture sideways because I was walking behind, but after ten minutes the whole line grew silent, and those in front began to listen in the muffled atmosphere, and to check the ground for tracks. Someone thought he heard a watcher ahead. Someone else discovered an arrow fresh-dug in the ground. In less than an hour we were at the site where we had left combs, scissors, strings of white beads, and a knife hanging from a cord between two stakes.

Many of the huts had been beaten down by the rain, and their banana-leaf roofs had been blown or washed away. The pumpkin creepers had spread over the square, and already smothered the skeletons of the huts with thick, pulpy, revolting leaves, like weeds from science fiction. They had even crept up the poles on which the presents had been hung; and for anyone who lives for months inside jungle, this is a more disturbing sight than any snake or jaguar; the speed at which your environment absorbs all trace of human endeavour.

When we had frightened the Kreen-Akrore away from this

village, they had left half a dozen stone axes made of the hard grey rock of the Peixoto rapids, ground into a cutting edge by incessant rubbing on rock and sand. A stone axe represents an immense investment of time and skill, and is a primitive Indian's most valuable possession. Yet though the village was a safe two or three miles from our camp, not one of these axes had been collected by its owner. Nor had any of the smaller axes with "penknife" blades so narrow that none of our Indians could guess at their use.

I looked at a child's mat in one of the huts, and a stake beside it where the little girl had tied her pig. One of the Txukahamei had shown me how the pig's hooves had beaten a circle into the earth; and as the sleeping mat would have been the right size for my daughter, I often thought of that little Kreen-Akrore girl being tugged by her pig down the trails of the jungle. No child and no pig had played here for six weeks or more.

With great thoroughness Claudio checked the presents we had left. Some scissors were rusted, a coloured magazine was ripped to shreds.

"It's not them." He examined the torn pieces of paper. "The monkeys have no shame."

We walked back to the camp in the rain. Behind us lay the channel of diplomacy by which we, the official ambassadors of a section of mankind based in cities, had tried to open negotiations with a section of mankind that for thousands of years had lived in the jungle. And though "diplomatic notes" in the form of clubs and beads had been exchanged, the "line" had been unused for weeks.

Yet what was truly curious was not so much our attempt to negotiate with the Indians, but that we felt certain that the Indians really wanted to come out, but were unsure how to do it.

"It will come," Claudio insisted, as he stumbled through the thick mud of a flooded stream. "Perhaps with *civilizados* I am not sure. But in the jungle with Indians, I understand."

As we re-entered our camp, we saw that the cook had dug a series of dykes to protect his fires from the brown flood that was now sweeping through our shelters. A wounded parrot brought in by a hunter was walking up and down, feathers wrapped round itself, stamping like a Victorian cabby. The rain was so heavy that it muffled voices, and the surrounding walls of jungle looked as dark as a catacomb. I remembered that there were watchers behind that screen, and that, naked, presumably they were colder than we were.

How could any group of Indians arrive at such a twisted mental state as to sit in the soaking undergrowth, day after day, probably only forty yards away—wishing to come out and yet unable to do so? The explanation that we offered was that their inherited fears had mushroomed in the darkness of the jungle into something monstrous and beyond all proportion, that they had been isolated for so many generations that even the concept of meeting a stranger had vanished from their minds. But though the previous weeks had increased our knowledge of the Kreen-Akrore, we could only claim that our theory was partly supported by the facts.

*   *   *

The plantations, villages and trails of the Kreen-Akrore lay all around our camp, and every day we found in them a different detail or piece of information. The first village consisted of six huts in a rough circle, with another two huts in the centre which were flimsier and without sleeping mats. These were probably men's "clubs", like those in a Txukahamei village. Counting the bedding mats and assessing the space, I calculated the village must sleep about forty or fifty people, though if some of the other villages under the trees were occupied at the same time, then the total would be greater.

In the main village, an open area roughly twenty yards wide formed a broad band round the back of the huts, where each household had its oven-circle of grey stones. These were heated by burning branches, which were then raked out so the food could be roasted. Behind that was the tribal rubbish strip, and searching through it one morning, I found Brazil nuts, jatoba nuts, peanuts, honeycomb and snails, fish bones, parrot and turkey feathers, and the bones of tapir, deer and monkey. There were also a stingray tail, one or two armadillo shells, and about forty shells from tortoises. This preponderance of tortoise sug-

[175]

gested that the Kreen-Akrore, like the Txukahamei, had a tortoise festival.

Outside the village, the plantations were large and laid out in the patterns of circles and ellipses we had seen from the 'plane, with bananas on the perimeter, and potato, corn and mandioca in the centre. Unfortunately none of them had the clear geometric design of the plantation we had discovered on our second flight from Cachimbo; this plantation was twenty miles to the north. Most, however, had urucu, cotton or calabash, and there were three crops which the Txukahamei did not have in their plantations—peanuts, cara, and a sort of creeper which the Txukahamei insisted was "ours until the Kreen-Akrore stole it away".

About a hundred yards outside the first village, Kretire had found a pile of ashes and human bones. He showed us how the thigh and shin bone fitted together in the knee joint, and said that these were not Kreen-Akrore bones; their dead were buried in the conical graves we had seen in the village.

"Only when they slaughter enemies," he explained, "do they leave them for the vultures to eat. Then they take the bones when they are clean and roast them in the village. They dance for a long time." Kretire said that he had not seen it himself, but that some of the older Txukahamei had spied on the Kreen-Akrore village and had told him about it.

A number of arrows and war-clubs had also been discovered in the two villages, and—according to Pripuri—these were exactly similar to those of the Ipewi who attacked at the River Teles Pires. Our tribe was thus proved to have a range of 350 miles across the Cachimbo rectangle, and we were now sure that they must have several villages. But what interested Pripuri was whether, amongst these groups of Kreen-Akrore, there could also be a friendly village of the missing Apiaka, who were relatives of his own Kayabi tribe.

One day, rooting around in the first village, Claudio had found the broken fragment of an earthenware pot, and this had surprised and excited him. The Kreen-Akrore carry their water in gourds or strange "baskets" of reeds and leaves, and do not know how to make pottery. In the two villages, there were no other earthenware fragments, and it was clear that the Kreen-Akrore, like the Txukahamei, only roasted food directly on a fire; there were no stones or logs to support a pot. The piece discovered by Claudio must have been traded or captured from some other tribe, and it looked very much like Tupi-type earthenware. We knew that the Apiaka were a Tupi-speaking tribe.

For Pripuri, this fragment of pottery was proof of his theory.

"Of course it's a pot of the Apiaka. They're friends of the Kreen-Akrore, and when we make contact they will tell me where my relatives live."

Our theory stood on not very different foundations.

The more we had examined the villages, the more the Kreen-Akrore had seemed to resemble the Ge-speaking group of tribes, which includes the Txukahamei, Suya and Xavantes. The graves, ovens, huts and sleeping mats of the Kreen-Akrore were exactly like those of the Txukahamei; like them the Kreen-Akrore did not know how to make canoes, pots or hammocks. Their baskets and hunting clubs were similar to the Xavantes; the rush circlets worn round their heads resembled those of the Suya. In fact, though the Kreen-Akrore had been at this site for at least twenty years, they still continued the rhythm of moving from camp to camp around their plantations; the whole pattern of their life seemed nomadic in origin.

But the most tantalising discovery was the fifty huge logs we had found scattered round the first village. They were comfortable as seats, and some of them had been pushed further and further into a fire until a whole log was almost consumed. But it was inconceivable that the Kreen-Akrore would haul these heavy burdens through the jungle just for seats or firewood. Branches are better for fuel, and you don't need fifty logs—each seating three—for a tribe of fifty at the most. One day, therefore, Claudio mentioned the log races for which the Ge-speaking Timbira tribes were famous, in which two groups of men raced each other with logs on their shoulders. He said that our logs were too heavy and bulky for a man to carry, but that the logs had obviously been trimmed with a hand-hold at each end. My guess was that perhaps they were used for a log race in which several men supported a single log, which would explain why there were two "racing" paths, only five yards apart, running out of the village to a clump of trees where more logs were found.

From that time, I always pictured the Kreen-Akrore through Curt Nimuendaju's description of a Timbira race:

> When the marchers have got to within forty or fifty metres, the singers raise their hands aloft, and stamp their feet until the opponents have reached the logs. Forthwith, four men from each team lift their own log to the first racer's shoulders, and he immediately dashes off in the direction of the village followed and surrounded by a tumultuous group of his fellows . . . At once a mad chase starts in. Yelling and inciting the racers to greater efforts, blowing trumpets and ocarinas, the Indians with their waving grass ornaments bound deerlike to the right and left of the log-bearers' path, leaping over tufts of grass, low steppe bushes. After a distance of about a hundred or so metres, a fellow member runs up to the log-bearer, who without stopping in his course dexterously twists his body around so as to transfer his load to his mate's shoulder, and the race continues without the least interruption. Thus it goes on madly down and up slopes of the hills in the torrid sunshine of the shadeless steppe.
>
> (From *The Eastern Timbira*, translated by Robert H. Lowie, University of California Press.)

Of course, there was no proof that the logs were used for a race, just as there was no direct evidence to connect the Kreen-Akrore with the ancient Timbira group. But in Claudio's theories about the history of Southern Amazonia, the Txukahamei and Suya tribes had been part of the Gorotire tribe until they splintered away and moved westward just before the turn of the century, whilst the Gorotire themselves may have hived off from the Je-speaking Gaviao or Apinaye, who lived on the western edge of the great Timbira group a hundred and fifty years ago.

In the early nineteenth century, the invading Brazilian cattle-men had launched deliberate wars of extermination against the lip-perforated Timbira tribes who lived in the barren interior behind the sea coast of Brazil.

"In 1816," Major Francisco de Paula Ribeiro recorded, "a bandeira [heavily-armed expedition] lured the Augutge tribe

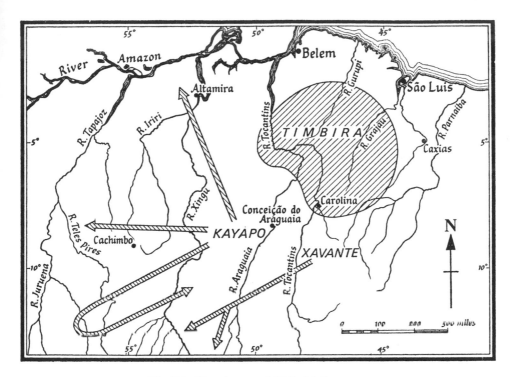

The Timbira Area and Tribal Migrations

into its power by mendacious promises, enslaved its members, and hacked to pieces the chief when he protested against such treachery. Part of the slaves were shipped to Para, the rest were sold to itinerant traders who sold them to Piaui."

On July 24th, 1815, another expedition murdered many of the Kraho tribe, and the leader's share of 130 slaves were branded with red-hot irons. A few years later, the Capiccran tribe were lured to Caxias during a smallpox epidemic, then flogged and driven away in order that the epidemic would be carried to the tribes in the jungle. And so on. Only four out of fifteen Timbira tribes survived into the twentieth century.

The question that intrigued us was whether one of the missing Timbira tribes might not have chosen flight rather than extinction. Could they have fled westwards like the Suya and Txukahamei and settled in the deepest, most impenetrable retreat in Southern Amazonia—the Cachimbo range? It would explain the Kreen-Akrore's diffidence with *civilizados*.

[179]

19

WAITING

Claudio swung slowly in his hammock, methodically justifying our tactics:

"As long as we are here, we are calling to them. In the emptiness of the jungle, our human nature is a magnet to theirs. In this way, human groups have always been drawn to other groups, till after thousands of years the whole of mankind now lives in a world civilisation. It's only those which are dominated by an extreme fear that remain outside and this is the sort of fear that thrives in the emptiness of the jungle. If people say that every month in the jungle shows its strain on me, then how much more on the Kreen-Akrore, who've been alone for hundreds of years? We must be patient and continue calling to them. Somewhere they are watching and calling to us."

*   *   *

Rain is the temper, or the black mood, of the jungle. And as we waited, rain either pounded on the roofs of our camp or wrapped us in a grey drizzle. We breathed, we ate, we moved in rain. Storms and the passing of storms were what marked the time of our waiting.

The little stream near the camp had been a foot wide and three inches deep in October, and only a tadpole could have swum in it. By December it had become a torrent ten yards wide, two yards deep, rushing so fast that anyone who tried to swim was swept away like driftwood. Hundreds of miles of jungle were already under water, and the whole character of the land had visibly begun to change. The animals had gone to higher ground, few birds sang, and it was the pintado and the triarao—the leopards of the water—that hunted under the trees.

It was not the first rain season I had had to spend in Amazonia, but this time we were stationary with no other purpose than to let our watchers watch. Under our nylon or banana-leaf lean-to huts we sat and stared as the rain poured down; during the dry intervals it was a relief to work. The air-strip was extended further, then further again. At first it had been only two hundred yards for the Helio-Courier or similar 'planes with stall flaps on their wings, but in case the Helio was withdrawn, Claudio had decided to lengthen it to four hundred yards so a Cessna could land. And since DC3s flew the supply route to Cachimbo, and there were no emergency landing-grounds in the area, the air-strip was extended once again, this time to five hundred and fifty yards. We all waited for Claudio to remember the Boeing 707s, flying thirty thousand feet up on their way to Miami.

"Put Claudio in the jungle," Orlando had once said, "and he builds an air-strip. If there is already a strip, he extends it. And if it is extended, then he goes elsewhere and starts another."

And as the rain fell, so the Kreen-Akrore watched. Late at night Claudio would rake the loose earth on the air-strip, and next morning there would be footprints, fresh on the dew. A new green arrow was found, dug into the ground.

"They are beating the trees." Pripuri came running up one day. "They are there, beyond the bridge."

"What have you done about it, Pripuri?"

"I have withdrawn myself, running."

So it went, to and fro, round and round, but without any physical contact, and therefore without any sense of reality. For a whole period of six weeks, not a present was taken; and then, quite suddenly, every present in the second village disappeared. The Kreen-Akrore had accepted what was for stone-age man the gift beyond price—a dozen steel axes. The same labour would now produce for them a fivefold increase in plantations, and, therefore, food. And in this sense, steel is the opium of the jungle. Once stone-age man has learnt to use it, he can never be without it again.

Our hopes soared and then sagged when the Kreen-Akrore seemed unimpressed with their luck. And the rain went on wearing away at our patience, like some spectre of Amazonia reaching for our minds and health. About once a week the usual drizzle worked itself up into a storm. Branches and trees hurtled to the ground. Once a hut was smashed by a falling tree, and we all just crouched there, helpless and resentful. Then, when it was over, the jungle caught us again in its padded cell, so that what had become the very real claustrophobia of rain and forest seemed increasingly to be turning us away from the material world and back into our own minds and the misgivings that lurked there.

During this time I sometimes doubted the existence of our watchers, and one day, with the squirrel-like instinct of an insecure TV producer, I decided to bury two biscuit tins full of bullets, medicines, books and fish-hooks against some hypothetical return in the future. We dug deep inside one of the huts, and then Bejai beat down the earth on top. He covered the surface with twigs and leaves so that it looked like the rest of the jungle carpet, and the rain was allowed to run over it for several days. Finally, we pulled away the central pillar of the hut, and the whole roof collapsed, bringing with it a rotten tree that had split in a storm and was leaning on top.

The pile of debris looked like the result of a storm, and it was impossible to guess what lay beneath. But a Kreen-Akrore must have been watching, for we heard later that the tins were dug up a few days after the expedition left (see Orlando's letter, p. 197). And it was probably this incessant, though unconscious awareness of our watchers that made me suggest to Claudio a journey to the plantations or a reconnaissance along the trail— in fact anything that would vary the fish-in-a-fish-tank sensation. Claudio always refused. He would not take any action, or adopt any more positive policy.

That he was right and I was wrong was brought home when the Helio-Courier flew in with supplies and newspapers. On the first page we read:

ATROARI INDIANS MASSACRE EXPEDITION
OF PADRE CALLERI

The Indian Foundation had sent an expedition to remove a tribe from the path of the road which was being built to the

Left The abandoned Kreen-Akrore village. (*Adrian Cowell*)

Right A Kreen-Akrore fire built among stones that preserve the heat for roasting. In the background, a Kreen-Akrore grave (p. 175). Both are exactly the same as used by the Txukahamei. (*Adrian Cowell*)

Left Working on one of the three air-strips built by the expedition. (*Adrian Cowell*)

Right One of the air-strips. (*Adrian Cowell*)

Brazilian parachutists check remains of a government expedition wiped out by the Atroarí Indians. Most of the skulls were fractured by war-clubs (p. 182).

Above A Brazilian boy demonstrates the straw wig taken from the village of the Cabecas Peladas. The wig reveals that the tribe was in contact with the Portuguese centuries ago. When the tribe fled into the jungle, they must have passed down this souvenir in their dances (p. 76). (*Jesco von Puttkamer*)

Below Imitations of axe, scissors, needle and knife left by Cinta Larga Indians as a 'shopping list' for the Chico Meireles expedition (p. 183). (*Jesco von Puttkamer*)

north of Manaos. The Atroari tribe had once lived close to a
Post and so understood a few words of Portuguese. But the
inexperience and haste of the leader—so far as the rescue
expedition could discover—had led the Atroari to club the
whole party to death during a visit to their camp.

Another newspaper had an article on a second FUNAI expedition, led by the very experienced Chico Meireles, which was
as bogged down as our own. For more than six months the
tribe Meireles had been trying to contact had been accepting
presents; they even left a regular "shopping list" in the form of
pieces of wood carved to look like knives, scissors or anything
else they wanted. But not once had they let themselves be
seen.[1]

The articles could not have been a more obvious vindication
of Claudio's policy, and we settled down again to the monotony
of waiting. Even Claudio sank into a period of depression as the
rains approached their climax, and this increased when the
supply 'plane brought news of a tragedy amongst the party of
Indians we had left to guard the air-strip up-river.

Mossoko, one of the cleverest of the boys in the recently contacted Txikao tribe, was dead. Orlando had brought him on
the expedition to widen his experience as a first step in training
him to work for the Parque. But newly-contacted Indians are
not safe with guns, and are never allowed to have them. One
day when the other Indians were out of the camp, Mossoko had
stolen and experimented with the gun of a Kayabi, and had
pulled the trigger. The shot went through his stomach and into
his pelvis. There was no radio to call for help, and it had taken
Mossoko three days to die.

After he heard the news Claudio seemed unable to move for
almost a minute. Then he walked laboriously over to the other
Txikao on the expedition, Caraiwa. We heard him speaking in
the terrible banality of pidgin-Portuguese.

"Mossoko. Gun." Claudio pointed to his stomach. "Gun.
Bang. Mossoko dead."

We watched helplessly as Caraiwa gave a sort of half smile,
and moved off with a sack of supplies. Fifteen minutes later we
all stood round as he sat crying, in the midst of people he could
not talk to, knowing that in a similar place Mossoko, his relative,

[183]

had died. He understood a gun was the cause, but everything else must have been inexplicable. Only a few months before, the most intelligent member of their tribe, Waggi, had died of pneumonia. The Txikao saw that the *civilizados* were sorry and had tried to help. Yet Caraiwa knew that neither Waggi nor Mossoko would be dead if they had stayed in the jungle away from *civilizados*.

After the news of Mossoko's death, Claudio grew more and more nervous, at the same time displaying increasing determination to hang on.

"Definitely it's no use to burst into a village," he would break out suddenly. "Truly, after twenty-five years, I know. It's not wise to confront them in a village. All they can think of is the women and children, and they just shoot or run."

At dusk we would see his hunched figure wandering aimlessly round the air-strip.

"Is that smoke over there?" he would ask, and his bearded face would seem smaller and more shrivelled. He became peevish if I suggested looking to see if the presents in the nearby village were still there, and indignant if Kretire made another of his expansive offers.

"The Txukahamei will arrange," Kretire would say cheerfully. "The Kreen-Akrore are just over there, and they are easy to grab. In three days we will capture you a nice one."

"Negative, negative," Claudio replied explosively. "Kretire, I will not have captives. Even if I have to wait ten years, they will come of their own choice." And he would plod off to the Kreen-Akrore plantations. These plantations had been freshly sown only two months before our arrival, and Claudio hoped that hunger would force the Kreen-Akrore to harvest the corn when it was ripe.

"On the Cururu trail it was the same," Claudio said as he walked. "When my Department sent me to cut the trail then stopped the food, Orlando's message said it was stupid to go on. 'The Department,' he said, 'is making politics with you.' But I said, 'What I have started I will finish,' and I did, though it took two years, though thirty mules died, though most of the men deserted, and though my Department never used the trail and it's now swallowed in the jungle."

From behind, Claudio looked nervous and frail, with skin that was grey with malaria. But his boots went through the mud with the same determination as his words, plonk, plonk, plonk, and I knew—to my cost—that he would go on doing precisely that for the next ten hours, and if necessary—sometimes I thought even if unnecessary—for the next thirty days.

At the plantation, the tall ears of corn looked yellower than before. They stood, hard and barren, unharvested by the men who had planted them. Back at the camp, I got into my jungle hammock, and for the rest of the day was alone with what was for me the most disturbing doubt of all.

In one sense, the object of our mission was so clearly worthwhile that there was a tendency to look at it in terms of black and white. Unless we contacted the Kreen-Akrore, their bows would confront the road-builders' rifles; and when they gave in, they would be racked by disease and their culture shattered by misunderstanding and scorn. But if the Villas Boas got to them first, they could be led away from the site of the road, trained to accept inoculations and medicines, and helped during the approaching years of shock and dislocation.

So obvious was all this that many visitors to Xingu—myself included—tended to regard the Parque as the shining force of good, and the prospectors and the road-builders as the dark force of evil. It was only when you met the prospectors and the rubber-tappers who actually did the shooting that you realised they were humble men driven by necessity to the jungle, and that they shot from little more than ignorance and fear. Behind them were fifteen million near-starving people in the north-east of Brazil, and no government could ignore their desperation in the interests of a few hundred Kreen-Akrore.

It was this that had led me to reflect that the same government that paid for the Parque's budgets also paid for the road that would destroy the Parque; that the Department which guaranteed the Indians' land in some cases shared the same building as the Department that lent money to "develop" Indian land. And that if charitable organisations supplemented the low budget of the Villas Boas, so the financial empires which created these foundations provided the resources that sent the prospectors to the jungle. The killing and the "saving" were, in

[185]

some ways, linked, and I had begun to wonder whether our expedition was an essential part of this process.

Since the first Europeans came to the Americas, from La Casas to Marshal Rondon, there have always been *civilizados* who were genuine friends of the Indians, fighting to protect them. Yet, despite them, the Indians have died at an appalling rate. The idealism of Rondon's[2] group of officers cannot be doubted, but in the cruel light of history, was not the bloodless acquisition of Indian land the final result of their heroism? And was it not at their Posts that the Indians were exposed to disease, without sufficient medicine to fight the disease? Once, when I had asked Rauni what the Txukahamei would do if they found a group of primitive white men in the jungle, he had said:

"Kill all the men and marry all the women."

What I now suspected was that we followed this evolutionary technique, but that our principles made it hard to speak of it with the honesty of Rauni. After all, how could we mount a humanitarian crusade to develop the jungle of Cachimbo in order to feed the poor, if this meant killing innocent Kreen-Akrore? And could a world civilisation, expanding across the globe to draw all men into a universal brotherhood, have as its by-product the slaughter of Indians? Perhaps it was the unconscious solution of our race to proceed with the ruthlessness of all evolution, but to send other *civilizados* to work against it— assuming that not enough men, and not enough resources, were sent to make any difference. In which case our expedition was little more than a ritual act to salve the conscience of society, as the Kreen-Akrore were robbed of the basis of their existence.

This is an extreme presentation of only one side of the case. But in the jungle, in the rain, it was the reason for confusion, or at least uncertainty, in my mind. I also suspected that something of this sort explained Orlando's occasional outbursts of great bitterness. When we had arrived at the village of Kararao[3] to find that, without a grain of medicine, twenty-one Indians had died of 'flu in the preceding week, that nearly eighty per cent of the tribe had perished in their first three years of contact, Orlando had said wearily:

"It would be kinder to machine-gun them at the start. Or would that be to soil our hands with their blood?"

[186]

And so, as I lay in my hammock during that last month of January, staring through the mosquito netting at the blank wall of jungle from which I knew a Kreen-Akrore was staring at me, this was the reason why, at one and the same time, I was determined to do what I could to contact him, and was also delighted that we had failed. Day after day, I thought with real pleasure of the wild people roaming their wilderness, of the little girl pulling her pig down the cool paths of the jungle, of the black-painted seven-foot leaders ruling the last unknown forest for a few weeks more. Claudio would not admit to similarly divided feelings, but it was the influence of the Villas Boas that had isolated Cachimbo during the previous decade, and that had given the Kreen-Akrore, still a separate atom of mankind, their last few years of peace.

Towards the middle of January, Claudio decided to relax the pressure for a few months, and the 'plane began to ferry the expedition out. Richard Stanley and I were flown to Posto Leonardo, while Claudio and a small party went back to cut the scrub on the Peixoto air-strip, and then clean the trail to the River Manitsaua. He said he would need both for the return journey.

Later, as I left Xingu, Orlando gave me a copy of the following statement:

Posto Leonardo,
January, 1969

This Administration plans to suspend for some time—two to three months—its activities in procuring contact through its expedition. Until now, the Kreen-Akrore Indians have rejected all approaches. We believe that despite the exchange of presents, it would be convenient to withdraw from the area to make possible a more spontaneous approach from the Indians. We intend to return to this work within two or three months.

Orlando Villas Boas
Administrator, National Park of Xingu.

NOTES TO CHAPTER 19

1. The Cintas Largas walked into Meireles's camp in the summer of 1969, but in spite of growing friendliness, no *civilizado* was allowed to enter their village during the next two years. Their distrust was expected. The tribe was bombed with dynamite in 1963, and later an overland party attacked them with rifles and sub-machine guns.
2. At the end of his life, a very disillusioned Marshal Rondon turned against his own Indian Protection Service and became a friend and ally of the Villas Boas.
3. Outside the Villas Boas area, near the mouth of the River Xingu, during a journey in 1967.

INDIANS MENTIONED IN CHAPTERS 13 TO 19

Bejai Txukahamei. Worked with film unit. Son of Matiban who was shot with Bebcuche in 1961.
Bebcuche Txukahamei, relative of Rauni.
Caraiwa From the recently contacted Txikao tribe.
Cupionim Son of the Kayabi chief.
Cuyabano Kayabi leader.
Dudiga Juruna. Previously on many Villas Boas expeditions.
Kaluana Accompanied author on a previous visit.
Karinhoti The Txukahamei who started the clubbing in Chapter 4.
Kretire Chief of the Txukahamei.
Maluware Karaja exiled to the Parque. He has since become the Karaja chief.
Mossoko Young Txikao boy killed in a gun accident.
Pripuri Kayabi leader, anxious to contact a related tribe, the Apiaka.
Quatara Kayabi. The expedition's cook for a time.
Rauni Claudio's right-hand man in the Txukahamei tribe, later to become one of the chiefs.
Waggi Txikao leader who died of 'flu.

III

The Aftermath

20

THE END

The Parque was intact when I flew out in January, 1969, and even now, at the time of writing (1972), the Villas Boas have still not resigned.[1] For nearly a year now they have been torn between presiding over the ruin of their own work, and the impossibility of deserting the Indians at a time of need. But there can be little doubt that what the Parque stood for has been destroyed in the intervening period. The road has made it impossible to control the arrival of civilisation in the form of disease, prostitution and the money economy. The annexation of half the land has undermined the Indians' confidence in the government's promises, and the future that depended on them. Some façade of the Parque will obviously be preserved—if only to placate public opinion—but the essence has gone.

Yet it has never been easy to define what that core or essence was.

The Parque began to come into existence in the 1950s as little more than a series of practical measures to slow down the death rate in Xingu. At the time, the Indian Protection Service admitted that of the 230 tribes in Brazil at the beginning of this century, 87 had already passed into extinction. And this estimate it says nothing of deaths in the non-extinct tribes—is usually balanced against Professor Paulo Duarte's claim that from two hundred thousand Indians in 1963, only eighty thousand survived into 1968.[2] Together, the two sets of figures give an idea of the appalling death-rate amongst the Brazilian Indians and the almost insuperable problem which faced the Villas Boas.

Half a dozen practical measures solved that problem. The brothers contacted the unknown tribes before the prospectors and rubber-tappers, and gave them assistance during the most critical years. They guaranteed land for the Indians' hunting

[191]

and fishing economy, and won a political battle when the Mato Grosso State Government sold title deeds to all the Parque's territory. They drove off parties of surveyors and prospectors armed with sub-machine guns, and restricted disease by insisting that visitors arrive at Posto Leonardo with government permits. Air-strips were built at every village so that the sick could be flown to the Parque's hospital, and the medical campaign was so successful that Xingu now has a rising population. (In many villages a third of the population is under the age of nine.) Finally, missionaries were banned, and the brothers taught only those aspects of civilisation which the Indians asked for. Today, Xingu's Indians are still the most self-confident and least demoralised in Brazil.

In 1967 and 1968, the Parque that we saw was the result of these measures, but the brothers never claimed that they had solved the Indian problem. They said they had merely kept enough Indians alive to have a problem about. It was a co-incidence that at the time of the scandal about corruption in the Indian Protection Service, the Ministry of the Interior began using the Parque as a show-piece. When foreign journalists arrived to report on "Genocide" or "The Dying Indians", the Ministry asked them to balance their story with a visit to Xingu.

"Look at the more positive aspects of the problem," the journalists were told. "See how the Indian can be saved."

"How can the Indian be *saved*?" Claudio would retort, after talking to a group of these visitors. "Animals can be *saved* from extinction because they are content to remain animals. But all humans recognise improvement, and desire the advantages of other men. As soon as there's a shop near here, Pripuri will load his canoe with mandioca flour and paddle up the Suya-Missu. After twenty trips he will buy an outboard motor and make his business more efficient. You will see, it will be the Indians themselves who will break the isolation of the Parque, who will destroy their tribal society. In this cultural sense, how can the Indian be saved from extinction?"

And in this sense, the Parque was already facing the second stage of the Indian problem. Once the life of jungle man had been preserved, he must be offered an alternative livelihood without his jungle. Over thousands of years his nature has been moulded to existence within the forest, and when *civilizados* tear and cut that forest away, it is not easy for the Indian to adjust.

The solution proposed by the integrationists—many of them missionaries—is to force the Indian to become a salaried, Christian rubber-tapper or carpenter as rapidly as possible. This is his destiny, and a savage act of surgery is kindest in the long run. But the Villas Boas recoiled from this. They felt that no one has the right to violate even a primitive man's nature, just as no one has the right to force a Jewish or Ibo minority to become identical with the majorities that surround them. They argued that why Amazonian Indians were notorious in the past as thieves, pimps and drunkards was that the missionaries destroyed their culture but offered nothing understandable in its place. In the Indians' first years of transition, tribal culture was an essential staff in the storm, a point of view in a bewildering universe. Orlando pointed out that three generations after the last Indian wars, many North American Indians were still unsuited to modern life. They drifted away from the cities back to the Reserves, neither Indians nor city men, bitter and discontented. And some Reserves seemed little better than human slag-heaps—a dumping ground for unwanted people.

Was this the future of Xingu? The brothers always avoided the question. They prophesied that the Parque would be destroyed when its land became of commercial value,[3] and that there was, therefore, no point in speculating on its future. The issue worried them, however, and their views came out when they discussed other matters. Claudio, for instance, often talked about the famous Reductions of the Jesuits. The main Reduction of Paraguay was across the watershed to the south of Mato Grosso, but there had been a small one two hundred years ago near the mouth of the Xingu. As in the Parque, the Jesuits had planned a defensive system for the Indian, even mobilising tribal armies—with cavalry and artillery—which could number tens of thousands. Claudio thought that in all the bloody annals of Indian extermination, the most idealistic counter-attack against the slavers and land-owners had been that of the Society of Jesus. Yet he pointed out that once the Jesuits fell from royal favour, the entire edifice crumbled. The Indians had been passive subjects of the Reductions, disciplined with the lash and organised for "their own good". The Reductions had no roots in Indian character, so naturally they vanished when the Jesuits left.

Claudio was determined that the Parque would play a less domineering part; and this is why the Villas Boas never forced any plan or system on the Indians.

"The only hope," Claudio would say, "is to preserve the core of tribal society and help the Indians graft on to it the more useful tools of civilisation. If an Indian asks for a metal cooking pot, then the request arises from his own needs. The use of the metal cooking pot is a natural evolution for the man and his group. It will produce change, but not the same disruption as if I ordered all Kamyura to abandon earthenware tomorrow. In this way they can grow towards civilisation, but in a manner and at a pace suited to their own nature."

Claudio would then describe the Parque as a filter for civilisation.

"The holes, to begin with, are small, and the least destructive things come through. The Indians live as they always have done, but with the tools of our world. Axes. Pots. Rifles. The old men use the guns—their sons, like Pionim and Mairewe, already know how to repair them. Their grandsons will be school and university graduates who will study the theories and science behind it all."

The concept was of a whole society evolving towards civilisation, but protected from abrupt change or dislocation. Claudio would add that the Parque possessed one remarkable asset denied to most other Indians—the strange harmony between the tribes of Upper Xingu. Most of these groups had fought each other when they originally came into the valley, but over a period of time they had learnt to meet and compromise, and to form a common culture centred on the Feast of Quarup. They had gradually merged their different ways of life, so that now they dressed, danced, and worked in the same way; their economy and social systems were similar, they traded, intermarried and had festivals together.

Could not this process continue, perhaps be accelerated by

the Parque? Eventually fifteen or twenty tribes might draw together in a "nation" of two thousand people, assisting and inspiring one another. Claudio cited the Upper Xinguanos, who had found their first contact with *civilizados* easier than isolated tribes down-river, simply because they were used to meeting one another. They were able to learn Portuguese quickly because they were used to learning languages from each other, and their minds were quick and receptive, sharpened on the rivalry between their groups.

"If Rauni's or Pripuri's children can accept our world," Claudio said, "if they can become doctors or engineers and disappear into the people of Brazil, then I am truly happy for them. But it is likely that some of those who go to the cities will find it impossible to adjust. And it will be valuable for them to have a living society in the Parque for a generation or two to which they can return—a sub-culture which will allow them to be part of our world, and yet feel they have an identity of their own."

Obviously this development was hindered by quarrels between the tribes, and the Indian's attitude to killing. And it was the reason why—at the time of Javaritu's murder—I had asked Claudio whether the key to the Parque's problem was the *civilizado* concept of charity, or what Claudio himself called compassion.

"That would be like missionaries," Claudio had answered, "pushing an ideal on the Indians. We never want to push anything that overturns the balance of his mind or philosophy. So nothing must be 'most important'. But when one of them is talking to me, I just say so-and-so is a nice old man. What do you want to kill him for? And then I suggest that when he is old himself, someone might think of murdering him. Sometimes they weep and agree. But, of course, I don't force them, and sometimes they go away and kill."

The paradox of the Parque has always been that it required a crusader's determination to fight off the predators of civilisation, at the same time as it demanded a self-defeating gentleness of touch to help the Indians without crushing them. And it is open to doubt whether anyone could have combined these conflicting rôles for long. But Orlando and Claudio Villas Boas had tried to do so, and survived in the attempt for twenty-seven years, and that is probably why I admired them so much.

NOTES TO CHAPTER 20

1. But see Postscript: The Attack on the Parque page 216 in particular.
2. Almost certainly an over-estimate. Unfortunately, the government is not forthcoming with properly documented figures for the death-rate.
3. They predicted the Parque would go, not in one gulp, but in several bites over a period of years. The vast reserves of the next-door Xavante tribe were nibbled away like this.

THE ATTACK ON THE PARQUE

After we flew out of Xingu, I spent the next two years working in England, Ireland and Thailand. But of course I was intensely interested in what was happening in the Parque.

As the road approached, and Xingu's land rose in value, letters and press cuttings brought the news from Brazil, and they are set out here to present what happened more or less as I saw it from Europe.

Letters from Orlando[1] Villas Boas:

April 24th, 1969

We are waiting for the supplies we asked for from the Indian Foundation to start the attraction of the Kreen-Akrore again. We asked, as an essential, for the loan of a 'plane for the work of transport and contact. The ideal would be the Helio-Courier of the University of Brasilia. But without a 'plane it is impossible to start the expedition.

June 23rd, 1969

Claudio returned to the Kreen-Akrore camp. The strip was all overgrown with jungle. Everything that he saw showed that the Indians were there. They had taken everything left on the paths and in the shelters. Everything that was in the camp was broken up by them. The things buried by you were dug up and thrown around—books, ammunition and other things. As on the first occasion, they broke all the mirrors. Some suitcases that were left behind were broken up by clubs, they did not want to touch them by hand. Everything indicates that they are aggressive—so ferocious that they smashed one of the drums of petrol we left on the strip, with their clubs. They beat it till the drum was

[197]

ripped open. They put obstacles on the path to prevent movement.

We have not started the attraction again because the University 'plane is not readily available. But from one moment to the next we could start, and when we feel the Indians are going to approach, we will let you know. Perhaps you will have time to get some extra sequences. Keep listening.

Letter from Orlando written from Posto Leonardo:

September 1st, 1969

The University has withdrawn the 'plane that was supplying us. They say the motor and the insurance have expired. They say that the overhaul of the motor and the re-establishment of the insurance would cost very much. It's better to lay up the 'plane. That is what they have done . . . Without a 'plane, it's impossible. We would have to go back to mule convoys, the long marches. We would have to open a trail from the Peixoto camp to our Kreen-Akrore camp. And this in search of an Indian who disappears, who does not leave a trail or tracks. Suddenly they appear at Capoto —two hundred kilometres in a straight line and four hundred by natural means of approach. Only with a 'plane can we have the necessary mobility.

*　　　*　　　*

Marina was the government nurse at Posto Leonardo, and for some time Orlando's friends had hoped that she would become—as Orlando put it—"my nurse, too".

Cutting from the newspaper *O Popular*, December 27th, 1969:

On the 23rd last, Orlando Villas Boas was married in Goiania to Srta. Marina Lopes Dias, for eight years a nurse in the Parque. The marriage was prepared and carried out in absolute secrecy . . . On the 22nd the couple took an Air Force 'plane with three children and came to

Goiania. In the Parque everyone assumed this was one of Orlando's usual trips to the Parque's São Paulo office.

*　　　*　　　*

There are not many ways that people outside Brazil can help the Indians, but I wrote from London to Orlando about one possibility:

April 20th, 1970

It's stupid to talk of awards in advance, but when the award means something to an international movement, then the issue is more than personal. I warn you in case there are political reactions.

One day in the jungle, it occurred to me that you and Claudio were the sort of people that are given Nobel Peace Prizes. But in the back-yard of the Kreen-Akrore, prizes don't have much meaning, and I only mentioned it to Maprim. I doubt I would have thought of it again, if now it did not seem that this was one of the very few ways we outsiders can help the Parque. The Nobel Peace Prize brings prestige, and this can be of use in politics, especially the Indian sort of politics, which deals more in responsibilities than in power. In fact, the Peace Prize has been given several times to support a leader under pressure—for instance Chief Luthuli.

So I contacted the new group of the Primitive People's Fund in London. Their interests are world wide, but with persuasion their vision narrowed. First they sent that £250 for medicine, and afterwards we organised a PPF showing of the film (before its TV transmission) for sixty influential people. They were very impressed with your work and it was not hard to launch the second stage.

The problem of the primitive peoples of the world is so complex that people rarely understand and invariably forget it. The world gives millions to save a species from extinction, but thinks nothing of human sub-species, like the Trumai and Nahukua. The reason is the public has no simple concept of the problem. The publicity linked with Martin Luther King or Gandhi did a lot for their causes.

[199]

Why not for primitive people? Once the PPF started looking, they were more or less bound to end in Xingu, and I am very happy that something I tried to do has worked at last. To help the primitive peoples of the world, the PPF has decided to nominate both of you for the Nobel Peace Prize for 1971, and following that for 1972. I hope—whether you get it or not—that you will sometimes remember that quite a few people—even myself—think you deserve it.

The English nomination was eventually proposed by Lord Boyd and Sir Julian Huxley, and supported by fifty other signatories. The French nomination was instigated by Professor Lévi-Strauss and the Societé des Americanistes, the American nomination by the American Anthropological Association. Many supporting nominations or letters came from other Latin American and European countries.

Orlando replied on May 1st, 1970:

Nobel. As you suggest, let us speak frankly. This is a great honour for us, but even greater is that we have friends who think of such a thing. There is no doubt that the scale and importance of such an award would give us doubled force in our work for the Indian. We thank the Directorate of the PPF for such a singular honour. And they can be certain that whether the Nobel recognition comes or not, we are always in the front line of the fight to defend the Indians and consequently to defend other primitive people as well.

At this time, the plans for the road released by the government showed it going through the village of the Kreen-Akrore but around the frontiers of the Parque. The River Xingu was to be bridged at the rapids of von Martius.

Cutting from *Correio de Brasiliense*, May 3rd, 1970:

MINISTER OF INTERIOR OPENS ROAD TO
INCORPORATE THE HEART OF AMAZONIA IN
THE NATIONAL ECONOMY

Exactly in the geographical centre of the country, SUDECO[2] started two months ago to open a road that will link the Mato Grosso capital, Cuyaba, with the Amazonian

city of Santarem ... by December this year the first six
hundred km. of pioneer road in the heart of Amazonia will
be concluded, on the following day the remaining nine
hundred km. will be started that link the distant settlement of Cachimbo to Santarem, almost in the other ex-
tremity of the great state of Brazil.

"The conquest of the legendary Amazonian region,"
declared President Medici in a recent discourse, "represents a desire of the whole Brazilian nation, and is the
foundation of the decisive action of the revolutionary
government in this respect. The rational occupation of
this area by the establishment of an integrated programme
of colonisation and regional development, constitutes the
primary goal of this government in continuing the efforts
of the previous governments of the revolution. This movement of the occupation of the West and Amazonia will con-
tribute to diminish the social tension of the North-east, and
will help in the expansion and strengthening of our internal
market ...

SUDECO is already constructing the road BR-080 (Brasilia
—Manaos) that will reach the Air Base of Cachimbo, crossing the Xingu at the falls of von Martius.

Leaving Santarem, on the banks of the Amazon, the road
BR-165 will also reach the base of Cachimbo.

This last road was the one that would pass close to the village
of Kubenkokre.

Note from Jesco von Puttkamei, May 6th, 1970:

In all the FUNAI politics going on, Orlando is wisely keeping himself out. But even so they are trying to diminish
the influence of Orlando, and I feel that at the moment
Orlando's influence is not very high, and he is being left
aside somehow.

The *Journal do Brasil* had an unexpected item on May 12th,
1970:

The President of FUNAI ... has stated that a few days ago
the withdrawal of the Suya (Beico de Pau) Indians from

[201]

the Rio Arinos to the Parque do Xingu has freed thirteen
thousand sq. km. of land for the Pioneer frontier.

A note came with it from Orlando:

The Beico de Pau arrived as if from a rigorous concentration camp—skin and bones. We were lucky. We cured and
fattened them all. Today they are happy and sing the
entire day with their relatives, the Suya.

A week later, the *Folha de Goiaz* for May 17th, 1970, added
to Orlando's note:

AFTER TWO CENTURIES
THE BEICO DE PAU ARE REUNITED WITH
THEIR BROTHERS THE SUYA

At the end of last year, without any justifiable motive,
in an operation which would normally be called a reconnaissance, an official contracted to FUNAI accompanied
by some journalists—one of whom was suffering from
severe 'flu—went to the village of the Suya (Beico de Pau)
on a tributary of the River Arinos, and contaminated the
whole village. The consequence of the irresponsibility of
the leader of the expedition who permitted the inclusion
of the sick journalist, or did not make him return when the
first symptoms appeared, was that some dozens of Indians
died, sixty-five in all, and their removal became a matter of
urgency to avoid new victims.

The forty-one remaining Indians of the Suya Beico de
Pau, accompanied by Padre Thomas, after a journey by
truck to Cuiaba and then by 'plane, disembarked last week
at Posto Leonardo Villas Boas.

My letter to Orlando, June 17th, 1970:

Sometimes we're on the verge of getting a 'plane for the
Parque, but at the final moment it becomes impossible
without some sort of official report. Charitable foundations
have to be careful with their money. What about the PPF?

They have seen that the Red Cross is doing a survey for a programme of medical assistance, and I am trying to encourage them to send an official representative to Brazil, I hope Robin Hanbury-Tenison, who organised your Nobel nomination . . . Of course they cannot match the Red Cross. But their report could channel money from the big foundations. Have you suggestions for any schemes or projects they could study?

Orlando replied on August 3rd, 1970:

It would be a good thing to have a representative of the PPF here in January. The Red Cross certainly plans to mount a great work in Brazil . . . And to organise a co-operation between the Red Cross and the PPF would be an important thing with far-ranging results.

The first President of FUNAI, Dr Queiroz Campos, has fallen. We now have a General who on his part has co-opted four other Generals and an Admiral. The thing gets more entangled each time. Poor Indian.

We don't know how they will act. They are changing everything. And not everything is being done with much wisdom. Many things smell wrong. The new masters don't believe in skill or experience—they prefer to improvise.

The moment now is very important. The new directors are altering, changing, transferring, creating, finishing.

The new President of the Indian Foundation, General Bandeira de Melo, did not have what could seriously be called any previous knowledge of or experience with Indians, nor could it be said that he was publicly known for his liking for Indians, or inclination to defend them.[3]

September 2nd, 1970—a paragraph from a letter from Dr. Peter Fry, an anthropologist at Campinas:

Claudio and Orlando are doubtless pulling their hair out with worry for the three thousand odd Indians who will suddenly find bulldozers ploughing through their territory. According to the *Estado do São Paulo*, which has been launch-

[203]

ing reporters into the region, some Indians have already begun a pathetic attempt to stave off the invaders.

Orlando confirmed this a month later:

Recently we managed to acquire from SUDECO a 'plane to continue our pacification of the Kreen-Akrore. Then when everything was ready, the new management of FUNAI ordered the 'plane to be transferred to Bananal ... The Cachimbo road continues. Soon it will be in direct conflict with the Indian. We have shouted, but no one pays any attention. As I have said, the 'plane we arranged was diverted to Bananal which can be reached by lorry, boat, the Air Force's weekly service and VASP [the commercial airline]. We don't know what they're up to ... We continue to believe that a small aeroplane for the exclusive use of the Parque is very important for this contact.

My letter to Orlando, September 29th, 1970:

The news from Brazil is that you're under pressure from the new Directorate, that the Indians of the Parque are too isolated, too primitive. That you may be forced to resign.

There were two replies from Orlando, both dated October 14th, 1970:

The information that has reached you is to a point correct. But we have been treated well by the new Directors. It happens that they are very optimistic but seem determined to speak absurdities. Pledged to economic development, they forget that FUNAI is essentially a welfare organisation and that a man is worth more than a bullock. What is happening now is a conflict between two types of politics— one of development without planning, smelling of politics and demagogy. The other is the tradition that cries through the humanism of Rondon.

The Trans-Amazonica road [Cuyaba—Santarem] is going

to pass through our Samauma air-strip, the one at the Kreen-Akrore village. Because of this we are going to start, or rather re-start, the Kreen-Akrore attraction. Obviously we have asked for a 'plane of the Cessna 180 type. But I don't think FUNAI will give the 'plane. They want us to do it on foot. Around the Parque in the way of the Trans-Amazonica we are going to work to contact five neighbouring and unknown groups. As you will want to know, I will enumerate: Miahao, Kreen-Akrore, the Indians in front of Poiriri (they made a lot of smoke this year), Awaike that have appeared on the Suya-Missu, and finally some lip-disc people that have appeared below the rapids of von Martius (very savage).

The new President of FUNAI, General Bandeira de Melo, used the Nobel nomination to defend his policies, as reported in the *Correio Brasiliense* for October 15th, 1970:

FUNAI WANTS NOBEL FOR VILLAS BOAS

With reference to the news of the nomination of Claudio Villas Boas[4] for the Nobel Peace Prize, General Bandeira de Melo, President of FUNAI, made the following declaration: "I have still not had official notification of the nomination, but in case it is confirmed and the prize comes to be conceded to Claudio by the Royal Academy of Stockholm in 1971, it will be reason for just pride and satisfaction for us Brazilians . . . just the fact that Claudio had been nominated by men of such repute in the scientific world represents a positive reply to those who for ulterior motives try to denigrate the Indian policy of the Brazilian government, of which FUNAI is the executor and in which Claudio is one of the key elements.

The magazine *Veja* published an article on November 4th, 1970:

At the same time as news and letters from friends spoke of a possible nomination of Claudio for the Nobel Peace Prize of 1971, confirmation arrived through official channels that

[205]

the Xavantina—Cachimbo road projected by the government will cut the Parque reserve for Indians. The confirmation of Claudio's candidature for the Prize—supported by such personalities as the anthropologist Lévi-Strauss and the philosopher-naturalist Julian Huxley—signified worldwide recognition of the work that he and his brothers Orlando and Leonardo started almost thirty years ago. But a road cutting the Parque (twenty-six thousand sq. km., approximately the size of the state of Alagoas) would be its negation. In the opinion of Orlando, "the penetration of the Reserve by a road would bring the Indian rapidly to destruction." And Claudio does not conceal his dismay. "If the road cuts the Parque, at that hour we withdraw from here."

O Popular, November 10th, 1970:

EXPEDITION SETS OUT AFTER INDIANS TODAY
FUNAI has placed an aeroplane under the orders of the expedition led by Orlando and Claudio Villas Boas which sets out today in the Xingu National Park for the village of the Jurunas. The Jurunas have reported the arrival of unknown Indians of hostile character in the interior of the jungle . . . The arrival of these Indians is an enigma, but one interpretation is the flight—for reasons unknown—of the Kreen-Akrore, original and traditional enemies of the Txukahamei.

On November 24th, 1970, the same paper reported:

VILLAS BOAS EXPEDITION ABANDONS SEARCH
FOR INDIANS
The Villas Boas Brothers have withdrawn their search for unknown Xingu Indians and already returned to a base at the rapids of von Martius, because rain had swamped the forest and eliminated the columns of smoke that acted as guides to direction . . . The explorer Acary Passos in charge of guiding the expedition by air, said that his own mission was frustrated because the rain prevented smoke rising

from the fires of the Indians. In consequence he was not able to give the signals needed by the Villas Boas to guide the expedition. "Now," explained the explorer, "nothing can be done. The expedition will only be able to work after the period of rains and *if the unknown Indians go back to giving signals.*

The Txukahamei Indians have been withdrawn from their village and taken to an area close to a Post in the Xingu National Park. The Xavantina—Cachimbo road will pass through the area they previously occupied and the withdrawal of the Indians—according to the explorer Acary Passos—has the purpose of avoiding conflict during the construction of the road.

Note from Orlando, January 2nd, 1971:

We were able to do nothing. The Minister and FUNAI supported the measure. It [the road] is without doubt the first step to the end of the Parque.

A postcard arrived from Orlando and Marina, dated January 15th, 1971:

Born—30th of last month—Orlando Villas Boas Jr.— mother and son well.

Abraco, Marina/Orlando.

Cutting from *O Estado de São Paulo*, February 26th, 1971:

FUNAI —THE INDIAN IS ASSISTED

"The Indian is not a museum item and his absorption into the nation has to be a gradual process, accomplished in such a manner as to permit his complete integration into the community," explained yesterday the President of the Indian National Foundation, General Bandeira de Melo. In his opinion the report of the International Red Cross upon the indigenous tribes of Brazil "rained on wet ground", since the measures suggested had already been largely adopted . . .

[207]

The acculturation of the Brazilian Indian is being carried forward with a rhythm of intensity, General Bandeira de Melo revealed yesterday. FUNAI is concerned to avoid that the Indian feels a trauma between two cultures, that of his tribe and that of the rest of the community. He committed FUNAI to the perfect integration of the Indians into the Brazilian community, because he would not permit the "formation of ethnic cysts". The President of FUNAI said he still could not agree with the criticisms relating to the construction of the road across Indian territory.

The same paper quoted Orlando in an interview, March 1st, 1971:

Obviously nobody could believe that this is an inopportune moment for the construction of the Trans-Amazonica. Everything that it does in Amazonia should be well received, with enthusiasm, even. What is needed is reconciliation of the interests of development with the purely human problem of help for indigenous man. Let us make the road, but make it humanely, with reference to the Indian. We must not, in the name of development, take the land of the Indian, massacre him—absolutely not! . . .

Many people ask me if my son, Orlandinho, will become an Indianist in the future. And it is with real sorrow that I say, if the present type of policies towards the Indians continue, twenty years from now there will be no more Indians in Brazil for my son to help. We will have the remnants of an extinct race, to provide for our curiosity and our folklore.

Inset with the interview, the *Estado de São Paulo* carried a personal note on Orlando:

His problem is his eyes. He is a man that likes to read, but can barely distinguish the headlines and titles of newspaper reports. He has a cataract that has ninety per cent blinded one eye and almost fifty per cent the other. He would like to have an operation, but the doctors say the time is still not right. Orlando is therefore restless and will return to the Parque do Xingo where he likes to live. The operation, set for some months from now, will take place after his next expedition.

O Globo, March 4th, 1971:

THE ROAD WILL FINISH THE PARK OF XINGU

The road that will cut the National Park of Xingu for a length of eighty km. will mark the end of the world's greatest experiment for primitive peoples, said John Dalgas Frisch, member of the Association for the Preservation of Forest Life, naturalist and ornithologist, who recorded the song of the Uirapuru. Criticising what he calls the "descasso" of the authorities and the official departments, among them the Brazilian Institute for Forest Development, Frisch demonstrated how the forest reserves have decreased in such a short time, and how the little that remains is wasted by illogical extraction for speculation or for unnecessary exploitation. In 1964, fifty per cent of the national territory was natural reserves; in 1968, one per cent; now only 0.20 per cent are virgin lands. According to him the Xavantina —Cachimbo road will put an end to the work of the Villas Boas brothers, who, disillusioned, are inclined to give up and resign from the conservationist struggle. The Indians were brought into the Parque Nacional do Xingu with the promise of protection, guarantees and assistance. "The road, however, will bring them alcohol, TB, prostitution, and all the vices of civilisation. Land-grabbers, salesmen, miners and money will arrive," affirmed the naturalist.

Next day, *O Globo* followed the earlier article with some quotes from Orlando:

"The Txukahamei are dispersed, walking by the recently opened road, abandoning their tribe, their village, their families. They roam the camp of the contractors, curious, looking at the machines, risking picking up the diseases of the whites ... This road could put an end to the Parque. And worst of all it is against the instructions of President Medici and the President of FUNAI, General Bandeira de

[209]

Melo, themselves. They decided that the Indians within the area of the Trans-Amazonica should be removed to the nearest forest—the Parque do Xingu. But with this road, there is nowhere left to take them. Little by little, they, the Indians, will mix with the whites to their extinction." Orlando spoke with great bitterness. He only heard of the road when it had already entered the territory of the Parque.

Soon after, Orlando was forbidden to speak to the Press, and the *Folha de São Paulo* could only report, on March 23rd, that Orlando "was advised by the President of FUNAI not to speak on the matter. Therefore, whatever information was required should be requested directly from the President of the organisation."

A letter from Orlando followed this, dated March 18th, 1971:

Recently FUNAI, for convenience or lack of interest in the Indians, has threatened to launch an Indian policy of the absurdest sort. FUNAI—that should fight for the survival of the Indians, increasing assistance to them and guaranteeing their isolation for some time—intends to integrate them rapidly into the national society, as if this had sense or was even possible. In their view, immediate integration is necessary in order that the Indians should cease to constitute an ethnic cyst within the country.

How can they speak of ethnic cysts in reference to people who, down the years, are rapidly disappearing? Cyst! The Indian? Is that not curious?

I include a newspaper cutting that sets out FUNAI's thinking. Sad that FUNAI, through ignorance, is becoming, without realising it, a vehicle for the extinction of the Brazilian Indian.

We don't believe that there is now, within Brazil, any internal force that can convince these people to the contrary.

It is clear FUNAI already includes us amongst the opponents of its new Indian policy. And so has already started to attack us . . . Frankly FUNAI is putting us to one side, and we have no doubt that we will be forced to leave here very shortly.

Cutting from *O Estado de São Paulo*, April 7th, 1971:

General Frederico Rondon[5] yesterday supported the extinction of the National Park of Xingu, which in his opinion is a hindrance to the Indian's integration with civilisation ... The General added, "I hope that the BR 080 (road) will really put an end to this Xingu National Park, which is already becoming prejudicial to the security and development of the country."

Orlando wrote from Posto Leonardo on April 21st, 1971:

Our plan is exactly what you suggest in your letter. We will stick it out. We will not resign ... Resignation will be the last step. We do not wish to throw away thirty years in the jungle—two hundred malarias. We have been charged to try the Kreen-Akrore again this year ... This week I descend with Claudio to see some Indians that are appearing near the Juruna. Perhaps they are Manitsawa. Others are appearing behind Diauarum, perhaps Awaike or Yaruma.

From *The Daily Telegraph*, May 4th, 1971:

General Bandeira de Melo, President of the National Indian Foundation, has himself made a surprising attack on the Xingu National Park. Using a time honoured Brazilian expression, the General said that Xingu was "para Ingles ver" ("for the British to see") meaning that it was just for show. When visitors left the reservation, the Indians had discarded their feathers and other ornaments and slipped on their "civilised" clothes. "The Indians are not museum pieces," the General went on. "They need freedom." He suggested that the publicity about Xingu was really aimed at winning a Nobel prize for its directors. The Director of FUNAI said that keeping Indians in Xingu was contrary to the government's policy of "national integration"—the latest slogan in Brazil. In other areas they were being gradually assimilated and taught trades.

The newspaper *O Estado de São Paulo* immediately warned that to attempt to turn Indians into plumbers, carpenters and motor mechanics "would be a kind of indirect genocide."

Letter to Orlando on May 18th, 1971:

Last week-end there was a meeting between Robin Hanbury-Tenison, Renée Fuerst [anthropologist with the Red Cross Mission] and Francis Huxley [anthropologist who studied the Urubu with Darci Ribeiro] at Robin's house. I could not go, but 'phoned twice and shouted for about an hour.

1. Robin's report will be released at a press conference around the 5th June. It tries to be moderate and constructive in tone but criticises the new integration policy, the attack on the Parque, the problem with the Nambikwaras, etc. We hope it will be released simultaneously in France, Switzerland and other countries, together with interviews by local anthropologists. The article I sent you will go out a few weeks later.

2. More important, Robin is discussing the report with the Brazilian Ambassador today, and it will be sent in advance to the Brazilian Government. Its general points have already been discussed and we know—unofficially—that the Brazilian diplomats in Europe regard the new FUNAI policy as damaging to the reputation of Brazil abroad, and have told the Itamarity.[6] In particular they have said that since you were nominated for the Nobel Prize and cited by the previous administration as the model for all FUNAI policy, it would look curious if you were now dismissed.

Letter from Orlando, August 27th, 1971:

Everything continues as before. All the Parque below the road to the rapids has been lost. In compensation they will give another area above the Kuikuro to the river 7th of September. This new region of the Parque, besides being much worse than that which has been lost, has intruders, ranchers, and is the entry point for many hunters. There we must transfer the Txukahamei, but it will be almost impossible to keep them in an area so different to their own in every way. In short the Parque was mutilated, and the situation every time is worse.

Dr Noel Nutels, one-time head of the Indian Protection Service, wrote on October 29th, 1971:

In my view the Parque is in the worst possible state. The Villas Boas are suffering under greater and greater pressure ... and as I think you already know, the part of the Parque that has been cut off was exactly the part intended for the Kreen-Akrore. Already various ranchers have installed themselves and are cutting down the forest for cattle.

Orlando's note at Christmas:

Powerful people are helping us to retire. Pray God, it will be soon.

*   *   *

As a conclusion to everything that happened in 1971, I was sent a cutting from the magazine *Veja*—a full-page advertisement by the Bank of Amazonia and SUDAM—the Superintendency of the Development of Amazonia of the Ministry of the Interior:

ENOUGH OF LEGENDS
LET US TAKE STOCK

Many people are capable of drawing benefit from the riches of Amazonia.

    With the praise and encouragement of SUDAM.

    With the praise and encouragement of the Bank of Amazonia.

Brazil is investing in Amazonia and offering profits to whoever wishes to participate in the enterprise.

    The Trans-Amazonica is there: the highway to a mine of gold. Start now. Make your choice through SUDAM.

[213]

Apply your tax deduction to one of the 464 economic projects approved by SUDAM. Or present your own project (if it is industrial, agricultural, or a utility service).

You will have all the support of the Federal Government and of the Governments of the States that make up Amazonia. There is a treasure awaiting you. Avail yourself of it. Take stock. Get rich with Brazil.

Information from the offices of SUDAM and the branches of the Bank of Amazonia.

*   *   *

The final *dénouement* to the Kreen-Akrore expedition described in this book was reported in a few brief paragraphs in *The Times* of February 7th and 10th, 1973:

LEGENDARY INDIAN TRIBE FOUND

Brasilia, Feb 6.—A Brazilian anthropologist has made contact with the fierce giant warriors of a legendary lost Amazon tribe.

Senhor Claudio Villasboas met the giant Indians of the Krenakores tribe, some over 6 ft 6 in tall, at his jungle camp in northern Mato Grosso state. The warriors handed over gifts of arrows and bows and were given steel axes, knives and kettles in return.

GIANT INDIANS DEMAND TRINKETS

São Paulo, Feb 9.—A Brazilian anthropologist has made an urgent appeal for more trinkets to appease the Krenakores, the legendary giant warriors of the Amazon who have evaded white explorers for decades.

Senhor Claudio Villasboas, one of the country's leading Indian experts, says he is the first white man to contact the 6 ft 6 in tall tribesmen. He sent a radio message yesterday saying excited warriors were hovering round his camp.

He asked Brazil's Indian foundation (Funai) to send more porcelain necklaces, small metal knives and axes because he was running out of gifts for the warlike Krenakores.

Indian officials here were making swift arrangements to send a special air cargo of beads and knives to Senhor

Villasboas's isolated camp in the north of Mato Grosso state where the first full-scale contact with the Krenakores was made on Sunday.

If the supply of trinkets runs out the Indians might become angry and attack the camp, the officials said.

Senhor Villasboas, who is 53, described his meeting with the Indians in a radio message to his brother Alvaro in São Paulo, after spending 382 days camped on the bank of the Peixoto river waiting for them to emerge from the jungle.

He was confronted by 25 Krenakore warriors on Sunday. They allowed him to embrace them and hand them gifts in exchange for bows and arrows during a 20-minute encounter.

Yesterday two more warriors approached the camp to shake hands and take more gifts.

"They were very excited. They took knives and necklaces and ran back into the jungle from which other tribesmen were peering out. After a while they came back for more gifts", the anthropologist said in his radio report.

He first encountered a naked Krenakore man and woman last October and held a one-hour sign language conversation with them from a distance of 30 ft. Months earlier he had to avoid a volley of arrows when the Indians made it clear they wanted nothing to do with white men.

The Krenakores, one of five tribes believed to exist in a permanent state of war with each other in Brazil's remote Xingu national park, are on average a foot taller than their neighbours.

The giant Indians are feared by other tribesmen, who also say the Krenakore women are just as tall and powerful as their menfolk. One woman is reported to have battered to death four enemy tribesmen with a war club 4 ft 6 in in length before 15 members of the opposing army put her out of action.

The anthropologist was joined yesterday by another brother, Orlando, probably Brazil's leading Indian expert, and a doctor who flew to a jungle airstrip cleared near their camp.

The doctor was flown in to ensure that none of the 38 expedition members passes on a disease to the Krenakores, who have no antibodies to fight white man's viruses. If influenza were to hit the Indians it would almost certainly wipe out the entire tribe, estimated at 500, according to Indian officials.

So far none of the 38 Indians from six neighbouring tribes has been able to understand a word of the giants' language. Senhor Villaboas said he believes the entire tribe will eventually turn up at the camp for their share of trinkets.

"If there are no gifts when they ask they will consider it an insult and it could be dangerous at this stage", an official said here.

Senhor Villasboas has asked for porcelain beads because the Krenakores will not accept the cheap glass or plastic variety. The beads must be coloured white, yellow, green or blue. The Stone Age Indians have refused red ones.

Senhor Villaboas and his brother Orlando, nominated for the 1971 Nobel peace prize for their 30 years' work among Amazon Indians, have resigned from the Government-run Indian agency because they say it is helping to destroy the primitive tribes.—*Reprinted by permission of Reuters*

NOTES TO POSTSCRIPT

1. Claudio seldom writes, and messages from him usually go in letters to Orlando.
2. The old Central Brazil Foundation.
3. Some anthropologists and Indian specialists have described General Bandeira de Melo's "qualifications", and the motives for his appointment, in stronger terms.
4. It was reported in Brazil—incorrectly—that only Claudio would be nominated.
5. No relative of Marshal Candido Mariano Rondon, founder of the Indian Protection Service.
6. The equivalent of Whitehall—it houses the Brazilian Foreign Office.

Appendices

THE EXPLORATION OF XINGU

In 1870, Karl von den Steinen led the first known expedition into Xingu, but there may have been others before him. The maps of Brazil already showed the "open hand" shape of the headwaters, and the Kuikuro tribe has an account of a slave-raider attack at some time in the past.

1870 Von den Steinen descends the River Xingu to its mouth. Meets the tribes of Upper Xingu.

1884 Von den Steinen's second descent. Meets the Suya.

1897 Meyer visits Xingu.

1890s American expedition wiped out at Diauarum.

1900 Max Schmidt's expedition.

1910 to 1940s A period of rapid decline amongst the Indians, with many villages passing into extinction. Epidemics either came with visiting expeditions or were brought back by Xinguano trading parties to the Bakairi tribe and the Indian Protection Service Post of Simoes Lopes.

1920 Lt. Ramiro Noronha's expedition.

1920 Colonel Fawcett's first expedition to Xingu.

1924 Heinrich Hintermann's expedition.

1925 Colonel Fawcett disappears in Xingu.

1926 The Rev. Emil Halverson makes several visits to Xingu over a period of years.

1928 Commander Dyott descends the Xingu in search of Fawcett.

1930 Italian expedition killed by the Juruna.

1930s Albert de Winton killed by the Kamayura.

1932 Petrullo lands in Xingu with a float-plane.

1940 Indian Protection Service expedition to Xingu. Two Kuikuro Indians taken to Cuyaba and taught Portuguese.

In this phase, all expeditions entered from the south by river. No attempt was made to establish a Post, or to stay in Xingu for any length of time.

* * *

1943 December. Claudio and Leonardo Villas Boas arrive at Aragarcas, and join the Central Brazil Foundation's Roncador–Xingu expedition.

1944 The expedition advances to the River das Mortes, and Orlando Villas Boas joins it.

1945 June 12th. The vanguard of the expedition, led by Orlando, Claudio and Leonardo, crosses the River das Mortes.

1945 July–September. The expedition cuts its way across the Serra de Roncador, harassed by Xavante Indians.

1945 December. An air-strip is laid out on the River Tanguro, at the headwaters of the Xingu River system.

1946 February. The expedition meets the Kalapalo Indians, visits their village, builds a Post and air-strip on the River Kuluene.

1946 December. An epidemic of influenza sweeps through the Kuikuro and Kakapalo villages. Twenty-five Indians die.

1947 The expedition reaches the River Xingu and builds an air-strip and Post at Jacare. Meetings with Kamayura, Meinaco, Aweti and other tribes.

1948 Marshal Rondon nominates the three brothers as representatives of the Indian Protection Service in the Upper Xingu. The idea of a National Park is first discussed with Brigadier Aboim of the Air Force, and anthropologist Eduardo Galvao.

1948 River Tanguro explored. A journey to the Waura village on the River Batovi.

1949 The expedition descends the River Xingu to the mouth of the River Manitsaua, and builds an air-strip at Diauarum. First contact with the Juruna tribe.

1949 October–November. The expedition ascends the River Manitsaua and constructs the Manitsaua air-strip.

[220]

1950 Trail opened from the River Manitsaua to the River Teles Pires, and an air-strip built on the Teles Pires. Meetings with Kayabi Indians. Aerial exploration of the Cachimbo Range.

1951 Orlando, Claudio and Leonardo crash-land on a patch of savannah in the Serra do Cachimbo. They build the air-strip of Cachimbo and see the first signs of the Kreen-Akrore Indians.

1952 Exploration of the River Teles Pires, River Javare and Serra dos Kayabi, and further contacts with Kayabi villages. The brothers build an emergency air-strip on the Serra dos Kayabi.

1952 The first expedition to the rapids of von Martius finds trails and huts of Txukahamei Indians. A post built at Diauarum for the Central Brazil Foundation, then the brothers return to their base at Jacare. The Txikao tribe attacks some Xinguanos and a Villas Boas expedition ascends the River Batovi, but fails to contact them. The first group of Kayabi Indians enters the Xingu region. Orlando and Claudio start their campaign to save the land of Xingu, and publish a series of articles in Brazilian papers.

1953 Leonardo is transferred to the River Araguaia, and leads an Indian Protection Service expedition which makes contact with the Xikrin.

1953 November–December. Orlando and Claudio contact the Txukahamei tribe.

1953 The State Government of Mato Grosso sells the land of Upper Xingu, and Orlando and Claudio launch a campaign of protest that also attacks the heads of their own Department —the Central Brazil Foundation—for accepting the sales. They are forced to leave the Post of Jacare, and build a hut on the River Tuatuari. An epidemic of measles comes from Xavantina, and kills 114 Indians.

1955 Orlando and Claudio manage to drive off many of the invading parties of surveyors and prospectors, and the Federal Government promises to create a National Park in Xingu. With the Air Force, the brothers organise an expedition to survey the River Liberdade, and an airstrip is built close to the Liberdade.

1956 The second expedition to contact the Txikao enters their camp, but is driven off by a hail of arrows. The Txikao retreat to the River Jatoba.

1957 The Villas Boas's base on the River Tuatuari becomes the Indian Protection Service Post in the area. Claudio starts to cut a trail from Cachimbo westwards to the River Cururu, and builds air-strips to S. Benedito and Divisor.

1958 Claudio's expedition reaches the River Cururu, builds the Cururu air-strip, and Claudio returns to Capitão Vasconcelos. An expedition locates the Geographical Centre of Brazil, surveys the River Xingu to the Serra das Coordenadas, and reaches a section of the Txukahamei tribe on the River Liberdade.

1959 The Villas Boas are forced to abandon the Post of Capitão Vasconcelos during a dispute with the Indian Protection Service over the rapid integration of Indians into Brazilian society. The brothers move to the Post of Diauarum, and contact the Suya tribe on the River Suya-Missu.

1961 April 14th. The Federal Government creates the National Park of Xingu. Claudio explores the River Ronuro. Leonardo dies in hospital in São Paulo.

1962 The Indian Protection Service returns the Post of Capitão Vasconcelos to the Villas Boas. It is re-christened Posto Leonardo in memory of Leonardo Villas Boas, and becomes the headquarters of the National Park. The Kalapalo, Matipuhy and Nahukua tribes move their villages into the area of the National Park.

1963 The nomadic Txukahamei tribe settles at Poiriri, and the Villas Boas start building air-strips by every Indian village.

1964 October. Txikao tribe finally contacted on the River Jatoba.

1965 Another visit to the Txikao tribe.

1966 An expedition brings a section of the Kayabi tribe from the River Tatuin into the National Park.

1967 The Txikao tribe is brought into the National Park to protect them from prospectors moving down the River Jatoba. An expedition fails to contact unknown Indians on the River Penetecaua.

1967 December. The Indian Protection Service is abolished and the National Park, which was an independent Department, is incorporated in the Indian Foundation, FUNAI.

1968 The Ministry of the Interior increases the area of the Park to twenty-six thousand sq. km., and an expedition to contact the Kreen-Akrore tribe enters their village; but the Kreen-Akrore remain in hiding. Air-strips built at Manitsaua, Peixoto and Samauma, and a trail cut from the River Manitsaua to the River Peixoto Azevedo.

1969 An expedition returns to the Kreen-Akrore village. No success.

1970 The Beico de Pau tribe are brought into the National Park and settled with the related Suya tribe.

1970 The first President of FUNAI replaced by General Bundelra de Melo, and FUNAI's policy gradually changes towards rapid integration for the Indian. An unsuccessful expedition up the River Arraias to contact unknown Indians.

1971 FUNAI permits a road to cut the National Park in half, and announces an accelerated policy of integration for the Indians. A campaign is launched to destroy the National Park, and anthropologists and leading neswpapers like the *Estado de São Paulo* and the *Journal do Brasil* rally to its defence. Second expedition to the River Arraias to contact unknown Indians. The northern half of the National Park (below the road) is annexed, and a poorer and already occupied area is promised as replacement in the south.
The road-builders bring an epidemic to the Txukahamei tribe, and their village has to be moved. The Txukahamei open fire on a party of road-builders.

1972 The Villas Boas lead another expedition to contact the Kreen-Akrore, this time advancing southwards out of Cachimbo.

1973 The Villas Boas achieve contact with the Kreen-Akrore. They resign from the Indian Foundation.

TRIBES OF THE XINGU AREA

1a TRIBES OF UPPER XINGU

The tribes in the Upper Xingu culture group look and dress alike, share the same festivals and legends, and lead similar social, economic and religious lives. They have different languages, but many individuals speak several besides their own. Their first recorded contact was with Von den Steinen, but more than a score of expeditions passed through Xingu in the early twentieth century, and the Indians made regular trading visits to the Indian Protection Service Post of Simoes Lopes. Orlando and Claudio Villas Boas opened the first permanent post in the area in 1946.

Tribe	Village	Population 1970
KUIKURO	On a tributary of R. Kurisevo	161
KALAPALO	E. bank of R. Kuluene near Posto Leonardo	85
MATIPUHY-NAHUKUA		60 (Von den Steinen grouped all the Karib-speaking tribes under the name Nahukua. In 1870 there were 9 villages according to his estimate)
KAMAYURA	On Lake Ipavu near Posto Leonardo	128 (4 villages at time of Von den Steinen)
AWETI	On R. Kurisevo	40 (1 village at time of Von den Steinen)
YAWALAPITI	About a mile from Posto Leonardo	47 (1 village at time of Von den Steinen)

Language Base	Notes
Karib	Von den Steinen believed the Karib-speaking tribes were the first in Xingu, and therefore the core of the Xinguano culture.
Karib	
Karib	The Matipuhy and Nahukua tribes lived originally on the main trading route to the Post of Simoes Lopes on the River Batovi. They bore the brunt of the epidemics that came with the trading parties and ceased to exist as tribes forty years ago. The survivors lived with the Kuikuros and Kalapalos, but recently the Villas Boas persuaded them to revive their separate tribal existence. Now they live partly in their own village and partly with the Kuikuros and Kalapalos.
Tupi	The Kamayura were one of the last tribes to arrive in Xingu and probably came down the R. Suya-Missu.
Tupi	Probably entered Xingu from the Teles Pires area.
Aruak, but confused with another language, possibly during the period they lived with the Kuikuro.	In 1947 the Yawalapiti were reduced to a few families scattered amongst the Kuikuro and Kamayura. The Villas Boas persuaded them to build their own village and revitalise their tribal existence.

Tribe	Village	Population 1970
WAURA	Near mouth of R. Batovi	95
MEHINAKO	On R. Tuatuari close to R. Kurisevo	63

1b OUTSIDE UPPER XINGU CULTURE GROUP

TXIKAO	Close to Posto Leonardo	51 (53 on 1st contact in 1964)

N.B. **Population**

1870   Von den Steinen's estimate for Upper Xingu's population 2,500–3000

1950   Eduardo Galvao's estimate (including Trumai excluding Txikao) 600

1970   Dr. Baruzzi's census (including Trumai excluding Txikao) 704

Language Base	Notes
Aruak	As the principal potmakers and traders in the area, they were the "diplomats" of Xingu in the past. Their mediation put an end to several wars and the trade in pots is one of the key factors in the feast of Quarup and the common culture of Upper Xingu.
Aruak	The only tribe in Upper Xingu which does not take part in the festival of Javari—potmakers like the Waura.
Presumed to be Karib based	In the 1950s the Txikao had 4 huts on the R. Batovi and made several raids into Xingu. Under the leadership of the Waura the Upper Xinguanos counter-attacked in 1961, and many Txikao were killed. They withdrew to the R. Jatoba, and the survivors only had one hut when the Villas Boas contacted them in 1964. To protect them from prospectors moving down the R. Jatoba and R. Batovi they were moved to Posto Leonardo in 1967.

N.B. **Tribal Names**
The spelling follows the convention of the Brazilian Anthropological Association.

2a THE TRIBES OF LOWER XINGU

Unlike Upper Xingu, there is no common culture in the northern area of the Parque. Most of the tribes were either hostile or unknown to each other until they were contacted by the Villas Boas.

Tribe	Village	Population 1967
JURUNA	West bank of the Xingu near the mouth of the R. Manitsaua	49
TRUMAI	1967 hut by post of Diauarum 1969 moved to hut by Posto Leonardo Many of the younger men remained with their Suya wives at Diauarum	22 (2 villages at time of Von den Steinen)
BEICO DE PAU	Moved from R. Arinos to National Park of Xingu in 1970 Settled close to the Suya near the Post of Diauarum	41
SUYA	On River Suya-Missu Moved lower down the river in 1968	67 (Roughly 80 on contact)

Language Base	Notes
Uncertain, possibly impure Tupi	The Juruna were first recorded in 1640 close to the mouth of the Xingu with a population said to be several thousand. In the early twentieth century they worked and fought with the rubber-tappers on the middle Xingu but were gradually pushed above the rapids of von Martius. They were contacted by the Villas Boas in 1949, but in the 1950s their population was down to 20 and their tribe was thought to be dying out.
Unrelated language	Probably entered Xingu down the R. Tanguro from the east between 100 and 200 years ago. They have largely been absorbed into the culture of Upper Xingu though they have not yet taken part in the feast of Quarup. They taught the other tribes the dances of Tawarawana and Javari and lived in Upper Xingu on the east bank of the R. Kuluene till they fled to Diauarum in 1960.
Jo	After 85 Beico de Pau died in a 'flu epidemic, the tribe was moved into Xingu. The Villas Boas believe the Suya originally belonged to this group.
Je	Roughly 150 years ago, the Suya entered Xingu down the R. Ronuro, and were met by Von den Steinen at Diauarum in 1884.

Tribe	Village	Population 1967
KAYABI	Several villages grouped around Diauarum	152
TXUKAHAMEI (Mekrenoti)	At Poiriri on the west bank of the Xingu about 50 km. above the rapids of von Martius In 1970, when the road entered the National Park they were moved closer to Diauarum	170 (When contacted by the Villas Boas in 1953 they had 2 villages. Kremuro's with 60 banana-leaf huts—i.e. at least 240 people—and Kretire's with

Language Base	Notes

In this period they alternatively fought and visited the Upper Xingu tribes and absorbed much of the Xinguano culture. They fled after a massacre by the Juruna to the head-waters of the R. Suya-Missu, and hid for two generations until contacted by the Villas Boas in 1960. The Villas Boas believe that the Suya may have split off from the Beico de Pau tribe in the area of the R. Juruena, and that both groups could have originally (like the Txukahamei) hived off from the Gorotire on the R. Araguaia.

Tupi

Originally lived in half a dozen villages on the R. Teles Pires where they were contacted by Indian Protection Service expeditions in 1924 and then met the Villas Boas in 1950. The first group entered Xingu in 1952, but others began working for the rubber-tappers who started pushing down the Teles Pires at this time. A few Kayabi still live in the Teles Pires area, but most left in a series of exoduses organised by Pripuri. The last was in 1966. Because of their contact with the rubber-tappers, the Kayabi are the most Brazilianised Indians of the Parque.

Je

Txukahamei is a name only used inside the Xingu park and means the men without a bow (in the Juruna language). Their own names for themselves are Mekrenoti and Mentuktire and they are a section of the Kayapo horde, originally united with the other Mekrenoti, Kuben Kran Kegn, Kararao and Gorotire groups. From the beginning of this century they were based 40 km. to the west of the rapids of von Martius, but made

Tribe	Village	Population 1967
	considerably more)	

2b RELATED GROUPS VISITED BY THE TXUKAHAMEI OUTSIDE THE PARQUE

(The Txukahamei are the only nomads in Xingu and the only tribe to make regular visits outside the Parque)

Tribe	Village	Population 1967
MEKRENOTI (of chief Bebgogoti)	Between R. Bau and R. Chiche	Roughly 200
MEKRENOTI (by post of Bau)	Below junction of R. Bau and R. Curua	Roughly 80
MEKRENOTI (of chief Kokraimuro)	On Xingu, well above Rio Fresco	Roughly 200
KUBEN KRAN KEGN	On the Riosinho (tributary of the R. Fresco)	Roughly 200
GOROTIRE	On R. Fresco	Roughly 200

Language Base	Notes
	long nomadic journeys from the R. Araguaia to the R. Tapajoz. They were contacted by the Villas Boas in 1953, and eventually the group of Chief Kremuro and parts of the groups of Chiefs Kretire and Ukakoro settled inside the Parque in 1963.
Je	Regularly visited by Txukahamei. In 1953 this group of Mekrenoti lived with those in Xingu, until they moved over to the River Iriri region after a "civil war" in 1958. They were recontacted on the Iriri by Francisco Meireles in 1958.
Je	Occasionally visited by Txukahamei.
Je	Occasionally visited by Txukahamei.
Je	There have been no visits to this cousin tribe since a group of chief Kremuro's Txukahamei were massacred at the Kuben Kran Kegn village about 1960.
Je	The parent group of the Mekrenoti, but there have been no visits for more than a decade. In 1968 Claudio flew the chief into Xingu for a short visit to the Txukahamei village.

N.B. The population figures are from Dr. Noel Nutel's medical survey in 1967 and are less thorough and possibly more of an underestimate than Dr. Baruzzi's figures for Upper Xingu. The figures outside the Parque are only rough guesses.

3. UNCONTACTED TRIBES
IN THE NEIGHBOURHOOD OF XINGU

Tribe	Location	Notes
*KREEN-AKRORE	Near R. Peixoto Azevedo, but probably several other villages	Kreen-Akrore is the Txukahamei name for the tribe which dominates the Cachimbo area.
IPEWI	Inland from the east bank of the R. Teles Pires	The Kayabi name for the group that used to attack them from the Cachimbo area. Almost certainly the same people as the Kreen-Akrore.
AGOVOTOKUENG	Between the headwaters of the Rivers Kurisevo and Kuluene	Constantly reported by the Kuikuro, but they may have died out or moved into another area. Agovotokueng means the other Yawalapiti, and presumably they speak the same language.
AWAIKE	Headwaters of R. Suya-Missu	Seen by the Suya when they lived on the upper reaches of the Suya-Missu. Reported to have plantations and canoes, and to wear urucu, short hair, necklaces and armbands.
MIAHAO	R. Arraias	Constantly reported by the Juruna. Said to have short hair. Possibly the same people as Kreen-Akrore.

* First contact finally achieved February 1973.

Tribe	Location	Notes
UNKNOWN TXUKAHAMEI	To the east of the rapids of von Martius	A splinter group from the Txukahamei tribe reported recently by the Kayabi and Txukahamei.
APIAKA	Headwaters of R. Tapaiuna (a trib. of R. Teles Pires)	A Tupi-speaking group who lived on the R. Juruna, but were driven inland by the brutality of the rubber-tappers. Since then they have had intermittent contact with the Kayabi. In 1966 a flight over their area discovered a village with 3 small houses and 1 large one.

4. EXTINCT TRIBES OF XINGU

Tribe	Site	Language Base	Notes
AIPATSE also called Tsuva	On trib. of R. Kurisevo	Karib	Related to Kuikuro, but wiped out by disease. Some descendants live with the Kuikuro.
NARUVOT		Karib	Wiped out by disease, descendants live with Kalapalos.
KUTENABU	R. Batovi	Aruak	Wiped out by disease, descendants live with Waura.
ARUPATI	R. Ronura	Tupi	Wiped out by Kamayura, women taken as captives.
ANUMANIA	Lake Itavununo	Tupi	Wiped out by Trumai, survivors merged with Aweti.
YARUMA	R. Tanguro		Wiped out by Kuikuro, remainder merged with Suya.
AUALATA		Same language as Trumai	Wiped out by Suya, survivors merged with Trumai
MANITSAWA	R. Manitsaua-Missu		Wiped out by Suya, but a small group may still live in the jungle to the west of the R. Manitsaua.
TONORI	R. Ronuro		Fought Kamayura.

These names and facts are based on Claudio's research among the existing tribes.

5. UNCONTACTED TRIBES OUTSIDE XINGU
(Only tribes mentioned in the text)

Tribe	Site	Notes
CABECAS PELADAS	Roughly 50 miles NW of Altamira between the Rivers Penetecaua and Jaraucu	Cabecas Peladas is a frontier nickname for a group that may be Juruna or Arara. Language probably Tupi-base. In 1967 they had 5 huts and probably 50 to 60 people. They were contacted in 1970.
ATROARI	North of Manaos in the region of the R. Alalau	A group of the Waimiri tribe which has had sporadic contacts with the Indian Protection Service. Karib language. Wiped out an IPS expedition led by Padre Calleri in 1968, but there have been peaceful contacts with subsequent expeditions.
CINTAS LARGAS	Area between R. Aripuana and R. Roosevelt	A general frontier term given to all uncontacted tribes in the area between the R. Roosevelt and R. Aripuana. Francisco Meireles made contact with a Tupi-speaking group in 1969, but the other groups may speak different languages.

6. CONTACTED TRIBES OUTSIDE XINGU
(Only tribes mentioned in the text)

Tribe	Site	Notes
MUNDURUCU	On the R. Tapajoz and R. Cururu	Pushed up the R. Tapajoz fighting the Kayabi in the nineteenth century. Are the north-western neighbours of the Kreen-Akrore.
XAVANTE	Serra do Rondacor	A Je-speaking tribe said to number 6,000 when contacted by Francisco Meirelles in 1946. Now 1,800 Xavantes remain, scattered at several missions and posts around the Roncador area. Raided occasionally into Xingu in the past.
BAKAIRI	Headwaters of R. Paranatinga	At the beginning of this century lived on the headwaters of the R. Kurisevo and regularly traded into the Xingu area. Most early expeditions to Xingu relied on Bakairi guides. A Karib group.
TIMBIRA	The region between the coastal strip and the R. Araguaia	A group of 15 Je-speaking tribes including the Kraho, Gavioes, Apinaye. Their nearest relatives are the Kayapo and a Txukahamei can easily understand an Apinaye speaking in his

Tribe	Site	Notes
		own language. Many of the tribes in this group are now extinct.
KARARAO	Junction of R. Jaraucu and Penetecaua	A Je-speaking group fragmented from the Gorotire. Contacted in 1965. Of the 46 members of the tribe there were only 8 survivors in 1967.
URUBU	Trib. of R. Gurupi	Tupi-speaking group.
KARAJA	R. Araguaia around the Ilha de Bananal	Have declined from 4,000 in the 1880s to less than 800 now. (Maluware who joined the Kreen-Akrore expedition has since become chief of the tribe.)
GOROTIRE KUBEN KRAN KEGN MEKRENOTI	See page 234	
NAMBIKUARA	Between head-waters of R. Jaraucu and Aripuana	Pacified by Rondon Commission in 1910.

DECREE GOVERNING THE PARQUE

(Decree No. 51,084 of 31/7/61)

The President of the Republic, in use of the functions conferred upon him by Article 37, Item I of the Federal Constitution, and in view of the decisions of Art. II of the Decree No. 50,455 of April 14th, 1961,

Decrees:

Art. 1 The National Park of Xingu (P.N.X.) created by Decree No. 50,455 of April 14th, 1961, with borders set out in its Art. I, will have the following attributes:

1. To preserve the original flora and fauna of the area—against whatever forms of destructive exploitation or de-characterisation as a sample of Brazilian nature which in scientific and landscape value represents a national heritage.

2. To guarantee to the indigenous population in the area of the Parque possession of the lands they occupy under Art. 31b of the Federal Constitution.

3. To provide the indigenous tribes with the medical, social and educational assistance necessary to ensure their survival together with the preservation of their cultural attributes.

4. To encourage within the area of the Parque research in all fields of natural and social sciences.

5. To control tourist activities in the area, avoiding prejudice of whatever nature to the indigenous groups, or anything that places the natural heritage under its protection at risk.

Art. 2 The executive direction of the Parque will consist of an Administrator-General chosen and nominated by the President of the Republic.

Art. 3 Within the competence of the Administrator-General:

a. in his rôle as special delegate of the Indian Protection Service, to carry out and fulfil in the area of the Parque Brazilian legislation protecting the Indian;

b. in his rôle as special delegate of the Forest Service and the Division of Game and Fisheries of the Ministry of Agriculture, to protect the flora and fauna and the natural richness of the area of the Parque in the terms of the special legislation concerning these matters;

c. to encourage respect for law and maintain order in the area of the Parque, being empowered for this purpose to requisition armed forces when indispensable for the protection of Indians, flora and fauna;

d. to authorise, after fulfilling the legal formalities, the entry of persons or groups into the area of the Parque and to take action to remove invaders;

e. to employ financial allocations for the Parque and to present accounts of their application to those entitled to them;

f. to represent the Parque actively and passively, judicially and extra-judicially.

Art. 4 The personnel of the Parque will be organised in conformity with the rules of Art. 10 of Decree No. 50,455 of 14/4/61, or through contracts or covenants subject to the Legislation for Labour.

Art. 5 In addition to the allocation for it in the budget of the Union [of Brazil], the Parque is empowered to receive donations from individuals and organisations private and public.

Art. 6 It is within the competence of the Administrator-General to sign agreements and covenants in its name with public and private organisations for purposes that are humanitarian, scientific, or connected with the protection of nature.

Art. 7 The base of the National Park in Xingu will be installed within its geographical limits.

1. The Parque will maintain a representative in the Federal Capital.

2. The Brazilian Air Force will sign a covenant with the Parque for the maintenance of services for protection of aviation installed in the area.

3. The Central Brazil Foundation will sign a covenant with the Parque for the maintenance of its advance posts located in the area under its jurisdiction.

Art. 8 For the purpose of administration, the Administrator-General will be assisted by personnel of his choice, for medico-sanitary assistance, administration, education and control of scientific activities in the area.

The Administrator of the Parque will choose his substitute from amongst his assistants.

Art. 9 The Parque will operate within the area of its jurisdiction through a chain of posts for vigilance, assistance, or scientific observation.

Art. 10 Incorporated in the property of the Parque are all the goods located within its area, except those that fall into the sphere of national security or that are the subject of a covenant.

Art. 11 The present decrees will enter into force on the date of their publication revoking any rulings to the contrary.

Brasilia. D.F.

TXUKAHAMEI EXPEDITION TO PACIFY THE KREEN-AKRORE, 1969–1970

The following excerpts are from letters written by the linguist, Micky Stout. She has spent half a dozen years with the Mekrenoti and Txukahamei, and probably knows them better than anyone else.

Poiriri, December 4th, 1969

Here we are in the village [of the Txukahamei] just watching the excitement walk away and leave us—namely with the war party. Just think, if you were here you would have gone along with them—and if anything could be more exciting to film than the Kreen-Akrore pacification it could only be the Kreen-Akrore "demolishment" by our good friends.

The Village has made almost an all-out attempt to hide the facts from us, but after all, we do understand a bit after all this time—not to mention the two or three adults and a few children whom we saw before they got the message not to tell us—or who wanted to be ornery. When they were setting out the guns in a line in front of the men's house where the war plans were being made, Krumare's little girl scowled at a younger one who told us what they were doing, and thinking quickly assured us that the guns were being counted up for "fishing"—well, at least she thought of something other than war. "Oh, yes," I said, "they must be out of fish-hooks again." To which she heartily agreed. Then there were the little-child stage whispers to mommies: "Mommie, don't tell that Daddy went to kill a Kreen-Akrore, they will tell Claudio on the radio." And the mothers, caught in such a fix, would always be quick to launch into a very well-

[246]

staged explanation of the things the men were going to get for the festival—feathers, honey and beeswax for the special head-dresses, sap for sticking on the eggshell, and the blue "ator" bird egg. We would play dumb and not mention the fact that the Kayapo are known to have included man-hunts for the pre-festival hunting trips.

I understand they mean to bring back a captive child or so—boys. I don't know if this is by special request, as it were, or if anyone who can get a nice one will of course want him. One man told us that the men from Bebgogoti's village aren't going back for this attack—just the Poiriri folk. However, I heard someone saying that Eketi—presently moved to Poiriri—is going along to kill another.

One man who didn't go on the war expedition yet is our friend Kremuro. He took chief Kretire's son Beptori to Diau-arum for treatment for a malaria that wouldn't let him go. You heard that Kretire died? I knew Kremuro was a hard, tough, rather invincible man once he sets his mind to a thing, but yesterday he accomplished what I call rather a fantastic feat even for him. He paddled from Diauarum back here in ONE DAY. Left in the early hours, he said, and got here by 11.30 p.m. Yes, you guessed it—only one thing would bring him back in such a haste—death. It was really a grief-stricken village that mourned Beptori as they painted his body during the rest of the night. My heart goes out to his poor mother, having lost her husband and of course her belongings such a short time ago. Beptori was a fine young teenager—so strong and healthy-looking that I can hardly believe he could go so quickly.

Poiriri, December 13th, 1969

Warrior helper boys returned yesterday—also a few men—bringing the news that some are very sick with malaria—but are too far out to come back. Seems they are still pressing on to the enemy. Stubborn Txuks.

Orlando sent word by Bejai, as soon as the pilot was available, to tell the people here to send a runner and bring back the warriors. He's unhappy about this—and Rauni, when he returns, will also be unhappy that he [Orlando] knows. Surely they didn't think they could keep it a secret from him!

[247]

Poiriri, January 16th, 1970

The Txuk. warriors have returned—late Sunday afternoon, Jan. 4th—tired and thin, and with no success to report. The men looked a sight with eyelashes, and even some "whiskers" on their thin faces. And poor things, as soon as they felt up to it, they had Beptori's funeral rites to perform. As Claudio put it, they had a huge and useless hike. However, I'm sure you won't think it useless to know that they went to two or three old villages of the Kreen-Akrore and found them completely deserted and grown in weeds, and only bananas left in the fields. They reported one huge burial mound, and one fellow said he saw a human skull in one village. The third village was not entered, it seems, when they saw that it also was overgrown and had no fresh paths. They said there was no trace of a path whereby the people might have left for another part of the jungle. However, I trust that at least some are indeed in some part of this vast jungle still.

The villages they found are those of the area where Bebgogoti's warriors went, not where the pacification was attempted.

I wish you could have heard our diplomat, Rauni, dictating a letter to Claudio. "We didn't go to kill the Kreen-Akrore, but to pacify [subdue] them". He could almost make one believe he's a true son of Rondon[1] himself. Claudio says, would that what the Txuks allege about pacifying was true.

Well, I guess everyone was relieved—Krumare visited Diauarum and came back reporting that Claudio didn't like it because "every city" knew about the planned attack and wanted to depose Claudio from being in charge of these warring Indians. It would be rather flattering if "everyone" had listened in to our one little radio message to Brasilia at the crack of dawn. We heard a lot of discussion amongst the Indians at different times about whether we sent a radio message to tell of the attack, or wrote on paper and knew by means of paper, etc. But they never directly asked us if we told it on the radio, not even when I asked Krumare how Claudio heard it. I'm very glad they're not angry with us. I told them that they seem to all of a sudden be ashamed of themselves, that at first everyone talked about it and no one said it was a secret. I said that in my country people who kill are killed in return, like they do to the

Kreen-Akrore, but that Claudio's compatriots don't do that.

Oh, one more bit about the warriors. They left Karinhoti way out in the jungle with a bad foot, and his brothers ("Snake Charmer") Kotokurti and Bepur and others went recently to get him. Hope he's OK. A stingray got him near the ankle. We sent penicillin pills for him. Pretty grim of his pals to leave him, we thought.

Poiriri, July 20th, 1970

Karinhoti, you may remember was left on the path when the men returned from their futile "war trip" the end of the year. It was great to see him alive and well. He has a nasty scar on each side of his ankle where the stingray tail went through. A six-inch sawtooth sting on a stingray larger than he could reach around. (And, no doubt, a few inches larger in circumference every time he tells it—and I can't blame him.) On the outside of his foot the scar is still an oozing wound I can put my thumb into. Can you imagine what it was like at first? And he must have been out there months, alone, in that condition. Karinhoti says four moons, and got back shortly before the rains stopped. He had four large rivers to cross, and crossed with fear of sting-rays. However, his two brothers, Kotokurti and Bepur, along with Inhu, reached him before the last three crossings. He said he had killed four jaguars. I asked how he managed to hunt with such a bad foot, and he said he didn't have to go far—and told me about the jaguars! The medicine we had sent (oral penicillin) for Karinhoti ran out just before they reached the village, and then shortly after, the motor boat came and took him out for treatment. Coincidence?

NOTE TO APPENDIX IV

1. Marshal Rondon's motto was, "Die if necessary, kill, never."

ACKNOWLEDGMENTS

After all that has happened to the Parque, it would be maudlin to repeat what I owe to Orlando and Claudio Villas Boas and to the Indians of Xingu. But I must thank Sir Lew Grade, Robert Heller and Robin Gill of ATV and ITC for backing the film and taking what was an unprecedented gamble. The money they channelled into Xingu was of help to the Parque, and many of the Indians still have an ATV rifle or ITC fishing-net.

Bruce White, Jesco von Puttkamer, Charles Stewart, Chris Menges, Gareth Heywood, Erno Vincze and Richard Stanley don't appear much in the book nor do Pilly or Boojie. But for two years we worked and travelled together in Xingu. Pilly left the jungle looking like a skeleton, and everyone, except Gareth, caught malaria. It would have all been impossible without them and their help; their views, observations and photographs form an essential part of the book. And if Claudio is patient in wait for an unknown Indian, Pilly can match him with a husband—who, unlike the Kreen-Akrore, can at least guess at what that patience involves.

Aruyave, Javari, Bejai, Mairewe, Neitu, Cocti, Kenmer, Reunier, Cagrire and Bebtok were attached to our unit at various times, and much of what we learnt came from their very grandfatherly teaching. Rauni and Pripuri dictated some of the notes for this book, and took a great interest in it.

Dr. Acary de Oliveira Passos kept our supplies moving in and out of the jungle—through Genario and Taxi-Xavante—and after solving a particularly difficult problem he would fly over our camps to drop encouraging but cryptic messages in plastic bags: "The sky is blue with little white balls in it."

Alvaro Villas Boas and Lorival Lucena ran the Parque's offices in São Paulo and Brasilia, and Jorge Garcia Quiroga, Marina Lopes Dias and Lotte Bauerb worked for the Parque in Xingu. They all helped us, as did Dr. Noel Nutels, Luigi Maprim, and the anthropologists Aurore Monod, Patrick Menget, Kenneth Brecher and Micky Stout. Micky translated many of the Txukahamei tapes, and according to a recent letter, has just denied "the latest Mekrenoti rumour that you have fallen off the moon."

Alvaro Villas Boas checked the facts in Appendix I, and the maps. Permission to publish quotations and extracts was given by Orlando Villas Boas, Jesco von Puttkamer, Dr. Peter Fry, Dr. Noel Nutels, and Micky Stout; also by *The Times*, *The Daily Telegraph* and *Reuters*.

John Moore and Louis Wolfers provided photographs from previous trips to Xingu.

Maureen Verity drew the maps.

Simon Goodenough and Janet Dunbar were of great help with the writing of the book, particularly Janet Dunbar, who very generously gave up a great deal of time to cut it down and re-structure it. The typing was painstakingly done by Chitrakorn Sundarapakshin, Mrs. O'Brien, Piyasuda Utokapachana, and Pilly.

Finally I must record immense gratitude to Robin Hanbury-Tenison and everyone connected with Survival International (36 Craven Street, London, W.C.2) for taking up the Parque's cause.

A.C.